The Spaces in Between

A poetic duo-ethnographical exploration of living well in curriculum studies, learning, and life

Carl Leggo

Kimberley Holmes

Dear Jen

Always remember the importance of living life well. Education is life — that magical space of living, breathing & well-being

ox
Kimberley

ISBN 978-1-64504-046-0 (Hardback)
ISBN 978-1-64504-047-7 (Paperback)
ISBN 978-1-64504-048-4 (E-Book)

Library of Congress Control Number: 2020937878

Printed on acid-free paper

© DIO Press Inc, New York
https://www.diopress.com

All Rights Reserved

No part of this work may be reproduced, stored in a retrieval system, or transmitted in any form or by any means, electronic, mechanical, photocopying, microfilming, recording or otherwise, without written permission from the Publisher, with the exception of any material supplied specifically for the purpose of being entered and executed on a computer system, for exclusive use by the purchaser of the work.

This book is part of the *Critical Pedagogies* Series

Series Editor: Shirley R. Steinberg

Table of Contents

Preface   ix
Kimberley Holmes

Invocation   1
Carl Leggo

Alliance   17
Kimberley Holmes and Carl Leggo

Requiem   271
Kimberley Holmes

About the Authors   287

Embrace your doubts

As you do knots in the fabric.

Caress your losses

as openings to honor the depths.

Reknit your life

to the landscape of cherishing

each fragment you live through

this is the material for sweetness

your bodyspirit made visible

in all the ways that you honor

the fibers of the collective

story we knit together

into wonder

Teaching Writing: Fragments of a Poet's Credo, Carl Leggo, University of British Columbia. Previously posted on Celeste Snowber's blog, bodypsalms.com

Preface

A preface introduces a book, typically stating its subject scope or aims. In the Christian Church the preface is the central part of the Eucharist, historically forming the first part of the canon or prayer of consecration. Consecration is the solemn dedication to a special purpose or service or an association with the sacred. This text is a consecration.

I don't know how it began or when. In fact, I don't even know if it had a beginning or it was a cycle which was amidst it's spiralling synthesis long before my own biology became a reality. Perhaps the kaleidoscope of colors, the strands of the interwoven threads began merging when the chromosomes of my parents collided, or maybe the real journey began much later or perhaps even much earlier. Perhaps it all began in those who travelled the pathways before me, who wove their memories through my DNA and whispered their stories deep into my searching soul calling for me to pay attention to that words that tumbled through my head whispering to be heard, recognized and shared. Respect, relevance, reciprocity, responsibility.

It is a bitterly cold evening in Calgary and the frost creeps up the window pane in icy fingers of oppression. Yet, this morning I heard the birds singing, in the frigid -28°c weather they were calling out to one to announce that they were still alive and ready to face another day. Life. We survive the bitter cold to recognize the recurrence of another spring as we cycle through the season of existence and being. When we are done the physical existence, we cycle into another type of being that I am yet to understand. I am reading a great deal these days, specifically about grief and the interplay between grief and praise. I am reading about educating the heart, mind, body and spirit and drawn to the wisdom of indigenous story work. These themes are circling together and creating new patterns. I am searching to understand the power of this knowledge specifically indigenous storywork because these teachings contain power. I understand this is part of my responsibility to continue learnings I have been taught for, "if one comes to understand and appreciate the power of a particular knowledge, then one must be ready to share and teach it respectfully and responsibly to others in order for this knowledge and power to continue" (Archibald, 2008, p. 15). I am learning how to continue to move forward in my work, in my learning and in my teaching to others. I am remembering how to breathe again as I know the heart of any pedagogical process is learning to breathe.

My learning was stagnated for a while as I was suffering an immense grief. Pretchtel (2015) states, "grief is what living beings experience when what or whom they love dies or disappears" (p. 3) This is a natural and necessary process that must be purposely done for "without both grief and praise, life is only hate and mediocrity." I have been living with mediocrity and in many ways living with hate. I have been angry things have been taken from me, possibilities did not work out and that some people I have loved are gone away, they have died. It has not been pleasant, but it has been part of my journey, a chapter in my story that has been awaiting a rewriting a type of reawakening to things I previously recognized and understood. While I was stagnated, I stopped sharing, and I stopped writing as I refused to allow myself to grieve. I since have learned that, "sharing what one has learned is an important Indigenous tradition. This type of sharing can take the form of a story of personal life experience and is done with compassionate mind and love for others" (Archibald, 2008, p. 2). Hence, it is time to share this text that I wrote with my beautiful and inspirational teacher. This text is about love and compassion. It is a literary love story between a teacher and his student. That teacher was Dr. Carl Leggo and I was the student. Our journey began years ago when I was a lost doctoral student confused in the world of hermeneutics, auto-ethnography, narrative inquiry, learning sciences and educational inquiry.

I understood very little and the towers of phenomenology, ontology and epistemology towered above my reach whispering to climb up and seek the light. But the tower was high, and I stumbled on the steps often lost in a sea of poetry as words swirled in a strangled struggle to be understood. My frustrated supervisor at the time tried desperately to help me find Hermes, to seek the meeting of the horizons and dive into the interpretive waters but I hesitated afraid to swim out beyond the familiar shore. Finally, he told me to send an "email to Carl Leggo and maybe he will understand what it is that you are trying to do". And I did. In the middle of the night, struggling with the darkness of my soul I sent a silent plea out to a teacher I did not know and had never met. I bared my soul and let the words fall freely to a stranger. It was a strange and cathartic experience but somehow my heart knew it was the right path. I pushed send and whisked the email out to this language and literary professor at the University of British Columbia and he answered almost immediately. The Universe whispered to both or us and our journey together began.

Eventually, Carl joined my supervisory committee and supported me on my doctoral dissertation. His love of language and words inspired me to find my own voice, to seek the nexus between writing and neuroscience and to move into various areas of experimentation, exploration and play. He filled my life with joy, always encouraging, always inspiring and always light. I was truly blessed to have him as my teacher.

Once my doctoral work was complete, we continued our correspondence. It was a relationship of words and stories as our connection was through email strands. We saw each other rarely and then only briefly. Our worlds were only interested by our words which wove together in powerful patterns. He guided me through the transition back to the classroom, the re-entry to the front line and the challenges of going back to the work once I had been immersed in the knowledge. He was always quick to respond, always passionate and always willing to be my guide. Whenever I needed to connect, he was there to answer my call.

Then on Oct 6, 2018, at 3:10 PM, Carl wrote to tell me that he had a brain tumour. I was frozen and terrified. My mother was currently battling her second round of breast cancer, illness and disease was no stranger to me. Yet, I knew that it was now time to write our stories together and try to breathe life into those moments when it seemed like there is no air. What follows is the transcript of that journey. Carl and I wrote daily about the events of our lives. We wove our stories together and soothed our fears through our words. We sought holistic healing harmony in a world that felt unbalanced and unpredictable. We sought a way to work our way through grief and keep our spirit alive.

As we wrote we contemplated what it was that we were doing together. Carl sent me an unpublished paper entitled "Invocation," which became our opening chapter. We recognized why we were writing, why we needed to write, and why we needed to write together. The power of writing to help and to heal was evident. As poets we called to one another, always answering, always seeking and always finding the words needed allow the struggling soul spirare and create a type of sanctuary from demands of reality. We breathed our words into the spaces in between.

On Feb 13, 2019, Carl received news from his doctor that the end was near and he wrote to me about "organizing for the transition of leaving." Those words have never left my head. I am constantly contemplating transitions, beginnings, endings and the process of leaving this earthly life, yet I have done this without any significant signs of grief. I did this as a protection mechanism as I did not know how to process the loss of someone so significant without failing to pieces myself. I was afraid to let sorrow soothe me as I feared I would drown in the tears of salt, sputtering desperately for air as I fought to regain a voice I had only recently acquired.

On February 15th, 2019 at 1:45 pm Carl wrote his final email to me. Shortly after, he suffered a massive seizure from which he did not recover. I was told he transitioned surrounded by family and filled with love. As he transitioned existence my family prepared to travel to Germany. My heart froze over at the loss of my teacher and I simply went on with the daily details of living life. I went forward without recognizing and praising the incredible gift that Carl blessed me with. Today, as I write this preface, I am acknowledging the need to grieve and to praise. Praise has a sound that "always moves and motivated but never ends" (Pretchtel, 2015, p. 4). Our lives are always morphing, moving and transitioning. Grief and praise are part of the cycle, tightly interwoven in the strand of life as they are part of the process of love. Grief and love are a tightly connected duo that breaks and heals the human heart. As I write this tonight, I show my grief for the loss of a brilliant mentor, but tears are not running down my face nor am I wailing in sorrow. I am writing, letting the words fill the page and continuing learning, growing and living. Prechtel (2015) reflects, "Grief is a form of generosity, which praises life and the people and the situations which we have lost. Grief that praises life shows the depths of our appreciation for having been given life enough to begin with, to experience both love and loss and that with all the mistreatment we humans give to the earth, we still have the amazing unlikely opportunity to actually speak and bathe in the Divine" (p. 59)

My teacher was love, pure love. He was the Divine, a sacred soul who taught others the beauty of the world through his mastery of words and his understanding of love amidst sorrow. I can hear his words echoing in my head now and sometimes feel his presence when I am teaching. Even in his darkest hours he taught me to seek for the light, to find the words and to reach to others. Tonight, as the temperature plummets, I think of my own frozen heart and recognize the need to thaw from the bitter cold of grief and loss. I see the need to pray, to cry, to weep, to heal, and begin to breath and write poetry. Although I lost my teacher in the physical sense of the world, he is alive in all that he touched, he is alive in me. He exists in these words set forth on the page and continues to call to Others to join the journey and become part of the story. Poets call to one another—and we always answer. I have come to recognize that continuation of knowledge happens only through a reciprocal relationship between teachers and learners. I need to foster these reciprocal relationships and travel between the role of the learner and the teacher. I need to listen to the prayer, to the songs, and to the poetry as I turn my face towards the sacred light and love.

Stories swirl slowly in vibrant braids of interconnected pulsating patterns
Calling from beyond the human dimension as birds sing in the darkness
Chirping the magic of being alive and hinting of the next part of the journey
As we transition from the frozen darkness into the spring of our lives
Succulent summers leading into the vibrant colors of fall that eventually recede
To the winter silent slumbering of rumination and rest
Respect, relevance, reciprocity responsibility
Patiently braiding the stories of our lives into tightly interconnected strands
That will sustain us through the darkest hours
Awaiting patiently the rebirth and the reawakening from the deep dormancy
Stretching our arms outwards towards the sky and reaching for the Divine

Kimberley

Deepest thanks to Lana, Carl's wife and muse, for giving consent and blessings to go forth with this work. Lana understood Carl's expressed wishes to be able to teach and mentor his students, knowing he would want us to finish this work. Through this text, we hope his legacy of living life poetically will live on as we all aspire to dwell in spaces of wonder, hope and love.

KH

References

Archibald, J. (2008). Indigenous Storywork. UBC Press. Vancouver Canada.
Prechtel, M. (2015). The Smell of Rain on Dust. Grief and Praise. North Atlantic Books, Berkley, CA.

Invocation

Carl

In *Why Poetry* Matthew Zapruder (2017) writes about "the experience of getting close to the unsayable and feeling it" (p. xv). He thinks that "it may be that true poetry is the only way we can begin to see each other again" (p. 224). On January 17, 2019, my favorite poet, Mary Oliver, died. At the age of 83 years, she died with lymphoma. No poet has ever touched me more. She has both rattled and soothed my imagination and spirit. No other poet has ever spoken in the ways that she has spoken. I have been reading and citing Mary Oliver for many years. I, too, am living with lymphoma—not at all sure what the result will be, but definitely feeling like cancer is my daily health risk! I am glad that Mary Oliver lived till 83, and that she continued to write her wonderful poetry until the end. I am 65 years old, and so I feel most days like cancer is at least a little premature! Nevertheless, premature or not, cancer is what it is, and I am living with cancer even though a part of me wants to write that I am dying with cancer. Right now, I dwell daily in the space between living and dying. Matthew Zapruder (2017) claims that "maybe poems are not to be read for their great answers, but for their great, more often than not unanswerable, questions" (p. 107).

A while ago, I presented a workshop to some teachers about writing, especially poetry. As I spoke to the teachers, I realized that I have been sharing the same ideas, practices, and lessons for about forty years. Either I have something worth saying, or at least I am convinced that I have something worth saying! So, in this paper I am going to offer some fragments and suggestions from my credo (what I believe, what I have given my heart to). I heartily agree with Jean Baudrillard (1997), who once wrote that "doubtless the final state of thought is disorder, rambling, the fragment and extravagance" (p. 118). I am not offering these fragments as definitive guidelines for organizing a writing curriculum. I offer these fragments as the kind of wisdom I have gleaned from years of teaching and writing and living.

Michael Ondaatje (2002) once claimed that "practically everything I write is a surprise to me, so in that sense, it's inspiration. I don't sit down with an idea or a plan. I sit down to write and see what happens" (p. 36). I have always loved language, words, the alphabet, the dictionary, the possibilities of spells and spelling. I cannot remember a time that I was not passionately in love with language. I love the accidents of accents, the intentionality of intonation, the sinuous bending of syntax, the glamor of grammar. Poetry is my favorite genre because it is the most capacious genre. Poetry invites music, philosophy, story, imagery, romance, tragedy, fantasy, and comedy. Poetry is playful and purposeful. Poetry invents worlds and teaches us how to live in them. We have not even caught a glimpse of the limits of poetry. We do not even know if poetry has limits. According to Matthew Zapruder (2017), "the energy of poetry comes primarily from the reanimation and reactivation of the language that we recognize and know" (p. 9).

As a graduate student in creative writing in the mid-1980s, I remember one significant incident. I was sitting at a table in the library at the University of New Brunswick, reading or writing or falling asleep, when a woman whispered, "Are you Carl Leggo the poet?" I looked up with a startled face and said, "Yes." I had been named, discovered like Lana Turner, and with the question and my response, I was creatively reborn—I was Carl Leggo the poet. And I am, still. As Hélène Cixous (1998) understands, "I wanted to remain faithful to chance, to mystery and above all to difficulty" (p. 159).

I stare at the blank page, and its whiteness blinds and intimidates and disorients like a snow blizzard that conceals all landmarks and reduces visibility to zero. I stare at the blank page, and I do not know where to turn, what to do. I am lost. Beginning. Scratching the first words in the whiteness, always intimidating. Where did I learn that I had nothing valuable to say? Even now I feel that way most of the time. Who wants to read my words? Why would anyone want to read my words?

The blank page is like a hospital bed sheet or a portal to the unknown or a salt desert or a prairie field filled with snow. The blank page is expansive. Even if I use large margins and double space, the typical blank page of eight-and-one-half inches by eleven-and-one-half inches can hold at least one thousand alphabetic squiggles. That is the problem. I must begin, and I must continue. Writing is plodding, one step after the other, one squiggle after the other, until the blank page is filled or I grow weary or I run out of squiggles. And that is the big problem: I never know where the squiggles come from, and I never know how many of them there are for me to use, and so I never know when they will end. I began in suspicion that I could never start, and I knew surprise that I had anything to write, and I continue in suspense about when the words will end.

Where did I learn the fear of the blank page? The page is not blank; the page is never blank. Instead it is scribbled over and over by all the writers who have gone before me, as it will continue to be scribbled by all the writers presently writing and all the writers who will write after me. My fear is not only that I have nothing to write; my fear is that I have nothing new to write. Others have said it all. Why say it again? In school I did not learn I had a word-making role in the world, or that the world ran only as long as I made my words. Instead of wavering with the anxiety of influence, instead of growing weary with the desire for something new, instead of propagating a myth that writing is individual and idiosyncratic and unique, I need to write an older myth that celebrates the communitarian dynamic of writing as corporate. Writing is a palimpsest. Writing is a wooden desktop that has been written over and over. Writing is layers of acetate laid on top of one another, a thousand miles high. Writing is tangled and criss-crossing.

a

According to John Ashbery (2002), "there is more to our story, more to the telling of it" (p. 97). Writing creatively is primarily about learning to live creatively in the world. The only question that concerns me these days is: How can we live well in the world? Writing is about health and healing.

b

Margaret Atwood (2002) understands how "there's one characteristic that sets writing apart from most of the other arts—its apparent democracy, by which I mean its availability to almost everyone as a medium of expression" (p. 25). I am glad when young people write, in any medium, in any language, including Facebook, slang, blogs, Twitter, and text-messaging. I trust that, if writers write, they will grow as writers. And young writers will attend to formal conventions when formal writing is expected and/or required. Students will want to learn all they can in order to make their writing as effective as it can be, and that includes paying attention to standard language use in those kinds of texts and situations when formal language use is expected and needed.

c

The most difficult part of assessing writing is using the standard approaches to assessment, which are negatively oriented to finding what is wrong with the writing and how it does not fit standards. Creative writing should be evaluated creatively, by acknowledging the value of writing and the writer, by recognizing what works and suggesting possibilities for revision. The ancient Greek philosopher Heraclitus (2001) once wrote:

"The rule that makes

its subject weary

is a sentence

of hard labor" (p. 53).

We are obsessed with assessment! If a grade must be given, assign a letter like Q or Z. (These are interesting letters that are almost never used in assessing!) Above all, creative writing should be assessed by how much it moves us, brings us to laughter or tears.

d

Elizabeth Hay (2011) once observed that "it's possible that a hidden symmetry is often at work as we stumble our way through life" (p. 292). As a writer I am a whirling dervish, a freestyle dancer, an interpretive dancer, a wounded dancer, a broken dancer. As a writer I want to be the adolescent dancer I once was, wild and free, listening to the music, interpreting in my own ways, oblivious to what was going on around me. I want to dance with wild abandon on the edges, without following somebody else's dictates.

e

When we become "better writers," do we become wiser? I sometimes complain that the biggest challenge of being a poet is that nobody reads poetry, but that is not true. Canada is full of poets. We are ubiquitous like Tim Horton's. We just aren't as popular. My biggest challenge as a poet is other poets who review poetry with a fundamentalist fervor for guarding their convictions about what poetry is, and can be, and ought to be. In my experience, most reviewers of poetry like what they like, which is generally what they (and their friends) write. We need to be more generous in our responses to the poetry of others. Linda Hogan (1995) reflects on her process: "Walking, I am listening to a deeper way. Suddenly all my ancestors are behind me. Be still, they say. Watch and listen. You are the result of the love of thousands" (p. 159).

f

Patrick Lane (2004) understands how he found his "place in the world with language" (p. 169). We need to care for the stories as we care for ourselves. We cannot exhaust the stories of childhood. How much can we know in stories? Stories shape experience. Experience is like the ocean. A story is a cup of the ocean. How do stories inhibit our growth as human beings? What are the stories we cannot tell? How can we learn to tell all our stories?

g

Octavio Paz (1999) thinks that "writing opened unexplored spaces for me. In brief texts in prose—poems or explosions?—I tried to grasp myself. I set sail in each word like in a nutshell" (p. 68). I am now living with cancer, and I do not know what the future holds. For a time, I did not write much, like I am scared of writing, frightened of remembering, eager to live in the present moment, perhaps unable to live well in forgiveness, accepting that the past is always present, always a part of my life, not only like a part that precedes, that holds "in the beginning," that comprises the first sequence of chapters. Instead, the past is still present. It is still being lived, or it is still alive, or it is still living. I want to say that the future does not count, has not yet been lived, and therefore does not enter into my storied universe. But I believe in the eschaton, the future, the hope—the future is then like the past, also present. Perhaps the future is the telling of the stories that are possible when we attend to the art and heart of storytelling. So, the future is the panoply of versions of stories that can be told to reveal the world. "Future" is a word. So, I am not talking about linear progress—I am talking about growth to freedom, growth in spirit, a keen sense of artful attending in the momentous moment.

h

To write well we must care about our writing. When we care about our writing, we write well. As Thomas King (2003) reflects, "We trust easy oppositions. We are suspicious of complexities, distrustful of contradictions, fearful of enigmas" (p. 25). May we continue to shape our words and send them into the world! The act of writing is efficacious and necessary. May we read the words that we find along the way and linger with them as we would linger with gifts that have been offered with hope. I am seeking cosmos in chaos and finding that chaos is omnipresent and primordial and all-encompassing. Chaos is the ocean I swim in. Cosmos is the line I swim, lines in all directions, intersecting and parallel and skew. I lay down a line of words and the words are ephemeral, aqueous, beginning in darkness, ending in darkness, always immersed in darkness.

i

There is no end to the information and knowledge I need to write my poems. For example, I need to know the names of plants, trees, flowers, birds, and clouds, but if I waited till I possessed the knowledge, I would never write a poem. So, I need to write about what I know and continue to learn more as I go. Nobody knows everything. Agnosticism is part of humility.

Mary Oliver (2010) once wrote,

"What can I say that I have not said before?

So I'll say it again" (p. 1).

j

Irving Singer (2009) thinks that "the humanities can benefit from science, but they suffer badly when reduced to its methodologies" (p. 118). When I start drawing shadows, I realize that they are far more pervasive than I had earlier thought. The shadows are everywhere, creating a dark counterpoint to the light green grass. The grass is light. I can actually see the blades as if they have been bathed in light. There is a silver color to some of the grass, as if the light is shining directly on the grass. I now see the shadow everywhere. Perhaps the sun is moving. Perhaps I am moving. I want to know shadows, to know the ways I can linger in darkness and know, not the absence of light, but the spaces only light and earth can make, fecund places of imagination. There is always so much that I need to write and talk about and explore, always so little that I understand, but, of course, I probably can never understand many of the experiences in my life—I do not have the memory or the records or the insights needed to make sense of my life. So, I seek to make my life sensible, to understand as much of it as possible.

k

Wendell Berry (1990) is convinced that "a good poem reminds us of love because it cannot be written or read in distraction; it cannot be written or understood by anyone thinking of praise or publication or promotion" (p. 90). What would happen if I really turned my critical eye to everything I witness? I think it is easy to live critically, to make fun of everything, to cast a satirical light everywhere. I do not think it is at all difficult to critique, dissect, and deconstruct. Of course, everything can be criticized. What does the word "criticism" mean? How hard is it to be naïve, to hold hope, to re/present the world with an optimistic spirit? This is my goal. All fears and demons and potentially hard memories can be cleansed and transformed, rendered in optimistic ways. The world of words is a remarkably lovely location for locution. Enjoy!

l

Roland Barthes (1977) once claimed that "one writes with one's desire, and I am not through desiring" (p. 188). Like Barthes, I revel in the realization that rhetoric reveals our reality. I love to play with letters because in play I learn who I am, who you are. Unraveling = revealing = reveling. I am happy to doodle and write nonsense. I love to make up words. I love to play with rhyme. I love to compose long lists. I love to mine the past. I never feel like I have domesticated words. They are always wild and fierce and wonderful.

One of the most important ways is to emphasize playing with language—a lot of my work as a teacher educator is about encouraging teachers to be playful in their approaches to writing. Many teachers think they are preparing students to write the government-sponsored final exams at the end of high school, and those exams are not only important because they are government-sponsored, but because they also act as gatekeepers to university entrance. So, the goal for some teachers is in preparing their students to write these ultimate tests. We become readers and writers by engaging with the spells and mystery of language. I think we ought to emphasize the mystery rather than the mastery of language.

None of us ever masters language. We can never rest assured there is nothing more to learn. If we embrace the mystery, the playfulness of language, then we remain humble.

m

I am sitting in a retreat with faculty members, and my colleagues and I are talking words like chewing and swallowing myrrh from a fir tree. I am always very unhappy when words are made fat and sweaty like they have walked too quickly up the stairs and squeezed into your office. Language is not necessarily lovely and beautiful. With language, so much always remains unsaid. How is desire connected with the unsaid? What is deafness? An inability to hear? An inability to understand? A way/stance of being puzzled in the world? A sense of separation? A confirmation of aloneness? Steven Pinker (1999) accurately observes that "language comes so naturally to us that it is easy to forget what a strange and miraculous gift it is" (p. 1).

n

Stephen King (2000) wrote about the writing process that it is "a disjointed growth process in which ambition, desire, luck, and a little talent all played a part. Don't bother trying to read between the lines.... There are *no* lines—only snapshots, most out of focus" (p. 18). My advice to young writers is relatively simple:

- Believe in your writing and yourself as a writer.
- Commit yourself to writing every day.
- Cultivate a keen sense of your voice.
- Seek to know the world in writing.
- Always read lots of other writers.
- Share your writing with others.
- Learn to listen to your heart.

o

About her writing, Jeanette Winterson (2011) notes that "it is a true story but it is still a version" (p. 229). How can we learn if we do not sometimes (perhaps most times) invite failure or the possibility of failure? Perhaps we should give A's to people who try, and take risks, and experiment, and seek the unfamiliar, and fail, instead of those who play it safe all the time, and only, at best, recapitulate what has already been done. Parents and teachers need to let their children and students fail. Failure is a good thing. It opens the way for learning, forgiveness, grace, humility, openness, caring, compassion, and beginning again.

p

The word poetry comes from the Greek word *poiein*, to make—so as a poet, I am a maker. I could be making sense, or making stories, or making lines of connections with others. I am always engaging in something that feels like composing, constructing, and making. I always want to write poetry that is accessible to folk who do not ordinarily read poetry. Jay Parini (2008) understands that "the poet quickens our sense of language, and our sense of life as well" (p. 38).

q

I promote life writing as a way to investigate lived and living experiences. If I stand bare buff in public, I no longer need to hide, to linger in fear and silence, to live pretentiously under the guise of pretense. So, the main challenge of writing personally is that some people will scratch you off their Christmas card list or refuse to befriend you on Facebook. The blessing is that others will learn to regard you as trustworthy, as ethical, as human. Writing with love is simply necessary.

A phrase which I have been using for a long time is *living poetically*—about learning how to live well in the world. All of my poems are about daily living; they are autobiographical, about growing up in Newfoundland on the east coast of Canada. What I am really interested in is writing poems that others can read and enjoy. I write poetry for readers who will be reminded that the world, for all of the messiness, is still a beautiful place to be alive. So I write my poems to remind people to enjoy being alive, to savor the sensual experiences of lingering outdoors, of being with others, of relationships. And I write my poetry to deal with challenging issues. I've written some confessional poems that speak to life experiences. I write these poems autobiographically and personally because writing helps me to make sense of experiences and also helps me to connect with other people.

About her writing, Hélène Cixous (1998) notes, "I advance error by error, with erring steps, by the force of error. It's suffering, but it's joy" (p. 22). So, when I write about living poetically, I do not mean that everything is perfect. I am actually writing about living well in the messiness of the world we live in. What I am striving to understand is that poetry is not only this eloquent and lovely use of language that gives us sweet thoughts and entertains us and moves us. It is that, certainly, but it is a great deal more, and it can move us to action.

r

I agree with Stephanie Dowrick (1997), who thinks that "each choice we make replaces other choices" (p. 92). I am particularly concerned that much teaching about writing perpetuates rules and approaches that sustain dominant discursive practices that actually impair, instead of support, the writing processes and practices of many students. I seek to interrogate seemingly natural ways of writing and teaching writing in order to promote other diverse approaches which invite writers to write in different voices and styles.

s

Lorri Neilsen Glenn (2011) claims that "poetry remains the erotic hearth we are drawn to, the deep river and nameless source" as well as "the grace we can find in the everyday" (p. 117). Language is game or play. To use language is to be caught up in discourse, in rhetoric, in the materiality of language, in a verbal performance, in a verbally wrought illusion or reality-effect, in producing and disclosing and constructing the world. I claim that the most effective way to use language with power, conviction, and confidence is to use language with play, pleasure, and delight in the potential of language for making together. The binary opposition between seriousness and play leads to misconceptions about writing, which is, after all, indisputably, inarguably, and unquestionably most serious when it is playful.

t

All my teaching of writing, both in school and university classrooms, is informed and generated by my practices as a writer of poetry, fiction, and scholarly texts. Hence, the ways I teach writing are connected to my own experiences as a writer. In turn, I encourage my students to pay attention to their writing processes in order to understand the complex ways that writing unfolds in individual practice. When I read many influential books about teaching writing, I find myself nonplussed by the advice that is provided because I just do not see my own processes and practices as a writer and teacher in the typical textbook advice. Take, for example, the important work of Donald C. Stewart (1986), who was an influential scholar of rhetoric and composition. I have paid close attention to his books, and I have always learned from him, but, nevertheless, I also have many questions about Stewart's views and advice. In *The Versatile Writer* he contends that "writers settle for nothing less than absolute honesty in their work. This requires a special kind of writing discipline because you have to learn to throw away whatever is false, no matter how much it pleases you" (p. 19). How do we know what is honest and what is false in our writing? How do we acquire our authentic voice?

u

The notion of convention has been constrained by defining the word as rules of standard usage. Convention does not mean custom. Instead of defining "convention" as a rule of conduct or constraint or control, thereby making convention a strategy of power, a more liberating notion of convention is the calling or inviting of a chorus or assembly, a carnival of conversation. Hence, this essay contravenes common conventions of composition in order to court continuing conversation and collaboration in the creation of meaning. You are invited to interact with the text, which is an open space where writers and readers come together. The text is open. The text eschews fixed meanings. The authors refuse the mantle of authority that authors are conventionally invested with in efforts to convene a less authoritarian spirit of openness where multiple meanings can be playfully and productively summoned. I admire Anthony Doerr's (2014) claim that "it's embarrassingly plain how inadequate language is" (p. 503).

v

V. S. Naipaul (2000) once wrote, "I wished to be a writer. But together with the wish there had come the knowledge that the literature that had given me the wish came from another world, far away from our own" (pp. 9-10). It does not matter how much I write or get published, I will never be satisfied—I always want more. I've been a writer (a poet even) since my later 20s, and I have evidence of writing poetry before that, too. I wrote several theses. Perhaps most of my writing has been writing for the wrong reasons. Perhaps I need to write for myself. To write what I want to write with little thought of the ways that the writing will be published and reviewed.

    I am a writer because I have created myself, written myself as a writer, and in the creating and writing, I have come to know myself. I have called the shape out of the stone, or the stone has spoken and guided me to reveal the shape. The block of rock, the granite—the sculptor releases and relives the shape that is held in the stone. I do not think we could breathe, or function, or be together without writing. I call the shape forth and reveal the shape so that I can then be/come in the world full of grace, not granite. I will write, and my writing will find a fertile soil, not a fallow soil, in which to grow, and bear fruit.

W

According to David Lynch (2006), "ideas come along in the strangest way when you just pay attention" (p. 77). In ancient times a family slave or servant called a pedagogue led the child (Gr. *Paidagogos*: paidos = child + agein = to lead) to the teacher. The pedagogue was not the teacher; the pedagogue was the one who led the student to the teacher. The alphabet leads the student to the teacher, but we have pretended that the alphabet is the teacher when the alphabet is actually only the way. Pedagogy, and by extension life, since pedagogy and life are one, are always at the end of the alphabet. Of course, the end of the alphabet is really the beginning, a recursive movement of circularity leading to a grand (w)hole, dark and mysterious filled with stars (like Alpha), a (w)hole that is not bound by fences. I want to interrogate the notion that ordered, logical, grammatical arguments fueled by a classical rhetorical stance are the only way to know, to be, to be/come. I want to understand that the alphabet has constrained us to a linear way of thinking. We need a way to juggle many divergent paths of knowing—to walk down many paths at once, to dance with many partners.

X

Steven Galloway (2009) once wrote that "there is no way to tell which version of a lie is the truth" (p. 33). In school I learned to be a timid writer. I lacked the courage to write with boldness and innovation. In school I learned to be a half-hearted writer, afraid of the rules of correctness. Writing was a nerve-wracking effort to remember the many rules that constrained the writing, and the even more nerve-wracking effort to remember the exceptions to the rules, because writing apparently had a way of refusing to be boxed. Writing seemed organic, dynamic, alive, ever-changing, defiant of conventions, and radical. Writing was no hobbyhorse that rocked back and forth in endless and futile mimicry of going somewhere. Writing was a wild horse that charged and jumped and ran in exciting ways if only the writer shared the wildness. In school, of course, I rode the hobbyhorse, year after year. I went nowhere, but back and forth.

y

According to Méira Cook (2003), "the world is, was, and ever will be full of wonder" (p. 81). Perhaps most writers write in the gaps and cracks and spaces of living. I must write in the cracks and gaps (gasps) of a busy life. Why do I want to be correct and clear? I feel muddled and muddied most of the time. I feel like a fragment, a run-on sentence, a rambling sentence, an overlapping construction. I am incoherent, but still coherent in my incoherence, or only coherent in my incoherence. I do not want to write sentences that are clear. I want to write sentences that meander sensuously here and there, finding the way (or ways) as the lines of letters are impressed in space and time, creating a universe of discourse which reveals what is otherwise unseen and unheard, a journey without beginning or destination, an explosion or strip-tease of revelation, in which the world is worded (the godly creative efficacy of words spoken and written), so you and I can know the world through the prism of language which disperses white light into countless shades of meaning, a dazzling and dizzying explosion of incoherence *in coherence*.

z

Luci Shaw (2003) understands that "no poem ends at the bottom of a page" (p. 72). In all my writing, I know I am not telling the whole story. I am writing a few fragments only, and the fragments are like bits of colored glass that refract light in entrancing ways—*entrance* (the verb); *entrance* (the noun). Writing is discovery. I love to be surprised in my writing. My calling as a poet is to write the poetry and to share it, and to send it out into the world. If it is not responded to, if it is rejected, if it is not liked, that is not my responsibility. My responsibility is to work with the words.

Convocation

Octavio Paz (1999) thinks that "perhaps true imagination, nothing to do with fantasy, consists in seeing everyday things with the eyes of our earliest days" (p. 103). I have lived sixty-five years, many of those years with my wife Lana. I will draw this essay to a close with a recent poem written for Lana's sixty-fifth birthday.

Love Is

(Lana, January 7, 2019)

Love is joking around,
even finding my way
in words when the words
are popping up like gophers

Love is walking a tightrope
of remembering and dreaming,
always tense with balance,
singing with rhythm

Love is the blank space
that just called out to me
to continue writing
whatever called out

Love is letting go with
a stream of green ink flowing
from my fountain pen like I can
row my boat to the earth's center

THE SPACES IN BETWEEN

Love is calling out, even quietly,

while I wait for an answer

that might never come, or

might come, full of surprises

Love is one more stanza, always,

a stanza like a dais, a platform

for shaping views so we can

see what needs to be seen

Love is knowing the mystery

at the heart of every tunnel,

with mazes here and there,

always hopeful for …

References

Atwood, M. (2002). *Negotiating with the dead: A writer on writing.* Cambridge, England: Cambridge University Press.
Ashbery, J. (2002). *Chinese whispers.* New York, NY: Farrar, Straus and Giroux.
Barthes, R. (1977). *Roland Barthes.* (R. Howard, Trans.). Berkeley, CA: University of California Press.
Baudrillard, J. (1997). *Fragments: Cool memories III, 1991-1995.* (E. Agar, Trans.). London, England: Verso.
Berry, W. (1990). *What are people for?: Essays.* New York, NY: North Point Press.
Cixous, H. (1998). *Stigmata: Escaping texts.* New York, NY: Routledge.
Cook, M. (2003). *Slovenly love.* London, ON: Brick Books.
Doerr, A. (2014). *All the light we cannot see.* New York, NY: Scribner.
Dowrick, S. (1997). *Forgiveness & other acts of love.* New York, NY: W. W. Norton & Company.
Galloway, S. (2009). *The cellist of Sarajevo.* Toronto, ON: Vintage Canada.
Hay, E. (2011). *Alone in the classroom.* Toronto, ON: McClelland & Stewart.
Heraclitus. (2001). *Fragments.* (B. Haxton Trans.). New York, NY: Penguin.
Hogan, L. (1995). *Dwellings: A spiritual history of the living world.* New York, NY: W. W. Norton.
King, S. (2000). *On writing.* New York, NY: Scribner.
King, T. (2003). *The truth about stories: A Native narrative.* Toronto, ON: House of Anansi Press.
Lane, P. (2004). *There is a season: A memoir.* Toronto, ON: McClelland & Stewart.
Lynch, D. (2006). *Catching the big fish: Meditation, consciousness, and creativity.* New York, NY: Jeremy P. Tarcher/Penguin.
Naipaul, V. S. (2000). *Reading and writing: A personal account.* New York, NY: New York Review Books.
Neilsen Glenn, L. (2011). *Threading light: Explorations in loss and poetry.* Regina, SK: Hagios Press.
Oliver, M. (2010). *Swan: Poems and prose poems.* Boston, MA: Beacon Press, 2010.
Ondaatje, M. (2002). The company of great thieves. In T. Bowling (Ed.), *Where the words come from: Canadian poets in conversation* (pp. 31-43). Roberts Creek, BC: Nightwood Editions.
Parini, J. (2008). *Why poetry matters.* New Haven, CT: Yale University Press.
Paz, O. (1999). *Itinerary: An intellectual journey.* (J. Wilson, Trans.). San Diego, CA: Harcourt.
Pinker, S. (1999). *Words and rules: The ingredients of language.* London, England: Weidenfeld & Nicolson.
Shaw, L. (2003). *Water lines: New and selected poems.* Grand Rapids, MI: Wm. B. Eerdmans Publishing.
Singer, I. (2009). *Philosophy of love: A partial summing-up.* Cambridge, MA: The MIT Press.
Stewart, D. C. (1986). The versatile writer. Lexington, KY: D. C. Heath.
Winterson, J. (2011). *Why be happy when you could be normal?* New York, NY: Grove Press.
Zapruder, M. (2017). *Why poetry.* New York, NY: HarperCollins.

Alliance

Practicing Writing – Weaving Together the Threads

Kimberley and Carl

The Process

Poetic inquiry is a process, a journey through time and space that allows us a portal to find our thoughts and, in a sense, reclaim our places of living and being in the world. It is a space where

> long held secrets bubble up, betrayals are noted, simple joys giggle up like teenagers; there is an unusual attention to the details of material existence and the experiences thereof, alongside a heightened awareness arising of the absolute intractability of our human independence, sabotaging the myth of autonomy. (Smith, 1999, p. xv)

We do not walk alone in this world; our stories are always woven together with those who share the journey with us. Our curriculum is our life stories, a montage of color and being that encapsulates study and research as we write our way through our beginnings and our eventual endings. Our writing is a type of research, a daily practice of learning, as we bring forth into the world what lies deeply within us. Alliance is a commitment between two poetic scholars to learn to live poetically in the spaces between life and death. These are often dark and frightening spaces, fraught with despair and frustration, yet it is the poet's credo to seek the sunlight through the darkness and find the flowers breaking through the cracks of the cement and reaching towards the rays of life. This is the poet's way, to seek what is calling to us from those spaces in between, where life appears but a shadow of reality, something that eludes the scrutiny of the human eye and requires illumination to lead us out from the darkness.

This section explores the use of poetic duo ethnographic inquiry as a tool to come to a deeper understanding of self, of others, and the interconnected role that we have on our Earth. We blend the use of duo ethnographic, narrative, and poetic inquiry to explore living well through the adverse conditions of human life. Through the reflection of the lived experience of illness, healing, and wellness, we seek a higher understanding of what it means to live a life well in the face of challenge. We explore how our place in the world, internally and externally, informs our perspective and the development of our identity, specifically around the awareness of self and the connection of that self to others and the greater human condition.

Written as dialogue between the two authors utilizing narrative and poetic verse, this prose aims to provide pre-service and practicing teachers with the lived experience of understanding "curriculum as lived experience" (Aoki, 1991). Through this process, the text hopes to open parameters for discussion around the quest to find wellness in curriculum and learning and how storytelling/story sharing can be used to strengthen wellness, compassion, and understanding around the complex issues of illness, healing, and living well. The text traces the researchers' experiences as educators trying to meet the demands of the profession and balance family, wellness, and health. It also unpacks the meaning of illness and the value of hope and love. It was written daily over a five-month time period while Dr. Leggo continued to mentor his student despite his cancer prognosis. It is a testament of raw commitment and love, speaking of those dark places and bravely stepping forward to embrace what might be and what is. It is a poetic call for connection and deeper understanding of curriculum studies, learning, and the complex process of life itself.

The Practice: October 5, 2018 – February 19th, 2019

On 2018-10-05, at 9:52 PM, Kimberley Holmes <kaholmes@ucalgary.ca> wrote:

Dear Carl,

It is a cool fall evening, and we are in our mountain sanctuary. There is snow on the ground in Fernie draping the majesty of fall in a blanket of white. It seems much too early for the earth to fall into winter slumber. Summer has morphed into winter without the brilliant transition, and I miss the vibrant colors that lead to the dark and silent nights. It seems the seasons are calling me into a contemplative space where there resides a need for deep reflective work to be undertaken.

I hope all is well with you and your family as it has been a while since we have written. I have been engaging in the educational neuroscience studies and have been briefly entertained. Yet the deeper I go into "scientific studies" the more my heart seeks to return to deeper ways of knowing and being. Science still seems to me a false god, claiming much more power and knowledge than it deserves, and the song of the poet is calling deeply to me to return. I believe the brain, the body, and the spirit all grow through our language and our connections.

I am still at a "high achieving high school" and surrounded daily with the drill and kill of school. It pains my heart and stifles my soul. I have a student teacher from U of L who is saving my sanity with her fresh ideas and her open and evolving wisdom. We are navigating this pathway together as we seek to bring the human back into the humanities.

<u>Literacy Poem</u>

A child sits in the chair by the fire
Fully encompassed within the embrace of one who loves
Safely on her mother's lap pages of the book turn slowly as the Universe begins
To unfold within the chapters of the story of life

The child takes its place in the classroom on the hard plastic chairs
Sitting inside a little box that draws tight lines around the imagination
And the battle with reading begins as words become enemies
Demanding definitions, explanations, and right answers void of emotion
The memories of the embrace and the softly turning pages
Slowly begin to fade into empty nothingness

The high school student puts a head down violently on the desk
Tears of frustration threatening to overflow upon the pages
Eyes tightly closed holding back the frustration and fear
Of the literature that demands so much of them
When they have experienced so little of the story of life

Earth, air, water, and fire
Dancing slowly in a ring while the fairies sing
The magic embrace of the mother slowly turning the pages
Opening the portals to the alchemy of the Universe
Only to be slammed shut by this place we call school...

K

On Oct 6, 2018, at 3:10 PM, Leggo, Carl <carl.leggo@ubc.ca> wrote:

Hi, Kimberley,

Lovely to hear from you! Your poetic and pedagogic voices are strong and vibrant, as always!

I want to let you know some personal news. In July I was diagnosed with a brain tumor. I am currently on medical leave as I undergo an extensive series of chemotherapy treatments. I now spend about 5 to 6 days in the hospital every couple weeks. The treatments will likely continue till the new year. I have excellent medical support, and I hope that the treatments will be successful in sustaining me for some time!

My wife Lana is a wonderful support, and she walks beside me with courage and love.

I wish you and yours much joy in this season of autumn and thanksgiving.
Carl

On 2018-10-06, at 7:19 PM, Kimberley Holmes <kaholmes@ucalgary.ca> wrote:

My dear Carl,

I am saddened to hear you are facing some challenging obstacles, but I know with Lana beside you with courage and love you may overcome. I walked this journey with my best friend a few years back as her mother battled a brain tumor. The path is thorny and the treatment harsh and I send you prayers and love. We are truly blessed to live in Canada and have access to such a phenomenal medical system. They can give you the gift of time.

My mother is currently undergoing chemo for breast cancer. It is her third battle with cancer, but she still faces it with a determination and grace that amaze me. Her tenacity and will to live have sustained her through many difficult times. I believe you possess the same spirit.

I often wonder what it is that the Universe is trying to teach us through this complex process we call the human life. My eldest son, Tristan, still struggles with seizures. This has been our story for almost 11 years now as he is reaching the age of 17. Unfortunately, the seizures have caused some cognitive damage. His memory is compromised and his processing speed slow. Sometimes he completely loses his language, which terrifies me for the future. And yet, I hold on to the hope that we are much more than our biology, that our Essence—the very spirit of our Being—can somehow transcend what science tells us are impossible odds, and that we find our gifts because of the obstacles. Therefore, I refuse to hold science as my god and grant it only secondary status to something much greater. I must believe there is more than the mere physical being, and perhaps this is the lesson that I need to learn. I need to believe in the power of Spirit to guide us along.

I cannot begin to understand what you may go through, but my heart is with you every step of the way. In many ways, you are my hero. I was a lost poet, alone in the world and unsure of how to survive in a world I did not understand. You reached out to me and lifted me to a place where I could find my voice and understand myself. I cannot find the words to express my gratitude to you, and perhaps that is what I need to do the most. Thank you for being my Muse and helping me to find my voice to make whatever small mark I can make upon this world. You told me that poets call to one another—and they always answer.

Poets Calling

A clash or chromosomes and a new life has begun
Genetics swirling, mixing, merging to become
A living, breathing Being that will walk the Earth
Absorbing the vibrancy of the soil
Reaching daily for the sun

different An infant, a child, a teen, a parent, a grandparent
The cycle of life continues to swirl in never-ending
Circles of life and spirals of hope
The chromosomes mixing and blending into patterns
Creating versions of the common Essence

Each soul manifests in a unique way as the experiences unfold
The days make their impact upon our hearts and time wrinkles our faces
Our body grows old and tired and sometimes turns on itself
In strange and vicious ways that challenge our psyche

And make us question all that is and all that will ever be
As the questions swirl like the chromosomes of life
My breath quickens and I feel the stammering of my mind
Like a staccato hammer pounding out a never-ending rhythm
Of the complex cycle of life itself beating into my brain
Of pain, of sorrow, of laughter, of love, and of acceptance

A single poet calls out in sorrow seeking a familiar
And a strong answer is heard through the staccato stammer of the mind
Spirits swirl, synthesize, and harmonize their voices creating a common energy
As they seek the words and wisdom of the human story
My poets heart beats strongly as I recognize what I have always known

The stammer stabilizes and the symphony begins to seek a root
Deep within my heart where my Essence lies awaiting the calling
To join with another in prayer for strength on the journey
The chromosomes of the Muse bind tightly with the Other
Sending strength love and vibrancy
And breath....

Much love,

Kimberley

On Oct 6, 2018, at 10:59 PM, Leggo, Carl <carl.leggo@ubc.ca> wrote:

Beautiful wisdom, Kimberley!

We need to promote a holistic approach to understanding human being and becoming. One of the main reasons I love poetry is that poetry is capacious—there are no limits. Poetry opens multiple and complex ways of understanding and translating and creating.

Always hold fast to poetry,
Carl

From: Kimberley Holmes <kaholmes@ucalgary.ca>
Date: Monday, October 8, 2018 at 8:11 PM
To: "Leggo, Carl" <carl.leggo@ubc.ca>
Subject: Re: Connecting

Dear Carl,

I do believe that a holistic approach is critical. Each part of our being impacts the other, and the emotional, social, cognitive, and physical need to work in harmony. I have learned that in my neuroscience studies of the vagus nerve. I find it fascinating as it appears to be a superhighway between the brain and the gut or the "brain-gut axis." It is an important control center of the immune system and so much of disease and illness is connected to immune issues. My son's seizures are connected to inflammation in the central nervous system, so I think somehow connected to his "gut." What I find really intriguing is that "since the vagal tone is correlated with the capacity to regulate stress response and can be influenced by breathing, its increase through yoga and meditation likely contribute to resilience and the mitigation of mood and anxiety symptoms" (Breit, Kuperberg, & Hasler, 2018). Our mental health is influenced by the health of our gut and our gut directly impacted by our environment in so many ways.

I speculate this is somehow connected to the "flight or fight response" and stress. I wonder if our body manifests physical symptoms as a response to environmental or internal stress. An Elder taught me to "listen to my gut" as they believe this is the primary way of knowing and being. I need to spend time learning about these traditional ways of understanding the body and its messages. It is something embodied deep within us, and I believe poetry opens portals for translating and creating new meaning.

Body Speak

A deep rumbling within my intestines

And the hair on my arms begins to rise

A sharp flash of lightning and the roar of thunder

And my head begins to tingle of the impending change

My body listens to the energy of the Universe and waits

A child catches a virus and loses the ability to breathe

Tubes down his throat his voice is silenced

And when the body finally heals the voice remains absent
Violent seizures wrack the body screaming out in desperate ways
Attempting to heal the trauma of the spirit that was broken

A daughter watches
her mother take her last breath
And the bonds of a dysfunctional family are forever broken
Family conflict over estates and cash turn ugly
Broken trust results in a tumor growing in the breast
As the body speaks to the need to nurture and heal the wounds

The rumbling in my intestines continues as the Universe keeps tapping
Deep into my embodied ways of knowing and being in the world
The poetry falls from my fingers sending a silent prayer
For wholeness, for healing, for breathing and becoming
My body listens to the energy of the Universe and waits

ox

K

From: Leggo, Carl <carl.leggo@ubc.ca>
Sent: October 9, 2018 9:52 AM
To: Kimberley Holmes; Leggo, Carl
Subject: Re: Connecting

Thank you, Kimberley, for all this poetic wisdom.

I love the notion of "the vagus nerve." That speaks well to my cancer story.

Your poem is a clarion call to pay attention. I especially like the line:

"My body listens to the energy of the Universe and waits"

My 5th cycle of chemo at the BCCA went well. I returned home yesterday. A recent CT-Scan indicates that the tumor is much diminished.

In autumn sunlight,

Carl

From: Kimberley Holmes <kaholmes@ucalgary.ca>
Date: Tuesday, October 9, 2018 at 8:18 PM
To: "Leggo, Carl" <carl.leggo@ubc.ca>
Subject: Re: Connecting

Dear Carl,

That is wonderful news that the tumor is much diminished!! I am glad the chemo is going well and not taking a toll on your spirit. Thinking about this I was intrigued by the origin of the root chemo. It can be traced to the meanings "chemical, chemically induced and chemistry." Chemistry has two meanings. One is the branch of science that deals with the identification of the substances of which matter is composed; the investigation of their properties and the ways they combine, interact and change; and the use of these processes to form new substances. The other is the complex emotional or psychological interaction between two people. I found this fascinating. If our bodies can combine, interact, and change, and this is somehow connected to complex emotional interactions between the Self and the Other, perhaps it is not the radiation that causes the tumor to shrink but the trinity of the body, mind, and spirit combined with our interaction with others. Even more intriguing is the etymology of chemistry. It appears to have been derived from the ancient Egyptian name of alchemy meaning blackness. Thereby, alchemy is the black art or a type of mystical transformation of one thing to another. Traditionally, literature, specifically poetry, takes us to a place of darkness prior to finding light, or hope.

I was struck by the phrase "your cancer story." I wonder if all illness is indeed an embodied story, perhaps of trauma or other conflict, that eventually manifests and actualizes itself. Griffin and Griffin (1994) speak of the connection between the alignments of the mind and those of the body. As our systems are so intricately connected these stories weave through the very fiber of our physical, emotional, and social being. If we "rewrite" that story, can we change the interaction that is resulting in the chemical interaction? Can we switch the chemical response of our bodies from darkness to light? The neurosciences opened my eyes to the concept of epigenetics, which literally means "on top of genetics." Our genetic code is hardwired in our physical being, but whether that code is turned off and on is completely determined by our environments and our experiences. Hence nurture can play a much larger role in our nature. Trauma in our lives results in unfortunate epigenetic manifestations, which often result in illness. I wonder if once we have turned on the gene we also have the power to turn it off? How much of our physical destiny is determined by our conscious will to survive and overcome? Can the body speak of our illness, and through the recognition of the voice begin to heal itself? Is this the essence of language and poetry—a portal to human healing?

Last night, under the glow of the full moon Tristan had the strangest seizure. He was aware it was happening and tried to talk to me through it. His body was sweating profusely, and his heart was racing. As he pulled himself out of it, he announced, "I am back." He then proceeded to have a detailed conversation with me about "observing" the seizure as it was happening to him. In theory, he has temporal lobe epilepsy, which should impact language and result in a significant amount of time where he was unresponsive. This was not the case. I am trying to understand how he could go from a full seizure to having a calm conversation about the experience only a few moments later. I am really starting to wonder if his body is simply processing his medical trauma in the only way it knows how. It almost seems like he "reboots" himself, as today he is bright eyed and engaged with the world.

Perhaps illness is a reminder to us to live. My mother is currently in Arizona for 3 weeks before she starts her next round of chemo. She decided she was "done with traveling" but changed her mind once the cancer returned and is off living her life. Perhaps illness only serves to help us recognize the beauty of the present moment and the body needs to "heal itself" to allow it to fully live. My thoughts are deep tonight under the glow of the autumn moon. It seems the moon is challenging me to recognize the cycles and seasons from brief to full manifestation.

A child arrives into this world and takes its first breath

Lungs bursting with pressure the glare of the world overwhelming

The small human that arrives to embrace all the glory of this complex

Journey we call the human story

Then the novelty begins to fade, and breath is taken for granted

Days fall into night and each precious moment does not seem so special

Life becomes a routine, a task, something to be completed

And the glory fades to empty nothingness

Out out brief candle shining on the softly lighted stage
A whisper, a breath, a sigh of discontent
And the stage is left to dusty darkness
Where all the actors fail to dwell

The wind whispers across the prairies
Calling out its lonely cries
Embrace each precious moment
It is a gift to be alive

The moon whispers her silent message
As she reflects the warmth and majesty of the sun
Beware the illusions of nothingness for nothing is everything
As everything soon becomes One

K

From: Leggo, Carl <carl.leggo@ubc.ca>
Sent: October 10, 2018 9:45:09 AM
To: Kimberley Holmes; Leggo, Carl
Subject: Re: Connecting

Fascinating, Kimberley!

Your etymological understanding of "chemo" opens many rich possibilities.

We need to understand more how "story" and "poetry" can heal our bodies and hearts and psyches.

I can only imagine how Tristan's complex experience occupies him and you and your whole family. Continue to record and research and interpret Tristan's story. I have been reading a lot about cancer, and it is fascinating to realize how cancer has been understood historically, and how cancer is understood today. I am grateful for contemporary cancer research and knowledge. As you write beautifully in your poem, "It is a gift to be alive."

With autumn rhythms,

Carl

From: Kimberley Holmes <kaholmes@ucalgary.ca>
Date: Wednesday, October 10, 2018 at 2:04 PM
To: "Leggo, Carl" <carl.leggo@ubc.ca>
Subject: Re: Connecting

Dear Carl,

Yes, Tristan's story impacts us all and is intricately wound with my own story. I did not realize when you have a child that your heart splits and begins to live in another body. The responsibility is daunting and the pain deep. It is such a raw human experience unlike anything else and daily takes my breath away.

I have a Zen den attached to my English classroom. It is a small room with fairy lights, a sofa, a soft carpet, and pillows. A salt lamp and a singing bowl are available as well as coloring books and other ways to unwind and release stress. Daily it is used by many students seeking solitude, craving warmth, and simply trying to find a sacred space within the complexity of high school. It is amazing how many of them gather in this small space and sit in silence together.

As I type this my son Tristan is sleeping in the Zen den attached to my English room while I quietly teach my English class about the human experience. He came to me half an hour ago with a severe headache wanting to go home. Instead I put him in the Zen den with earplugs and a blanket.

I wonder what associating school as a "safe place" will do for his overall health and wellness. For many years school has been a hostile and unwelcoming environment. Many students at Abe use our Zen den, but this is Tristan's first visit. Perhaps a coincidence, perhaps a message for me to pay attention. I cannot help but think of Gadamer

and his thesis that "understanding begins when something addresses us." I am strongly being addressed by the need for wellness, the need for wholeness, the need for safety, and the need to find a space and place to belong. This is the world we need to create for our children and for ourselves.

My grade 10 class is watching The Way as we have just finished reading The Alchemist. I am trying to get them to understand the journey and the precious nature of each day. The refrain "gather ye rosebuds" keeps running through my head, and the irony that my first-born sleeps in the "Zen den" attached to my classroom is not lost on me. I need to do this work.

Imagine a world where everyone is cared for
When the cries of sorrow are clearly heard
When pain in the body and the mind is clearly recognized
And acknowledged as part of our human journey

Imagine a world where grades did not matter
And children embraced the magic of learning just because
To understand the pilgrimage of life itself
Without worksheets, stress, tests, and constant evaluation

Imagine a school where we care for each child
As if they were all our own flesh and blood
As each spirit grew and found the patterns of their lives
Their bodies, their minds, their spirits
Imagine
I sit silently and wonder and listen
Waiting for the voices in my head
To speak

K

On Oct 11, 2018, at 12:08 PM, Leggo, Carl <carl.leggo@ubc.ca> wrote:

I am glad, Kimberley, that you live with family and students and colleagues in creative and hopeful and heartful ways. I am intrigued by your creation of the Zen den. We all need such spaces. Continue to live with the conviction that we can create possibilities for healing and health in the world. I admire your spirit!

Onward, Carl

From: Kimberley Holmes <kaholmes@ucalgary.ca>
Date: Thursday, October 11, 2018 at 9:08 PM
To: "Leggo, Carl" <carl.leggo@ubc.ca>
Subject: Re: Connecting

Dear Carl,

My family and students are indeed creative and hopeful, but alas my colleagues still a work in progress. They are too tied to the traditional ideologies of the factory model and unwilling to recognize the teaching of the heart. There are small pockets of hope that breathe life into a tired system each day, so I need to remind myself to nurture those pockets, to fill them with breath, and to bring them to life. Education is filled with bitterness and disillusion, which takes a toll on the heart of those who understand the true essence of pedagogical power. It is important we seek others who understand and connect with an ideology of hope and creation. I am reading David Smith's (2014) work *Teaching as a Practice of Wisdom* and am finding new energy. In the introduction he asks, "If education and teaching basically concern the stories we tell the young about life, what are the stories that need to be told today?" What story needs to be told about wellness, about wisdom traditions, and about what it means to live well in a convoluted, complicated, and chaotic world? What investigations about the mind and its role in human suffering need to be undertaken, and how can we protect the Spirit from the illusions of the matrix of the mind? Such a complex story and yet one so worthy of being whispered around the circles of a community. What is the story of wellness and wisdom, and how shall we ensure that the ending is vibrant? So many stories I seek to understand, to embody the connection between the story and the body in order to seek a place of sanctuary and healing.

The Zen den is a remarkable space. It was created last year by two of my grade 12 students who both suffered from serious anxiety issues. For both, the anxiety was a direct result of medical trauma. They wanted to create a safe space where students could retreat and breathe. It is used daily for stress, panic attacks, and sometime quite severe trauma.

The young lady who claimed sanctuary there today is one week out of serious brain surgery. I am struggling to comprehend why she was even at school, as she clearly is still impacted by pain and filled full of drugs. With glassy eyes she tearfully told me she was "worried she would get behind in her studies and needed to push herself to get going." Her parents, both educated professionals, had gone to work, and I needed to phone them to remind them their daughter needed care and should be home resting. I am struggling with this immensely. What type of society have we created where we feel school is more important than recovering from life-threatening surgery? The young lady has put this immense pressure on herself as she needs to maintain her "perfect" status. Her beautiful long hair covers the scar that runs from her spine to the top of her head. The perfectly fashionable cashmere hat covered all signs of the surgery, and she looked as if she had just walked off the pages of a magazine. The image was a stark reminder of what can be hidden inside the physical form, as her pain, her sorrow, and her post-traumatic stress was clearly bubbling frantically around her soul. We sat together on the sofa of the Zen den and cried deep tears, and then she settled down for a nap in our sacred space. I was struck by the fact that my own son slept on the same sofa just one day prior, also with issues of the mind and the brain. Schools need to be sacred spaces where brains not only can grow but can heal....

These are the messages that come to me daily, so I must continue to live with the conviction that we can create possibilities for health and healing. I must continue to believe, to create, and to care; otherwise I shall slip into the "empty nothingness of the stage of life."

I have no poetry at my fingertips today other than some Shakespearean refrains. My eyes are heavy and my spirit tired. I have spent the week caring for my own family and for those who needed me. Today, I have given all I have to give, and the poetry is silent. I shall draw the warm waters of a bath and release myself into relaxation. Tomorrow is another day, and I must keep myself strong to be able to help heal Others.

I admire your spirit and your courage as you face your own adversity. You have inspired mine.

Bravely paying careful attention to the messages,

Kimberley

From: Leggo, Carl <carl.leggo@ubc.ca>
Sent: October 12, 2018 10:08:52 AM
To: Kimberley Holmes; Leggo, Carl
Subject: Re: Connecting

Hi, Kimberley,

Your compassion for others is a wonderful gift! Always live with this generosity of spirit!

David Smith is an immensely wise voice in education scholarship. We need to hold fast to David's wisdom.

Continue to nurture the Zen den—every classroom needs such a space and opportunity for contemplation.

With care,

Carl

From: Kimberley Holmes <kaholmes@ucalgary.ca>
Date: Friday, October 12, 2018 at 3:05 PM
To: "Leggo, Carl" <carl.leggo@ubc.ca>
Subject: Re: Connecting

Dear Carl,

I have just looked up the root of compassion, which is *pati*, which means to suffer. Alas, I fear it is the world of the artist to suffer immensely, as we see all the things in the world that are dark. It can also mean you have feeling or sympathy, and in the Catholic Church, the Passion refers to the suffering and death of Christ by crucifixion. This signals the rebirth if you remain pure and true. A rebirth is what I am seeking.

Yesterday, as I was teaching Timothy Findley's *The Wars* and the allusion to David and Goliath, I realized some significant gaps in interpretive discourse. Hence today we began viewing *Narnia*. My students are rapidly picking up the connections and excited about their new understanding of complex literary texts, and I am realizing the significance of hermeneutics. Our ability to translate and interpret our world is such a way of being. Perhaps it is time for me to review the work of Aristotle and other philosophical works to seek the signs of truth. Perhaps we need to go back instead of rushing blindly forward in a frenzied race to an unidentified destination.

Today my staff met with our Superintendent. He is leaving the system, so his answers to complex questions were raw, authentic, and mindful. When queries about grades and validity were brought up his response was "to get over it and go forward with the work." I could barely contain my glee, but the message was lost. A chorus of "grades do matter" was heard through the crowd, specifically strong from the math and science people. The concept of learning and authentic intellectual work was lost, and hence I return tonight to the work of Smith, Steinberg, Friesen, and yourself to guide me. Critical pedagogy is calling me.

I want to live my life poetically, with passion, and with wonder, but the cave dwellers keep smothering me underneath the shadows. I cannot help but remember that Socrates was eventually killed on his quest to bring humanity to an understanding of the light, yet the spark in my students calls for me to keep the flame alive and burning strong. It is difficult work, and I find myself retreating to my own mentors seeking answers or perhaps affirmations of what I already know to be true. I also find myself drawn to the new generation of teachers who see the world differently than the current regime, and I hope that soon they will take the front line. I hope.

Push yourself to the limit to achieve that perfect grade

While knowledge and wisdom of the deeper meaning will continue

To elude you

Hold tight to the shadow and believe they are your God

While the sunlight dances complex patterns just outside the entrance

Do you really believe that grades have caused you to be successful?

Have you considered what it is that you have learned?

Do you find your heart is still yearning for some answers?

That we still have so much more to learn?

Take me back into the mystical forests of Narnia

And help me avoid the temptations of the Queen

Although hot chocolate and Turkish delight excite me

The world is not always what it seems

Lucy remind me of the magic of the world we hold deep inside

The poetry and the patterns of all our lives combined

Hold fast to that vision and keep the perpetual dream alive

Dreams and imagination are what keep the soul alive

I shall think more about contemplation and the role it plays in education. I shall think more about the need to examine my life.

K

From: Leggo, Carl <carl.leggo@ubc.ca>
Sent: October 13, 2018 10:29:13 AM
To: Kimberley Holmes; Leggo, Carl
Subject: Re: Connecting

Hi, Kimberley,

I have now spent 60 years in schools, as a student and a teacher, and I have learned that I cannot change the typical culture of education. I offer what I am called to offer, and I live what I am called to live. Many of my colleagues disagree with me, as I disagree with them. My calling is to speak in a voice that is creative, critical, compassionate, and courageous.

We have perhaps spoken about the connections between trauma/wound/blessing. Gregory Orr (2002) writes about the connections in his memoir The Blessing.

Here are a few notes from Orr, who teaches me constantly:

"In French, the verb blesser means to 'wound'" (3).

"... the Old English bletsian which meant 'to sprinkle with blood'" (3)

"To wound, to confer spiritual power, to sprinkle with blood" (4).

"... stories are where human meanings begin" (28).

"... irony, that mode in which the head mocks the heart and bares its intellectual teeth at what it sees as a hostile world" (128).

"a yearning for intimacy" (140)

"... what I felt when I wrote my first, clumsy poem was that the words were creating a world, not describing a preexisting one" (143-144).

"I understood some things now, but also felt I understood nothing" (204).

"... this is art's way of fighting—to stand very still. This is art's way of fighting—not to do battle, but to concentrate emphatic being in an object" (207).

Hold fast to your poetry and to living poetically!

Carl

From: Kimberley Holmes <kaholmes@ucalgary.ca>
Date: Sunday, October 14, 2018 at 7:12 PM
To: "Leggo, Carl" <carl.leggo@ubc.ca>
Subject: Re: Connecting

Dear Carl,

I have spent the weekend reflecting on your thoughts. It struck something within me, and as I look out at the pink candy cane swirls of the evening autumn sunset, I am ready to respond. Sixty years in schools and I wonder how much has really changed. When I think of my own 47 years in schools, I wonder if children today are doing much as I did or something entirely different. The novel choices and readings on the curriculum remain much the same, yet the context is vastly different. Yet perhaps some of us always were and always will be writing poetry.

My need to express what "I am called to offer and live what I am called to live" is very strong. I fought school from a very young age, the box was too tight, the pace was too slow, and the rules too rigid. As a teacher, I fought to break all those binding elements of my childhood. It too is my calling to use my voice in creative, critical, compassionate, and courageous ways. I often feel my heartbeat quicken and my body respond when I know I need to speak. I almost feel like I am shaking right down to my soul, bursting forth with words that need to be uttered and actualized.

The trinity of the connections between trauma/wound and blessing speak to my poet's soul, and I often think of words as bleeding on the paper. I have never questioned my use of the metaphor, yet now I wonder if somewhere deep inside I understood the essence of the undertaking. When I work in poetry it does dig into old wounds, bring things to the surface of my consciousness, and sometimes metaphorically and physically brings me to my knees. A part of me weeps my Essence through the fingertips and into the words as they spiral in patterns of often unrecognized meaning.

Stories have always called to me. Joseph Campbell spoke to me as an undergrad, and much later I realized the connection to the yoga teaching and the wisdom philosophies as I sought other ways of understanding the human journey and ways of being in the world. This is where it all began for me as my heart overruled my head in a deep type of yearning, which I now recognize as the powerful call to intimacy. It was a yearning that I do not understand, and even as the words materialize on the paper, I am unsure of their meaning and their power. I just know they need to leave the sanctuary of my body and actualize in the world somewhere, somehow.

I have ordered The Blessing and look forward to unpacking its messages. In the meantime, I shall finish Smith and perhaps revisit Aoki. I feel as if I am seeking old friends, rediscovering meaning, and trying to make myself somehow whole. Yet perhaps before this can fully happen, I need to bleed. I think I shall write a found poem tonight.

The Passion

When I was a child my emotions ran deep and violent
Terrified of being left alone and filled with a passion far beyond my age
The emotional hurricane threatened to overcome my small being
And I hid under the magic cover of my sheets until the swirling winds subsided

When I was a teenager my thoughts and energy flew
Rapidly around rooms in a never-ending frenzy of seeking something
That somehow seemed beyond my reach and unlike any Other
And although surrounded by many Others I often walked alone
Within the raging fluctuations of the mind

When I was a young woman, I thought that I had all answers
Running was my God as the physical exhaustion stomped out all demons
Rote regurgitation and mindless memory tasks filled the contemplative hours
The emotions often hidden with only occasional violent rages
As I thought the tempest tamed and the mental toil endured

When I became a mother, I understood "the ways the head torment the heart
And how my "intellectual teeth" could not fend off the hostile world and I began to bleed
My children are my blessing yet also my deeply embodied wound
As every time they struggle "tiny sprinkles of my blood" gather in painful puddles on the floor
As my mother's heart beats the patterns of our interconnected stories

I can no longer hide beneath the covers, seek shelter in my books, or run into the rage

As I begin to recognize the spiritual power that comes from such emotion

That allows me to "sprinkle my blood" upon a deep infested wound

And allow the blood of Life to grant harmonious and heartfelt healing

Now instead of hiding I reach for that intimacy knowing it may wound me

Understanding that I may understand but feel I understand nothing

That if I stand very still and listen to the careful whispers of the Blessing

Bitter battle will no longer be required and my "head will no longer mock my heart"

With voice, with poetry, with acceptance

K

From: Leggo, Carl <carl.leggo@ubc.ca>
Sent: October 15, 2018 9:51 AM
To: Kimberley Holmes; Leggo, Carl
Subject: Re: Connecting

Hi, Kimberley,

You have packed a lifetime of living/questioning/examining into your words.

As a person who is almost 65 years old, especially a person now living with cancer and an uncertain future, I find that many of the questions I once lingered with are no longer as pressing as they were. I am now more contemplative, still, quiet, even complacent. I know little changes, but that does not stop me from promoting possibilities for change. I admire your commitment to reaching for "intimacy." Perhaps that is what we are always seeking in our commitment to living poetically—how to live intimately in our relationship with others, with the land, with schools, with colleagues, with students, with parents, with children, etc.

In the pursuit of living intimately, Carl

From: Kimberley Holmes <kaholmes@ucalgary.ca>
Date: Tuesday, October 16, 2018 at 8:30 PM
To: "Leggo, Carl" <carl.leggo@ubc.ca>
Subject: Re: Connecting

Dear Carl,

My questions seem to bubble over all at once, and then I am left with silence. I can only observe what it might be like living with cancer. My mother is currently somewhere in Arizona, perhaps Vegas, between her chemo treatments. I hope she is living her life to the fullest and enjoying the time she has left—the future is indeed uncertain. I have done some research on the roots of cancer. I did not realize how long it has been part of our human story. It seems to be much like the brain, in that it is a complicated thing that is impacted by a diversity of factors both internally and externally. I speculate I too carry the cancer crab in my genetics so perhaps it is time to let go of some of the things that I ponder and turn more inward. I found your use of "complacent" striking. I wonder how I would live my life differently if I remained unaware of any dangers or deficiencies. How much of our life is governed by our use of language, and our intent? Maybe intimacy is what requires my focus now. The building of close relationships, the gathering of tribes, and the creation of communities. Yet that intimacy also comes with a deep vulnerability. I think the vulnerability is what I am afraid of because somehow my cultural experiences have taught me that it is a weakness.

I just finished a soccer match with my senior girls' team. They were lacking a coach, so I took them for a season, as many years ago I was quite accomplished at the sport. I had forgotten the energy that can be created as a pack of young women work together to accomplish a goal. As we scored the winning goal to take us to the city final, they leaped into each other's arms and danced with joy. It is just a game, but the players are a type of tribe. They belong to each other, to their school, and to their community, even if it is only for that magical moment that will be etched into their human memory for an eternity.

No poetry tonight. I have spent too much time in my head thinking. Tonight, I need to sit quietly with my family.

With reflection,

K

From: Leggo, Carl <carl.leggo@ubc.ca>
Sent: October 17, 2018 11:06 AM
To: Kimberley Holmes; Leggo, Carl
Subject: Re: Connecting

Your message is full of poetry, Kimberley!

Poetry is everywhere! We just don't always recognize it.

My granddaughter Madeleine has been part of a soccer team for several years. Her dad is the coach. All my granddaughters are athletic and active and enthusiastic for play.

May we all learn to be more vulnerable in the ways we need to be.

With heart,

Carl

On 2018-10-17, at 7:27 PM, Kimberley Holmes <kaholmes@ucalgary.ca> wrote:

Dear Carl,

Yes, I suppose I do communicate in poetic transcripts all the time. It has become my way of walking in the world as I play in the possibility of word and images. My awareness of the imaginative pull of the images, my call to patterns and rhythms, is not something I learned but somehow something that is transcribed deep inside of me. For whatever reason my senses are attuned to this method of communication.

I wonder how one might learn to be more vulnerable. We are not naturally inclined to open to any type of aggressive action, and this is what I think of when I think of being vulnerable. I think of it as a type of exposure, rendering us defenceless in the world. I have spent many years building up my armor around me, to protect from those that might destroy. The heart of the poet bleeds deeply, so it is quite susceptible to wounds. Yet, we have uncovered a wound that in fact can be a type of a blessing, which leaves me somewhat perplexed.

We finished studying *Narnia* today in my grade 12 class and were reminded, "he who is not a traitor cannot die on the stone tablet" and that "things always work according to their nature." Tomorrow we return to Findley's *The Wars* to reflect on the ideas of life, as when Rodwell writes to his daughter, "I am alive in everything I touch. Touch these pages and you have me in your fingertips. We survive in one another. Everything lives forever."

I think I shall focus my week on touching....

Reflecting on being alive,

K

From: Leggo, Carl <carl.leggo@ubc.ca>
Sent: October 18, 2018 10:23 PM
To: Kimberley Holmes
Cc: Leggo, Carl
Subject: Re: Connecting

Hi, Kimberley,

I am in the BC Cancer Agency for a 6th and final chemo treatment. I will then spend much of November and December in the hospital as I undergo a stem cell transplant process.

I am very vulnerable, and I have no sense of control or authority over my vulnerability. Instead, I embrace my vulnerability. I am growing old, and embracing vulnerability impresses me as a wise way of living. (Check out the etymology of vulnerable.)

Continue to teach your students Lewis and Findley—the kind of authors who can guide us in precarious times!

Reveling in autumn possibilities,

Carl

On 2018-10-19, at 10:27 PM, Kimberley Holmes <kaholmes@ucalgary.ca> wrote:

Dear Carl,

I am glad to hear that you are in the final round of chemo but sad you will spend much of November and December in the hospital. Yet I know these are places we go to heal the festering of a wound, and all will be well again soon. I find it intriguing the term hospital originally referred to "a shelter for the needy" and "an institution for sick or wounded people." Hence a place where we go seeking shelter to heal the wounds of the body, the mind, and the spirit.

This thought flashes me back to 11 years ago when I spent much of November and December in the Children's hospital with my then 6-year-old son who was struggling to breathe. I can still hear in my nightmares the gasping wheeze as he fought to keep his small body alive. We were admitted on November 18th, ironically his 6th birthday, and were released sometime in December. I don't remember what day it was as time stood still for a while, my whole concept of what was important was drastically altered, and days merged into weeks without any semblance of rational or logical thought. All that was previously deemed significant rapidly represented empty nothingness in the face of true adversity.

The one thing I do remember is that the day we were released to go home somehow the main floor of the hospital had morphed into Christmas. It was like some sort of bizarre holiday special storyline that Tristan and I had become the characters of. I remember thinking how cliché it all was, yet my faith in the magic of Christmas temporarily helped me work my way through the wounds that were deep in my heart, wounds that still bleed. That promise of some type of magical renewal helped me move forward, although it was slow and careful movement.

I realize now the impact of stress that echoes endlessly throughout my body. I still wake in the night with my heart beating rapidly, my mind stammering in panic, and the urge to rush to my son's bedside and verify that he is indeed alive. This was magnified by the onset and the continuation of the seizures. Today we were at the Children's hospital for his monthly IVIG. Once every 28 days, he receives the purified blood of others to keep him strong and stop the inflammation from attacking his brain. The "cure" for his illness lies in the "bleeding" of others to aid in the healing of his wounds. It is human life blood that gives us back our lives and makes us both less vulnerable. For this gift, I am eternally grateful yet remain cautiously vulnerable. I cannot yet embrace vulnerability.

Perhaps we are all vulnerable at points in our life and need to make a conscious choice regarding how to face the demon. My mother and you now face a frightening nemesis who threatens to consume you both. Yet, I watch you both embrace the beauty of life and bravely face the lack of control, the endless medical appointments, and the uncertain future. I observe your collective faith and fortitude. I find this awe-inspiring in the truest sense of reverential respect and a sense of wonder. Perhaps one day I shall reach this point of wisdom but not yet. I am not yet ready to go that deep, my wounds are not yet healed, and the rawness still threatens to consume me. Hence, I seek for ways to control my world, even though I know in my heart I cannot.

I cannot help but ponder how often I have tried to control the future, to maintain a sense of power and determine outcomes that were far beyond my ability to manipulate. I am not ready to embrace my vulnerability but perhaps to reflect on its role in my story.

Vulnerability is a state of being exposed to the possibility being attacked, physically or emotionally. The origin, *vulnus*, is a wound. Hence it is a state of wounding, hurting, of injury. To embrace vulnerability would be to embrace the pain suffered from the affliction of the wound, to remember that feeling pains means that we are still very much alive. The fact that we are alive is a remarkable thing, but often we forget what a precious gift it is to simply take in a deep breath and accept what each moment has to offer us. We forget that this is all there really is, and all that will ever be. Hence the need to have literature to guide us through uncertain times, to remind us that there is always hope, and that in spite of the darkness, somewhere in the shadows hidden deep lies a glimmer of everlasting light.

My high school team won silver tonight. There were tears of disappointment, there were hugs of support, and there was laughter. I remembered my own high school days of glory, the teammates I shared them with, and the memories that we created. We are alive. I sent an email to old high school friends tonight and let them know I thought of them, and my memories brought me joy.

Alive

The goal crosses the finish line and the screams of the crowd reach a frenzy

While the opposing team falls to their knees in horrified despair

As they feel the victory falling from their fingertips

And their glory fading into but a memory of what could have been

The IV tube drips slowly and the machine continues its droning beep
The chill in the air is palpable and the aroma of depression strong
The mind begins to stammer, and the spirit begins to slip
As the glory of what could have been merges into the shadows

The defeated team gathers in a circle arms embraced around each other
Sweat dripping from their efforts and the defeat still a sharp sting
Yet the victory is now something much much greater than a goal
The glory beyond the pitch into an interconnected memory

The IV tube is filled with the essence, that luminous liquid gift of life
The chill in the air begins to slowly warm as illumination glows
The mind begins to brighten, to reset, rejuvenate, and to renew
The shadows of darkness slowly slipping into the embrace of the sun
Sending you sunbeams and healing,

K

On Oct 21, 2018, at 9:31 AM, Leggo, Carl <carl.leggo@ubc.ca> wrote:

Hi, Kimberley,

Have you considered writing a memoir with your son about your lives with illness?

As James Hillman knows, it takes a long time to grow into our characters.

We all live with vulnerability. We all need to determine how we are going to respond to vulnerability. I choose to look at the wound. I have no choice.

I think your soccer team was quite successful. We can't all win all the time, but if we play with conviction and enthusiasm, we play with the spirit of winners.

I admire your notion of "interconnected memory." If we could focus on the interconnected memories of all creatures and all creation, we could learn to live together with hope and dignity and love.

Hold fast to the energies of intellect and heart and body and spirit, the energies that fire you with devotion in both words and world.

Carl

On 2018-10-21, at 9:28 PM, Kimberley Holmes <kaholmes@ucalgary.ca> wrote:

Dear Carl,

I have pieces of memoir work braided in almost everything that I write. My words are not disconnected from my story, and one feeds the other. I did a "novella" in a class with David Jones when I was just starting my doctoral journey. The writing is primitive as my voice had not yet emerged, but the memories encoded for future visitation. Kara and I braided our teaching stories based on our lived experiences, and the publication should be almost ready to be actualized in Emerald Journal. This was the piece we wrote for the Creative Curriculum conference, and we would one day like to "perform" it, as it is truly oral learning. It requires human voice to capture the essence of the experiences.

I would love to write with Tris, but language is one of the areas that are of challenge. Both oral and written exploration are a struggle for him due to possible damage sustained from ongoing seizure activity. This breaks my heart in many ways as language is my portal to help others. For the moment, this portal is limited for us, but perhaps I could try to bring his own voice out through my own. His loss of language has been a deep struggle.

I have strong cynicism for both education and health care in my story. Perhaps, I am seeking a resolution of some sort around this, which is why I also hesitate to write my memoir. A part of me craves a happy ending, and there is not one for this story. The struggle is still daily, the pain still present, and the battle continues to rage on against the injustice of a badly broken system. But then again, happy endings are not real. Real life is vulnerable and a struggle and yes, I need to determine how to respond to that struggle in a way that feeds my spirit. I need to take the darkness and lead towards the light somehow, but currently the shadows still threaten to smother me.

Interconnectivity in memories and experiences is something I crave. So often I feel I walk alone, in charge of situations and experiences that I have no control over. The vulnerability is immense, so I hide behind my costumes of clothing, make-up, and bravado. It is my armor that protects all that is soft and fragile within me. My writing exposes all that is fragile within. Then I might break into a thousand tiny fragmented pieces and be unable to care for those who need me. Responsibility stops me from going too deeply into my thoughts. If I shatter, those I care for might shatter with me.

I am not familiar with James Hillman. I shall look at his work and see if he can help me grow into my character and help me find the courage to tell my story. The story does need voice, yet I still feel too vulnerable. If I actualize its existence, my costumes may no longer protect me. I shall need to find stronger alchemy to take me through this part of the journey. Perhaps I will revisit my original memoir to see if it will foster the growth of the real one...one that explores living with hope, dignity, and love in vibrantly interconnected webs of life.

Living with illness is a deep and complex process. It terrifies me in many ways, and I believe I am afraid to give the illness voice. Yet, it does speak—it is part of our story.

Nasty migraine today. Not sure if it is living with crazy Calgary weather fluctuations or my body's way of telling me I need rest and deeper connection.

I will write memoir soon. It will fall from my fingers in pieces, and then I will braid the strands together to seek meaning. It will be hard.

K

From: Leggo, Carl <carl.leggo@ubc.ca>
Sent: October 21, 2018 11:07 PM
To: Kimberley Holmes
Cc: Leggo, Carl
Subject: Re: Connecting

Hi, Kimberley,

I appreciate your concerns and reservations and hopes and desires for your researching, writing, teaching, and parenting. You are invested in "living poetically," and this way of living will always hold challenges and blessings. All your writing is threaded through and inspirited by your living stories. I think you should always focus on who you are as you write about the ways you navigate the world in words. I know you are always writing about who you are, but I encourage you to write with an abiding sense of confidence and conviction in your wisdom, generated in a lifetime of loving scholarship.

Your voice is needed!

Breathing autumn rhythms,

Carl

From: Kimberley Holmes <kaholmes@ucalgary.ca>
Date: Monday, October 22, 2018 at 8:00 PM
To: "Leggo, Carl" <carl.leggo@ubc.ca>
Subject: Re: Connecting

Dear Carl,

I am invested in "living poetically" in a world more interested in efficiency. The oxymoron present between my way of being in the world and the world I live in often exhausts me. Calgary is such a corporate frenzy where the need to climb to the top circumvents wellness. We seem to avoid any type of authentic human connection by keeping perpetually busy with tasks that signify very little. Perhaps why the level of disengagement and unhappiness is so high.

I need to write daily and carefully reflect upon the complexities of my journey, yet time is my nemesis. It is always evening before I have time to reflect, and then my energy is low. It seems like I am needed in so many spaces and places by so many people that there is just not enough of me left over at the end of the day. I crave lazy mornings, strong coffee, and time to sit at my computer and birth what needs to emerge. There is something pushing deep inside me that needs to evolve and actualize.

I know this is something that I need to do, and I am focusing on finding a way to clear some space for creativity and renewal. For without poetry and art I am not truly alive. Only when I am writing and teaching about writing do I feel like I am closer to my purpose for being. I have looked up James Hillman and will spend some time with *The Soul's Code*. Perhaps this will aid me in the process of my voice's emergence as I read, seek, and wonder.

Today my English 30 class focused on what does it mean to be alive and what does it mean to be a human being. They struggled to answer these questions as we have taught them to memorize interconnected bits but never asked them to consider who they are. It comes as no surprise they are a lost generation seeking community and connection.

Where does one start a memoir? Where does the memory begin, and how do we know where to end? There are so many pieces, so many threads that I am not sure which one to pick up and explore. I need to sit in silence for a while and listen for my voices to speak.

With reflections on the moonlight,

K

From: Leggo, Carl <carl.leggo@ubc.ca>
Sent: October 23, 2018 9:43:00 AM
To: Kimberley Holmes; Leggo, Carl
Subject: Re: Connecting

Good-morning, Kimberley,

Yesterday I returned home from my 6th and final cycle of chemotherapy at the BC Cancer Agency. Much of November and December will be occupied with preparations and processes for stem cell transplanting. I am hopeful that I am on a healing journey!

Continue to seek ways to write in the midst of your busy life. We will almost always find time. It seems insufficient for our purposes, but, of course, the time we have is the time we have. I am currently on medical leave, and I have so much more time than I typically have, but I am also much more tired, and so I sleep much more than ever. Also, I find myself in strange situations like yesterday where I spent almost 7 hours waiting for doctors to attend to me. I sat quietly in anticipation, but I did not have the will to read or write. Time moved slowly, and I floated with it.

Our calling is to live with the kind of commitments that sustain us and those who are close to us.

Carl

From: Kimberley Holmes <kaholmes@ucalgary.ca>
Date: Tuesday, October 23, 2018 at 8:06 PM
To: "Leggo, Carl" <carl.leggo@ubc.ca>
Subject: Re: Connecting

Dear Carl,

I am glad to hear you have finished your final cycle of chemo. I am intrigued by the stem cell transplanting. I was just researching the process and again am struck by the ability of the human body to heal itself. Your new healthy cells will indeed put you on a path to healing, much like the donated blood plasma heals my son.

Are you using your own stem cells, or do you have a donor?

As I reflect on the full moon outside my window, I wonder about all the possibilities we have for healing and going forward. The moon is luminous in her appearance tonight and seems to be sending me silent messages of hope, of connection, and of strength. I feel the need to bathe under her gaze and take in the wisdom that seems to be pouring off her surface.

In Ashtanga yoga, we do not practice during times of the full and the new moon. They are observed as holidays or "holy days" where we take rest. It is a day to rejuvenate and contemplate. On the days of the moon, the sun and the moon are aligned in such a matter that they exert a greater gravitational force on the planet. This force affects us as human beings and can impact us mentally and physically. As human beings, we are comprised of a great deal of water, and all things affected by water are affected by the phases of the moon.

Honor your body's need to rest and be still. You are preparing for the next phase. Earth, air, water, and fire are all part of an intricate balance. Your chemo treatments have put you through a literal and metaphorical fire as you fight this parasite that has entered your being. Now you need to move slowly and float while you wait for homeostasis to return.

The elements of life surround us all. Earth, air, water fire....

From: Leggo, Carl <carl.leggo@@ubc.ca>
Sent: October 24, 2018 1:32:52 PM
To: Kimberley Holmes; Leggo, Carl
Subject: Re: Connecting

Thank you, Kimberley, for all these wise and hopeful words!

I love the moon—a poet's companion in countless ways.

I just learned that I will spend Christmas this year in the hospital. I will spend at least 3 weeks as a patient in December. I might get home close to New Year's. During the transplant process, my stem cells will be harvested and then returned to my body. The process sounds almost sci-fi!

Living with hope,

Carl

THE SPACES IN BETWEEN

From: Kimberley Holmes <kaholmes@ucalgary.ca>
Date: Wednesday, October 24, 2018 at 8:04 PM
To: "Leggo, Carl" <carl.leggo@ubc.ca>
Subject: Re: Connecting

Dear Carl,

As I gaze at the illuminated face of the moon outside my window, I must agree she is my inspiring companion. She seems to whisper to pay attention, to say what needs to be said, and to address the issues in the world that need acknowledgment. She encourages me to speak with passion, conviction, and authenticity in hopes of a brighter world where the shadows may fade into the darkness. She shines brightly through the darkness, reminding us that a glimmer of hope always provides the needed radiance for wonder to actualize. Her luminosity reminds me to be well in spite of the unwell that often threatens to overpower me.

I am sorry you will spend Christmas in the hospital but wonder about the mystic nature of that particular coincidence. As your own stem cells are harvested and in essence "rebirthed," you will be celebrating the birth of the Christ child and the quintessential essence of hope. When they return your cells to your body, perhaps you will be once again born unto this earth to bring forth your gifts. You have so many gifts still to offer the world, so many words that still need to be written, and a powerful voice that still needs to be heard.

Although it does sound very science fiction it also is very mystical and magical. What a wonderful blessing to be given the gift of life once again and to be bestowed that gift from the cells of your very own body. It certainly seems to me to be a type of alchemy far beyond our science.

Science and mysticism are a fascinating combination. One cannot live without the other. Although science offers us many portals to salvation, I do believe that it is the power of the human spirit that ultimately brings us into our essence of Being.

A child is born unto this earth wrapped in the waters of the mother

The waters break the precious sack and the child tumbles out into the air

Gasping for breath, reflecting on the process, and beginning the incredible cycle

Of this complex and remarkable process of human life

Seek the sunlight amidst the shadows always swimming in the turbulent seas

Find reflection in deep and dark mysteries of the night

Gaze with wonder on the world with all its warts and blisters

Our reality is based on what our mind perceives

With reflections on the mystic moon,
Kimberley

On Oct 26, 2018, at 12:54 PM, Leggo, Carl <carl.leggo@ubc.ca> wrote:

Lovely, wise words, Kimberley!!

I have attached a recent poem. I will soon celebrate a 65th birthday, and everyday life is growing more and more precious! I am definitely feeling more robust than I have for several months.

Revelling in the joys of autumn,

Carl

<u>Advice for Living the Quotidian</u>

for sixty-five years I wish I had known

how short life is, too short, impossibly brief

how to live each moment as momentous,
alive in each moment with hope for possibility

light and shadow dance a tango, everything
in flow, everything likely or unlikely

this poem reminds me to listen carefully,
to remember with the body's story

everything is heightened, everything is dull,
cancer refracts light in unknown ways

THE SPACES IN BETWEEN

a poet begins with sitting, perhaps
on a bench or a rock, under a tree

our first poem is the heart's beat, breathing
is the ancient language we must always hear

each day requires sensual attending
and taken-for-granted assumptions

I now seek to maintain a balance
between intensity and relaxation

if you want people to smile, smile at them
if you want a hug, offer a hug

above all, be sure to untangle the knot
of fear that threatens to strangle you

a poem is a response to silence,
the quiet resonance that lingers

poets are not scared to know the sacred, each
day brings blessings like disguised challenges

learn to lean on uncertainty,
know the journey is a mystery

be open to surprises, the stuff
of creation, new beginnings

hold the whole of life,
holes and all, heart-wide

always move with rhythm
like a carpenter's sure swing

if you want to know how to live
then live with love's tenderness

waiting with autumn patience for
the fullness after emptiness

this is all the wisdom I have to offer,
a broken body knows a life time

the mortal dances with the immortal,
heaven and earth in a kingdom of joy

From: Kimberley Holmes <kaholmes@ucalgary.ca>
Date: Sunday, October 28, 2018 at 9:07 PM
To: "Leggo, Carl" <carl.leggo@ubc.ca>
Subject: Re: Connecting

Dear Carl,

I have printed out your poem to remind me to savor the beauty of life. We need to feel strong and grounded to be able to embrace the fluctuations of the cycles of human life. My mother starts her final round of chemo tomorrow. At dinner tonight she was feisty and argumentative and somewhat annoying to all of us. This is excellent as she is preparing to fight. We have been told the end of this round will be challenging and she may become very ill, listless, and tired. She shall be finished in 6-12 weeks, depending on the outcome. She put up her Christmas declarations today, so she is ready to resume living as soon as possible.

We put out our witches and skeletons today. I love the spirit of Halloween and the Mexican idea of "Day of Dead." I like to think the spirits are all around me this week, giving me strength and showing me glimpses of what might lie on the other side. I am not afraid of the shadows, and in a strange way find them somewhat alluring. I often wonder if I might have been a witch in a previous existence, as I am drawn to the connections of the elements, the majesty of Mother Earth, and often feel the need to dance in the moonlight. I also have a deep terror of open waters that has no correlation to the life I live now in the dry and dusty prairies. I wonder what memories our cells hold, how our ancestors' stories are embodied deep within my own Essence via the epigenetic links. Epigenetic studies sparked my interest this summer, as I found it fascinating that the cells in our body can carry the genetics of many past generations. It is our environment and our lives that determine how those genes will be activated or silenced. Our life stories can bring us to a space and place of Enlightenment or make us very ill. I choose light that seeps around the edges of the darkness, the illuminations calling me to dance around the shadows and leap into the moonlight.

As we feel the need to dance in the light, I believe all will be well.

With dreams of dancing amongst the shadows,

Kimberley

On Oct 29, 2018, at 9:52 AM, Leggo, Carl <carl.leggo@ubc.ca> wrote:

Strong wisdom, Kimberley!

May we always dance "amongst the shadows"—even as the light sweeps around us.

I hope your mother's chemotherapy goes well. The cancer story is both life-occupying and life-centering!

I have attached another poem which is part of a sequence devoted to thinking about the quotidian.

Happy Halloween!

Carl

Sanctuary

most of my adult life I have spent Sundays
in church, but cancer has consumed my spirit,
so I now spend Sundays at the Sanctuary,
a coffee shop a few minutes up the road
Tim built the coffee shop, especially for cyclists,
where Coffee Cycle Culture is the slogan and highlights
of Tour de France races are presented on a big screen
hung over the coffee bar, a gathering place

for cycling groups from all over the Lower Mainland
who arrive in happy numbers in spandex and cleated
shoes with expensive bicycles and camaraderie
to drink coffee and eat raspberry and lemon scones

Tim remembers people's names, asks about their stories,
he knows I am now often in the BC Cancer Agency
and he is always glad to see me, glad to hear treatments
are working, I might actually have some future left

perhaps I will ride a bicycle again, one day, as I often did
in Corner Brook, and one Christmas bought a Raleigh
ten-speed and had it shipped by train across Newfoundland,
with anticipation of riding it in the spring after a long winter

*I look forward to returning to church on Sunday mornings
but for now I will sip coffee at the Sanctuary where
I can relax in the predictable pleasures of cycles of stories
that continue week after week, a simple air of repetition*

From: Kimberley Holmes <kaholmes@ucalgary.ca>
Date: Tuesday, October 30, 2018 at 9:33 PM
To: "Leggo, Carl" <carl.leggo@ubc.ca>
Subject: Re: Connecting

Dear Carl,

I love the idea of a coffee shop sanctuary. My family and I attempted to cycle the islands this summer, but in spite of my efforts to stay on my bike, I did find myself in many a coffee shop. My fancy bike and gear parked outside while I reclaimed my sanity by inhaling the fragment aroma of caffeine and cookies, transporting me back into the safety of my grandmother's kitchen. Cycling Vancouver Island in the summer was not a relaxing Zen experience as anticipated but a pulse-jumping adventure, especially while trying to manipulate the pathways around Victoria amongst the frenzy of tourists. We shall have to try it again during a quieter season.

The ideas of community and connection resound in your words. This is something that keeps speaking to me of late—how does one build vibrant and caring communities?

It seems essential that these connections thrive as they seem to sustain all human life. What are the essential connections that bind us to the beating pulse of life?

My mother's cancer lump has shrunken immensely while she was on holidays enjoying life. She gets to stop taking her "poison pills" and has a shorter round of chemo. Healing is happening, and life is beginning to resume its familiar patterns. The holiday I believe was essential to the birth of healing cells and rejuvenation.

Tomorrow the little trick or treaters shall wander through our front yard graveyard, and I shall delight in the costumes and the magic of childhood. These are the things that we hold on to; these are the moments that matter.

I shall teach my classes dressed in black wings and a beautiful mask tomorrow representing "The Raven" or perhaps anticipating the evolution to "the Crone." The myths and stories abound around me tonight, calling me to listen to the messages.

With reflections on connection and transformations,

Kimberley

On Oct 31, 2018, at 12:23 PM, Leggo, Carl <carl.leggo@ubc.ca> wrote:

Hi, Kimberley,

I am very glad to hear the good news about your mother!

May we always seek connections and community and healing!

I always enjoy Halloween—the costumes, the treats, the lively sense of communal celebration! Four granddaughters will spend the day in costumes, and they will come to Nana and Papa's house with eager anticipation.

Love,

Carl

From: Kimberley Holmes <kaholmes@ucalgary.ca>
Date: Wednesday, October 31, 2018 at 8:06 PM
To: "Leggo, Carl" <carl.leggo@ubc.ca>
Subject: Re: Connecting

Dear Carl,

I hope your granddaughters had a day filled with magic. As I write this, I watch my almost 17-year-old out in "the graveyard" in his Dracula costume. His excitement with the magic of Halloween is clear as he delights in amusing the little people that skip up our sidewalk. Among the bones, the skeletons, the flaming jack-o-lanterns, and a few scattered witches, laughter abounds. Symbols of death are juxtaposed with sounds of life. A scream of terror is followed by heartfelt giggles and authentic laughter of kids simply having fun by being scared. As the adrenaline surges through the body we all are reminded how wonderful it is to simply be alive. How incredible it would be if we could always simply laugh in the face of fear, if joy would bubble up inside of us instead of anxiety and stress. Tonight, I am going to focus on manifesting joy in all that I do. As the season of darkness begins its long days, which shall threaten to overcome me, I shall seek the magic of the night!

All Hallows' Eve

The tiny little creatures are out to play
Amidst the terrors of the night they find joy and glee
As their brightly colored capes swirl around them and candy falls in bags
The mystery of the night holds a special kind of magic
That often can only be discovered by the children and the poets

The Raven called to me today as I wandered through the park
Her harsh cry echoed through the trees and reverberated through my bones
An echo of a memory long held deeply embedded in the cry
A black and mysterious messenger singing stories in the sky
Its deep and luxurious feathers glistened in the sun and spoke of secrets

The magic of the Universe unfolds around us as we take each precious breath
It calls for us to recognize it before we step too close to death
Death's dark and dusty pathways can be cleared to allow for emergence of the light
For when the threat of death is looming reality and illusions merge into patterns
Of complexity, of connection, and of being in the world together

Each moment that we walk soundly and solidly on earth upon the sacred ground
The Raven calls to us in the hypnotic cawing call and melodies intertwine
These are the patterns to be recognized and honored by the complex labyrinth
Interconnected neuropathways of the vast landscape of the human mind
Synthesizing our human stories and winding the threads tightly together
Seek and you shall find the answers slowly swirling in the wandering wind

Mystery and magic spinning spirals in the sky that radiate out in synergetic patterns

Opening portals and pathways far beyond our human dimensions

Stardust rapidly spinning outwards building connections of life

With thoughts of alchemy,

Kimberley

From: Leggo, Carl <carl.leggo@ubc.ca>
Sent: November 1, 2018 9:18 AM
To: Kimberley Holmes; Leggo, Carl
Subject: Re: Connecting

Hi, Kimberley,

"All Hallows' Eve" is a complex poem that dances light and dark in an alchemic performance. Superb!

You understand Halloween intimately.

Lana and I had fun last night as we handed out treats to a parade of children. We live in a townhouse complex where there are many young families, so there are many children to enjoy Halloween.

I have attached a recent poem about attending. I am eager to devote more attention to being present in each day, present to the wonders all around me.

With heart,

Carl

Snow Geese

at the Steveston Hotel Café
Laura and I discuss poetry
loss   trauma   blessings

Laura asks, are those seagulls?
silver birds with dark wing tips
hover outside the expansive window

(perhaps ducks, I wonder how many
birds live near the Gulf of Georgia)
Laura notes, they're snow geese

just the day before I had walked
to Garry Point, everywhere snow geese
I didn't see, or at least didn't look

even though I grew up with
Dick's reminding Sally
Look, look.
Look up.
Look up, up, up.

gap of poetic awareness
caught up in whirling busyness
saturated   inattentive   senseless

knowing how little I know,

will ever know, I will heed

Dick's wisdom and look, look

From: Kimberley Holmes <kaholmes@ucalgary.ca>
Date: Thursday, November 1, 2018 at 8:08 PM
To: "Leggo, Carl" <carl.leggo@ubc.ca>
Subject: Re: Connecting

Dear Carl,

This idea of looking up and paying attention seem to be a recurring motif. Just as you did not notice the Snow Geese, I daily walk by the Ravens, ignoring their chatter. My head is down, and I am often checking my email or running through the tasks of the day. It is amazing I don't trip over my feet in my urbane slumber, ignorant to the patterns of the world as they swirl around me. The black and brilliant creatures seem to be demanding that I stop and pay attention, and their annoyance at my avoidance is evident. Today, their call was almost mournful, and I did pause and just listen to the melody they chanted into the skyscape. Pay attention, pay attention, pay attention....

Today was an intense day in my English 30 class. My students have been tasked with Project Me, a reflective piece which challenges them to reflect on who they are. They are asked to present a small piece to the class. The stories have been powerful, authentic, and raw. Today one student spoke of her little sister who has epilepsy, autism, and Rhett syndrome. She spoke of how this illness will impact her sister's ability to speak, walk, eat, and breathe. She spoke powerfully of her fear of watching her sister die. Tears flowed down her face and the faces of many of her classmates. A somber silence invaded the room, and their breathing became unified. I have two other students in the room who have autism, and I watched their responses carefully to try and monitor what was going on inside. My heart bled with all my students, and our stories spun together, braided, and then strongly intertwined. Her presentation was followed by a classmate who is currently being treated for serious depression. The second student shared a poem about the death of her best friend from a brain tumor. Again, the tears fell freely as the pain and suffering was set free. The class was frozen in a moment of compassion, of caring, and incredible human connection. Afterwards the two girls and another classmate retreated to the washroom where I found them sobbing into each other's arms. We held on to each other and then made our way to our guidance team to gather more support. Today wounds fester, bubble up, and bleed, but I am hopeful that

THE SPACES IN BETWEEN

healing also has begun. Our world can be so painful that we need to find ways to release that pain, to connect with others, and to find strength in our shared humanity. We need to pay attention to pain.

My son was classified as a para swimmer today. His epilepsy has caused many struggles and much pain and suffering but now offers him a gift. He has the opportunity to travel all over the world and perhaps one day represent his country in the Olympics. Sometimes our struggle allows us to ascend to remarkable places, and sometimes it ends in silence. Such is the complexity of this human journey and the ongoing spirals of birth, life, and death. I hope for transcendence but also recognize that in the end, "all that remains is silence."

I feel myself struggling for breath today. Emotions have run deep, and I am intensely tired. These are the days that I don't want to be the teacher, that I seek a teacher. These are the days I must pay attention and take rest.

Raven

The human essence of the mind is a complex and frighteningly fragile thing

Electrical currents surging through a fleshy mass of interconnected circuitry

Often resulting in brilliance, in interconnectivity, and in poetry

But sometimes splintering into a thousand broken strands

Melting into puddles of empty nothingness

The flicker of the candle is but brief as the flame sways in the wind

The opposing elements of nature allowing it to burn

Or to suffocate slowly out of existence

Signifying all that ever was and ever will be

Earth, air, water, fire swirling in the atmosphere as Life unfolds

The bird song sounds through the air and shatters the silence

The trees sway in the breeze holding out their arms in an embrace

Nature synthesizes its patterns in interconnected rhythms

Some will laugh, some will cry, some will thrive, some will die

All will be, K

On Nov 3, 2018, at 12:05 PM, Leggo, Carl <carl.leggo@ubc.ca> wrote:

Beautiful, Kimberley!

Your experiences with your students represent significant learning and growing and becoming. Very hopeful!!

Congratulations on your son's being classified as a para swimmer! As an adolescent, I competed in local swim meets and worked as a lifeguard. I have always loved swimming and especially the experience of being in water. I hope your son knows much success in his swimming.

I love your poem(s) about ravens. Clearly you are connected to ravens in ways that can heal our lives and our living in the earth.

Heartfully,

Carl

From: Kimberley Holmes <kaholmes@ucalgary.ca>
Date: Monday, November 5, 2018 at 7:11 PM
To: "Leggo, Carl" <carl.leggo@ubc.ca>
Subject: Re: Connecting

Dear Carl,

The temperature has dropped in Calgary and the nights already seem long and ominous. I am trying to gather my energy to do some writing, but my desire to crawl under a blanket and begin hibernation is very strong. My physical body aches with exhaustion. Good thing my children have sports, which will force me to go out, otherwise I might retreat into my house regularly. It is a challenge to participate in life sometimes, but one must always step forth to join the game even if you don't really feel like playing.

I have hope perhaps this will be a change of cycles for Tristan and for myself. I have been waiting to finish my book about our experiences as I want some type of a hopeful ending. I have given up on happy but will settle for hopeful. So much of our literature is focused on dark and depressing spaces where I would like to contribute some light. We need voices that speak of sorrow yet find a way to preserve sanity and ascend to brighter places. Perhaps if things shift for us, I will be able to finally find the words to bring our experience alive for others in some sort of hopeful discourse.

Ravens call to me in so many ways. They speak of transformations which I am still seeking to understand but know somehow; I must find a way to

THE SPACES IN BETWEEN

heed their call. I need to continue to grow and evolve, which is so challenging in this season shift when my body calls for me to slow down and sit quietly. The night moves slowly, and the darkness seeps into my pores. For now, I shall listen for the birdsong and wait for the awakening. It is difficult to craft words when my days are so consuming and the nights so long.

Seeking sunlight,

Kimberley

On Nov 6, 2018, at 9:09 AM, Leggo, Carl <carl.leggo@ubc.ca> wrote:

Good-morning, Kimberley!

Your experience of autumn and winter dark, or lack of light, speaks to me in acute and profound ways. I grew up in a world of long winters where the sun and streetlights shone brightly in the months of snow. I now live in a world where it almost never snows, but where the rain and low gray skies can challenge even the most hopeful heart.

I have attached some notes from James Hillman's *The Force of Character*—the notes might be useful. I have also attached a poem titled "Cancer (on) Ward."

I live with hope. Today I am going to see my lymphoma specialist, Dr. Sehn, and I hope to learn about plans for the stem cell therapy. I have recently had a second MRI and a second bone marrow biopsy. So, I have been well-tested and examined! I hope my body is continuing to respond well to the chemotherapy.

Seeking the light,

Carl

"So, why *do* we live so long?" (p. xiii)

"The last years confirm and fulfill character" (p. xiii).

"What does aging serve? What is its point?" (p. xiv)

"The old become strikingly memorable, ancestral representations, characters in the play of civilization, each a unique, irreplaceable figure of value. Aging: an art form?" (p. xv)

"Authors are characters in their own fictions" (p. xxiv).

"You can't get rid of your character in anything you write" (p. xxiv).

"... living a long life serves soul-making by bringing to life the psyche's amazing collection of adjectives" (p. 11).

"the confabulation of memories into stories" (p. 17)

"Longevity enthusiasts neglect to mention that bad characters last, too. So do the helpless and the useless, the miserly who gather it in and store it away like fervent ferrets the longer they live. Sadistic cruelty may become ever more tyrannical as years eliminate other avenues of pleasure, and ambition does not necessarily moderate in later life" (p. 18).

"Saturn, god of misers and misery" (p. 19).

"What preserves character? What helps it last?" (p. 20)

"Character is characters; our nature is a plural complexity, a multiphasic polysemous weave, a bundle, a tangle, a sleeve. That's why we need a long old age: to ravel out the snarls and set things straight" (p. 32).

"I like to imagine a person's psyche to be like a boardinghouse full of characters" (p. 32).

"Access to character comes through the study of images, not the examination of morals" (p. 34).

"To be only a mean old man, or always a list of complaints, or a record-breaking centenarian of 105, or a head flowing with long white hair and issuing long tales of cautionary experiences is to reduce the uniqueness of character to the unity of a caricature" (p. 49).

"Alchemists were workers in metaphor, like good psychoanalysts, and also like poets and painters" (p. 83).

"Memory is always first of all imagination, secondarily qualified by time" (p. 89).

"Life review is really nothing other than rewriting—or writing for the first time—the story of your life, or writing your life into stories. And without stories there is no pattern, no understanding, no art, and no character—merely habits, events passing before the eyes of an aimless observer, a life unreviewed, a life lost in the living of it" (p. 91).

"Life review doesn't belong to earlier years. Memoirs, autobiography, and the deep investigations of long-term psychoanalysis probably shouldn't be touched before sixty. Yet kids in high school are asked to write their memorable experiences and extract a lesson learned. Their therapies review their childhoods, which ended scarcely five years prior; their bull sessions and chat rooms focus on family difficulties and influences. Premature life review produces inflated subjectivity, not character, the empowerment of one more big fat 'me' graduating from high school into a world that, already crowded with expanded egos, rather needs the modesty and reticence of the apprentice embarking on an adventure" (p. 91).

"Forgetting, that marvel of the old mind, may actually be the truest form of forgiveness, and a blessing" (p. 93).

"There are more hearts than the one that shows up in clinical imaging" (p. 119).

"A recent statistic revealed that one third of all adult males in the United States, and one quarter of all adult women would choose to stay *permanently* at the ages between fifteen and nineteen: a life sentence to high school" (p. 125).

"Correcting course all day long: This is the beginning of wisdom. It is a practice, a quiet noticing of where you actually are, not of being right on, but of being slightly off" (p. 128).

"We look at each other to see into each other" (p. 151).

"You may little suspect the fullness of someone's character just from reviewing your memories. Your father's character, say, goes on unfolding and you go on learning about him, from him. He returns to mind in flashbacks and reveries. As you age, and you become more like him, he often feels nearer. A glimpse in the mirror, a dish in a restaurant, a joke in an old movie, and traits of his light up, never having been noticed before. Under scrutiny, the images reveal more and more, revising the obituary, nuancing impressions, teaching still" (p. 157).

"The easy path of aging is to become a thick-skinned unbudging curmudgeon, an old buzzard, a battle-ax. To grow soft and sweet is the harder way" (p. 163).

"Character is refined in the laboratory of aging. You don't get it right the first time. Each day brings another opportunity to strike the right mix, neither too malleable nor too rigid, neither too sweet nor too dry, giving the older character its power to bless with a tough-minded tenderness" (p. 163).

"We would begin to see again what we saw before abstractions claimed our minds: Life as lived is completely characterized. Adjectives and adverbs are the actual forces at work in perceiving the world and in our behavior" (p. 170).

"Language would be creatively imagined to equal the imagination of the creation" (p. 170).

"I differ from them [Socrates and Freud] inasmuch as their path of insight is analytical, mine imaginative" (p. 179).

"Ethics emerges from character not as virtue or vice, but as/ each character's particularity, and peculiarity" (pp. 180-181).

"Character forces me to encounter each event in my peculiar style. It forces me to differ. I walk through life oddly. No one else walks as I do, and this is my courage, my dignity, my integrity, my morality, and my ruin" (p. 181).

"I do not consider imagination to be a mental faculty only" (p. 182).

"More than a faculty, imagination is also one of the great archetypal principles, like love, order, beauty, justice, time" (p. 183).

"The aesthetic imagination is the primary mode of knowing the cosmos, and aesthetic language the most fitting way to formulate the world" (p. 184).

"Where imagination focuses intently on the character of the other—as it does between opposing generals, guard and hostage, analyst and patient—love follows" (p. 185).

"Without imagination, love stales into sentiment, duty, boredom. Relationships fail not because we have stopped loving but because we first stopped imagining" (p. 186).

"One of the poet's tasks is to bring a community to its senses and wake it up, and to do this by aesthetic means that are hardly distinguishable from moral chiding" (p. 194).

"Perhaps history lives in the world's memory beyond human rememberings" (p. 201).

Cancer (on) Ward

in July I was diagnosed with
Diffuse Large B Cell Lymphoma
which at least sings with poetic rhythms

I am now sipping a hot chocolate
   in the BC Cancer Agency

I have joined the circle of the elderly,
   perhaps prematurely,
while I wait patiently, a patient patient

Lymphoma Canada claims DLBCL
responds well to treatment with a high rate of cure

I am now cancer, pervasive, everywhere,
flowing blood cells, normal and abnormal,
I am aswirl with blood cancer

cancer is the uninvited guest you do not
want but do not know how to refuse,
a spectator who haunts every moment
like a noxious scent sent from far away

I am now Carl with Cancer, a character,
   illness journey   illness story
   illness trajectory   illness adventure

I just drank a Marble Slab Creamery
   strawberry milkshake, satisfied

   regarding cancer, constipation,
   consternation, I want conversation

   will I get porridge in the morning?
   French fries are coming for lunch

   Lana in a white summer dress
   ready for the Mayan Riviera or here

   the nurses are generous
   like elementary school teachers

   I have received many texts and prayers
   and love notes, glad and guilty,
   when did I become so popular?

   rather odd to arrive at a place
      where I am almost content
         how does that happen?
            how do we become happy?

   time moves slowly
      just like always

   I miss my granddaughters flowing
   with stories to be written and lived

THE SPACES IN BETWEEN

I fell this morning, crumpled supine
on the floor, TC gave me a walker

Lana and I lie on the narrow bed,
play Scrabble and Yahtzee

Peter and his wife chat behind their curtain,
  Peter coughs, his wife whispers

carpenters cleaners clerks cooks
counselors diagnosticians doctors
educators electricians managers
nurses pharmacists plumbers
providers specialists technicians

machinery beeps   purrs   alerts
a barrage of memos regarding healing
  processes and possibilities

coming and going
  murmuring and mumbling

any nausea? bowel movements?

why are salmon pink curtains
  popular in hospitals?

my granddaughters are faraway, now on
their own adventures where I cannot join them,
I love them, and I hold them fast in the light
of the heart, but they are on their journeys,
and I am mostly absent, holed up in a hospital

I am very tired today, just slept
at least an hour this afternoon

second round of chemo, platelets too low
to begin on Wednesday, so we went home
and returned on Thursday when I had
one platelet more than the minimum,
and it is now Saturday afternoon and
the chemo transfusions should be over
by about 8pm tonight, and I will rest
in the Agency on Sunday and hopefully
be discharged on Monday or Tuesday

I must continue to learn to flow with the story
that unfolds, I really know nothing, each day
composes a story and I learn from the story
(I hope I can learn what I need to know)

I pee at least every hour
    I pee a lot
I am learning the familiar rhythm

THE SPACES IN BETWEEN

Lana is doing a crossword puzzle
or knitting or sending messages to family

enjoyed coffee and a berry scone
    at Elysian

good news today! Dr. Sehn told us
    the chemo is working
and the tumor is much diminished
and she used several modifiers
I can't remember, but they were all
filled with confident encouragement
and I am beginning to relax
with the hope that I might really
have some more time left
to work and play and enjoy family

on the cancer ward I am tethered
to tubes transfusion bags monitors
which I drag here and there
on a kind of coat rack on wheels

the woman in charge of the kitchen
is from Fiji and remembers the brown sugar
she mixed with oatmeal as a child

my metatrexate level is 0.09
(happily below the level it must be)

I am especially eager
for some physical exercise

Disneyland, here we come!

in the BC Cancer Agency we all have cancer
    and every cancer is different,
written with fear and hope

we all have stories on the cancer ward
and all our stories are different,
especially when they are really the same

From: Kimberley Holmes <kaholmes@ucalgary.ca>
Date: Wednesday, November 7, 2018 at 10:04 PM
To: "Leggo, Carl" <carl.leggo@ubc.ca>
Subject: Re: Connecting

Dear Carl,

I am contemplating both the words from Hillman's work and your poetry. They speak to me in profound ways, and I am simply sitting and listening to the many messages that call for me to address them. It is a new moon day today. In my yoga practice this signifies a day to plant intentions, to ground them deeply in the earth so that they may grow and actualize. I am sitting silently contemplating what I may seed and how the words and ideas you have shared will take root in me. I am waiting for the stories to begin to spin their strands and interconnect the complex details of my history.

I am glad you are well-examined. I think this is an important reflection. An Elder taught me never to frame a thought with a negative as that will help the negative to actualize. Hence instead of illness perhaps a physical adventure that one is undertaking to reach a stronger, more enlightened state. A type of physical metamorphosis where cells are spinning, dancing, and rejuvenating in new and unexpected patterns, allowing something new to emerge from the shadows.

My mother's chemo is also progressing. I know she is sore, and her skin burns painfully, yet she still delights in the joys of her new puppy. She now has two puppies in the household. One arrived in July, following her cancer diagnosis, and a second one just last week. Watching them chase and frolic around the room is quite the delightful expression of life. Their vibrant energy is overcoming the shades of darkness. They prance with the unlimited joys of puppy glee and then fall into a deep and peaceful slumber. Eat, play, sleep. Perhaps a very simple recipe for happiness.

My students were freaking out this afternoon over a rather taxing math exam. Emotions were high, and the frenzy was building. I reminded them that they had clean water to drink, food to eat, and nice homes to return to. I also told them I failed math in my first year at University and somehow managed to turn out okay, even though I thought it was the end of the world. Our "first world" problems are so minor in this complex human story. What is truly important is that we are alive and that you can still see our breath in the frosty winter air.

Sitting silently under the sliver of the new moon,

Kimberley

From: Leggo, Carl <carl.leggo@ubc.ca>
Sent: November 8, 2018 12:18:34 PM
To: Kimberley Holmes; Leggo, Carl
Subject: Re: Connecting

Hi, Kimberley,

Thank you for all your generative and wise words—just what I need right now! I received good news on Tuesday re. the next stages of my cancer treatment, but sadly I received challenging news on Wednesday! I was looking forward to beginning stem cell therapy in December, but unfortunately I received a phone call from the doctor in charge of the stem cell therapy, and she informed me that my recent bone marrow biopsy indicates that I still have too much lymphoma to proceed at this time with the stem cell transplant process. So, I am back in the hands of Dr. Sehn, the lymphoma oncologist, who will determine a new course of action to address the lymphoma in the rest of my body. At least the brain lymphoma is currently under control! A very disappointing setback, but I will hold fast to hope!

Continue to be a bright light in your students' lives! They need you!!

In November sunlight, Carl

From: Kimberley Holmes <kaholmes@ucalgary.ca>
Date: Thursday, November 8, 2018 at 9:40 PM
To: "Leggo, Carl" <carl.leggo@ubc.ca>
Subject: Re: Connecting

Dear Carl,

I am sorry that your stem cell therapy has been delayed and the lymphoma is still active. I have been researching, and it is overwhelming how many types of lymphoma exist. I find the patterns between our "illness stories" quite striking. Risk factors for Hodgkin lymphoma include infection with Epstein-Barr virus, which was one of the potential catalysts under consideration for Tristan's seizures. We know the seizures are connected to some type of autoimmune disease, which is also the root of my migraines. This process of inflammation is a perplexing one. If I go to the root word of inflammation I find "excessive redness or swelling in the body part" or the direct Latin of inflammation: "a kindling, a settling on fire." Literally it could be taken as "the act of setting on fire."

When the enigma of Tristan's seizure was at its peak, I found a book entitled *Brain on Fire: My Month of Madness* (Cahalan, 2012). It begins with a quote by Nietzsche:

"The existence of forgetting has never been proved; we only know that some things do not come to our minds when we want them to."

Susannah Calahan explores the bizarre impact of a rare autoimmune disease which wreaked havoc on her mind, brain, and spirit. It was diagnosed as a rare type of encephalitis. Autoimmune diseases both terrify and fascinate me. They are this abnormal response of our immune system, which is supposed to help protect us not harm. It is our body literally attacking itself in some type of internal battle against an unknown force, resulting in a complex manifestation of various physical outcomes.

They can be genetic or trigged by infections or environment. This "setting on fire" must have some type of deeper purpose, and I cannot help but think of the interconnected elements of earth, air, water, and fire. Findley tells us in *The Wars* (1977) that "Robert Ross was consumed by fire." At the end of the novel he is a burned and tortured soul, his physical essence destroyed beyond all recognition, yet the "baptism by fire" seemed to inspire life. When offered death by the nurse he replies, "not yet." In that statement is the essence of Robert Ross and Findley's powerful message to his readers. When we are consumed by fire, we must continue to hold the breath of life steady.

When death taps us on the shoulder via inflammation, violent seizures, or destructive cancer we need to whisper to ourselves in powerful and reflective ways, "not yet." We need to still see our breath in the winter air and as the cycle of elements continue to circle, affirm that this complex journey is not over. There are still words to write on the page, thoughts to ponder and contemplate, and people to love deeply and passionately with everything our hearts have to offer.

Today, we had our Remembrance Day assembly at school. It has been 100 years since that significant event, and most of this year's graduating class were born in 2001, the year we began our war with terror. My "9/11 babies" and I were deep in thought and contemplation around the interconnectivity of these patterns. We were silent, and we remembered, and we questioned. In class we discussed if we should still be involved in war and if perhaps war could be waged in different ways than a physical battle, outraged words, and violent and hostile discourse. We discussed "education as a weapon" and how that might change our future from one of war to one of peace and love. We hoped for a future where we no longer lived in fear but lived in light.

Perhaps we should think of illness not as a war we are fighting, something we are battling, but something that might need to be done to cleanse our body and remind our spirit of the powerful essence of human life and our need to always seek the light. Earth, air, water, fire, juxtaposed with the four strands of the life writing braid. As our stories intertwine, so does our breath and our spirits. Together we are all so much stronger, and our voices will always be heard through our stories, our singing, and our poetry. "Look you can see their breath—and you can" (Findley, 1999).

I wrote a short poem today about my work with my complex students:

Reflections on Teaching

Give me the unteachable, the unreachable, and the defiant
Bring me their problems, their sorrow, and their rage
Tell me it's impossible, unachievable, unmanageable
Tell me your illusions and let me defy what you say

I shall seek the dreamers, the wonderers, and the mystics
I shall unpack the stories and read them with care
I shall touch the untouchable and feel all the rage
I shall work with the wisdom that arrives at this stage

I will give you the artist, the architect, and the poet
That is hidden deep within these unteachable Sages
I will find the essence that lives deep within them
I will shatter your illusions and contradict what you say

Each soul has an Essence that a teacher shall spark
Through the process of teaching we eliminate the dark
Each child a story wound in epigenetics quite deep
Let me slowly listen to the chapters of each child's life
Let me find each unique soul and invite in the light
Sending you light, love, and healing

OX
Kimberley

From: Leggo, Carl <carl.leggo@ubc.ca>
Sent: November 9, 2018 10:05:10 AM
To: Kimberley Holmes; Leggo, Carl
Subject: Re: Connecting

Wow, Kimberley! Stunning wisdom expressed in remarkable writing!

You have so much to offer others on the journey.

Your commitment to your students is extraordinary! May we always "invite in the light."

I have inserted a few quotes below from Wendell Berry (2001) who writes with your spirit:

"Thoughts in the Presence of Fear" (1-9)

Written as a response to 9/11, this essay presents 27 thoughts, each numbered with a bold Roman numeral.

"In a time such as this, when we have been seriously and most cruelly hurt by those who hate us, and when we must consider ourselves to be gravely threatened by those same people, it is hard to speak of the ways of peace and to remember that Christ enjoined us to love our enemies, but this is no less necessary for being difficult" (p. 6).

"What leads to peace is not violence but peaceableness, which is not passivity, but an alert, informed, practiced, and active state of being. We should recognize that while we have extravagantly subsidized the means of war, we have almost totally neglected the ways of peaceableness. We have, for example, several national military academies, but not one peace academy" (p. 7).

"The key to peaceableness is continuous practice" (p. 8).

"Education is not properly an industry, and its proper use is not to serve industries, either by job-training or by industry-subsidized research. Its proper use is to enable citizens to live lives that are economically, politically, socially, and culturally responsible. This cannot be done by gathering or 'accessing' what we now call 'information'—which is to say facts without context and therefore without priority" (p. 9).

"An economy based on waste is inherently and hopelessly violent, and war is its inevitable by-product. We need a peaceable economy" (p. 9).

Always live with heart, Carl

From: Kimberley Holmes <kaholmes@ucalgary.ca>
Date: Monday, November 12, 2018 at 7:45 PM
To: "Leggo, Carl" <carl.leggo@ubc.ca>
Subject: Re: Connecting

Dear Carl,

My apologies on the delay in responding. I have been completely out of commission with a horrific throbbing headache since Friday evening. My body was warning me all week with excessive tiredness and aching muscles, but in my usual fashion I continued with my daily tasks of life until my head screamed out in rage. The sledgehammer pounding in my left temple left me motionless in pain, unable to even leave my bed, victim to fits of vomiting, sweating, and psychedelic nausea. This continued until early this morning, when finally, the demon passed through my system. I could not help of thinking of "being consumed by fire" as my temperature rose, and the intense vibrations continued relentlessly in my head. Migraines are a type of hell I would rather avoid, but once they pass, I am eternally grateful to feel good again. I need to learn to heed my body's messages before it strikes me into this nasty inferno. Next time I take rest when needed. When my body speaks, and I ignore it, it sends me a violent message to pay attention.

Thank you for your kind words on my writing. It makes me smile to think I have stunning wisdom when most days I am confused about where I have parked my car. Perhaps this is the juxtaposition of age itself, the onset of wisdom combined with the aimless wandering, searching for something you have left somewhere and need to eventually find. My children think I am daft when it comes to interpreting the newest gadgets of technology, and frankly I am. I just want to push the on button and not require a multitude of passwords and key settings to achieve my objective. To them, it is simply another language and to me an enigma that eludes the grasp of my wisdom. I hope we will be able to share our "collective knowledge" about how the world works to find new ways to bring peace and joy to our world.

Berry's work made me think of Shakespeare's words in relation to Romeo and Juliet: "much to do with love but more to do with hate." Hate is such a vicious and violent emotion. Connected to spite, envy, malice, and hostility, it is all the horrid creatures that escaped from Pandora's box. I am so grateful that it is intermixed with hope. Hope is to wish for something, to have confidence in the future and the faith that humanity will rise above its ugly heart of darkness and evolve into the radiance. If we stay in our primitive heart, and brain, we are destined to become nothing but violent reptiles fighting and biting our way towards dusty darkness. I hope the human brain will continue to evolve into our higher-level pre-frontal cortex where empathy and compassion are the champions. This is our challenge as educators, to work in ways that bring brains into those higher levels of consciousness.

THE SPACES IN BETWEEN

I wonder how different our world would be if we trained peace academies in contrast to military academies. This speaks to my work in mindfulness and my caring heart. We need to practice our attention and attune our breath to the patterns of the Other. Only then, when we recognize that we share the same essence, will we be unable to be violent towards one another. This is the heart of our educational praxis—a curriculum of hope, of peace, and perhaps even miracles. Our current neo-liberal market approach is only breeding more competition, more anger, and more hostility. It is a desperate drive to the top regardless of consequences, and the ultimate prize is money and the market. Souls are crushed daily under this model, and all hope of peace fractured. It allows the human heart of darkness to emerge and to reign. It feeds that dark heart, giving it power yet leaving it alone and empty, devoid of any human connection, only surrounded by a greater amount of useless possessions signifying nothing. We are truly an economy based on waste and consumption, and daily I think of Huxley's dark dystopian warning to us all. What would it look like to have a world not based on consumption, competition, and the market? What would an economy of peace look like?

If

If money was not the objective to learning and school not a competitive game

If we believed that children mattered and recognized that not are all the same

If we taught for understanding, wisdom, and with mindful focused care

Would we ever have a vicious and violent war waging in the dark and dusty air?

Would children ever throw grenades across the blistering blue and smoky sky?

Would mothers weep through silent nights questioning through their rage?

Would fathers march their children through the ranks only to watch them die?

If we truly taught for wisdom and made people wonder, why?

Can we teach a curriculum that is filled with peace and love?

Can we change a hundred years of human history hearts embroiled in dark?

Can we rewrite the stories of our lives and let words spiral out in light?

Would that make a difference in our current age and stage?

I believe it is possible to educate the kind and gentle heart

I believe there is magic woven deep and powerfully in the liberal arts

I believe in innocence, hope for humanity, and all that glitters brightly

If we believe peace is possible and care compassionately for all humanity

With hope,

K

On Nov 12, 2018, at 8:44 PM, Leggo, Carl <carl.leggo@ubc.ca> wrote:

Hi, Kimberley,

There is no need to apologize for a delay in responding. You are one of the most diligent writers I know. I am sorry to hear about your headache. My wife Lana, and our son Aaron, and our daughter Anna have all suffered often with terrible headaches. I am glad you are now feeling better, and I encourage you to listen carefully to your heart, spirit, and body!

I am on medical leave, and so my days are often lived more slowly and meditatively than I have ever lived. After almost 65 years, I have finally learned to listen to my body, to sleep when I need to sleep, to sit quietly when I need to sit quietly. I am finally learning lessons I wished I had learned decades ago.

I took my family to a local hotel yesterday where we stayed in fancy rooms, and went swimming a few times, and ate at the buffet restaurant, and celebrated my birthday with cake. Everybody had a lovely time, and I was much loved and appreciated! Family is the core of my life!

Continue to write about hate and love and hope—knowing that we will always find sustenance in a focus on love and hope. In her moving memoir *Gently to Nagasaki*, Joy Kogawa (2016) asks, "Do we write to be free of our ghosts or to welcome them?" (p. 190) For Kogawa, the world is "an open book embedded with stories. We hear them if we have ears to hear" (p. 149). She knows that her "story is from the belly of the dark" (p. 47). She is both "forbidden to tell it and commanded to tell it" because she knows "that to speak is to slay and not to speak is to slay. What is needed is right action" (p. 47). Therefore, she concludes that "for my part, I hold with a fierce and painful joy my trust in a Love that is more real than we are" (p. 42).

Let's write more about peace! This is the kind of poetry we need—a passionate poetry that refuses to be silenced by all the horror that breathes into every day. Poetry can breathe peace, even, especially, in the midst of all the forces that threaten peace.

With hope,

Carl

From: Kimberley Holmes <kaholmes@ucalgary.ca>
Date: Tuesday, November 13, 2018 at 5:18 PM
To: "Leggo, Carl" <carl.leggo@ubc.ca>
Subject: Re: Connecting

Dear Carl,

Warmest wishes for a happy, harmonious, healing and joyous birthday! I am thrilled you spent the day with your family celebrating the journey of your life thus far. My husband celebrates his 52nd birthday tomorrow, and Tristan celebrates 17 on Sunday. Time indeed does pass quickly, especially when one is dealing with the obstacles of life. So much of Tristan's life has been a challenge, and I wish for him at 17 a future filled with joy and with laughter. He lost so much of the magic of childhood due to illness and challenges that we need to embrace the magic of life itself regardless of age and stage. We need to celebrate the remarkableness of simply being alive and present to the small beauties of daily life, good food, beautiful spaces, family, and friends.

You get a double response today as I took time during my day to write—a lovely choice and much better use of time than the busy work generally done at school. I was inspired by the idea of "living life more meditatively and slowly." I crave the time to sit silently, hence that is what I did while my students were engaged in their own writing process. The silence and the space were delicious, and time went by quickly as I was engaged in the beauty of creating. The words dropped from my fingers without effort and the process felt right. The signs are speaking to the need to find silence and space in my world. Without silence and space my head throbs in pain, and I am sidelined for days in a cruel torture. I am sorry to hear Lana, Aaron, and Anna all suffer the same plague. It is a cruel and unusual punishment, much like the short story of Harrison Bergeron where thoughts are disrupted by a violent scream within the mind. However, the headache eventually ends, and life resumes its patterns. Perhaps if I learn to listen to my body and sleep when I need to sleep, they will be less frequent. In all my readings, the reference to sleep to heal the brain is quite significant. The brain needs sleep, silence, and solitude to find sanctuary from the complex conundrums that vibrate around our head and threaten to consume us.

I shall look for Kogawa's memoir. I think we write to welcome our ghosts, to bring them into our conscious essence, and identify their purpose in our lives. These shadows are all part of our stories, and although they may haunt us, they are also an interconnected piece of the greater whole of our being. Joseph Boyden, when he spoke at a teacher's convention, said the key to writing is to "listen to your voices." This message touched something deep inside me which reverberated with a powerful yes. I am ready to say yes to my adventure and listen to things that are calling to me.

My voices speak often and powerfully when I give them space to be heard. They come from a deep embodied space somewhere between my mind and my gut, perhaps the mysterious vagus nerve that connects these ways of knowing. My voices have a passion that I know not from where it comes; they often speak in poetic tongues that are even unfamiliar to my conscious self. They speak of deep ways of knowing, of dark spaces and primitive ways of living and being in the world. They speak.

I refuse to be silenced by "all the horror that breathes into each day." The horror is deep and exists within the world and within our own Essence. I believe we need to meet our dark masters and allow them to be consumed by the frenzy of fire that can be stoked with the power and passion of words. The demons need to be purged through our fingertips and dance in the alchemy of words on the page in a frenzied formation of images, illusion, and identity. Once the fire has consumed all the rage, all the inflammation, and all the illness, then the healing of the heart and soul can begin. Then there can be peace in the world and acceptance of the obstacles. Perhaps it is time to address the demons in my story and allow them to be consumed by the fire and finally freed.

A student pointed out to me today that if we replace the "I" in illness with "we" it becomes wellness. We need to join our mysterious voices together and seek passionate love and caring through the power of our poetic muse. We need to be well.

Poetry of Peace

I sit watching my students reflect as they contemplate their essay

In which their chosen text reflects the interplay between resiliency and empathy

In doom and gloom English 30 the characters often painfully, pitifully, perish

Trapped within the darkness of their own emotions and experiences

Their empathy and compassion limit their ability to survive choking their breath

Overcome by the tragedy of the complex circumstances of their human condition

Tim O' Brien is a coward for in the end "he went to war" and sacrificed his soul

His contemplative time upon the rainy river forever etched into his memory of failure

An act of cowardice to fight viciously and violently for something he did not believe

Chris believed in the power and magic of his dreams as the nightmares continued on

And eventually they could make him march but he did not live inside his body anymore

His spirit disappeared from his physical form and only a sunken shadow remained

Hamlet was a philosopher who contemplated deeply yet Ophelia felt his rage

His hatred towards his mother, his uncle's betrayal, and his academic training

Unable to explain the complexity of his emotional and social experiences

In the end signifying nothing and all that was left was the shattered and shocked silence

And the remnants of blood, brutality, and bullshit are all that are left upon the stage

Out out brief candle that struts and frets then is heard no more tales told by idiots

Yet Guido continues to believe that life is beautiful in spite of all the sorrow

The horrors of the war are eclipsed by the love of a father and the sanctuary

Of human love, of hope and passion to overcome the darkest hour.

And Robert Ross whispers to the call of death, "not yet" as he has seen the reason

That every human experience has a season and after dark the light shall rise

Christmas shines its bright light in the middle of winter and Narnia awakens again

Out of the ashes rises the Phoenix amidst the ash and ruin of deep and dark decay

The brilliance of the sunrise continues to greet and inspire yet another day

The cycle of life continues to spiral around us in interconnected, complex ways

We find words and poetry to overcome the silence and speak in deep and powerful ways

This I wish for you my students as you contemplate this complex conundrum

Empathy may destroy us, or it may empower us to magnificently rise into the light

From: Leggo, Carl <carl.leggo@ubc.ca>
Sent: November 13, 2018 5:29:22 PM
To: Kimberley Holmes; Leggo, Carl
Subject: Re: Connecting

Marvellous, Kimberley!!

May we always attend to our voices! I wrote a PhD dissertation about voice in writing.

I love the notion of changing the "I" to "we" in illness.

Celebrate the birthdays in your family!

Let us seek the dreams behind the sanctioned stories and models and paradigms!

Joyfully, Carl

From: Kimberley Holmes <kaholmes@ucalgary.ca>
Date: Wednesday, November 14, 2018 at 8:11 PM
To: "Leggo, Carl" <carl.leggo@ubc.ca>
Subject: Re: Connecting

Dear Carl,

I shall need to spend some hours looking at your PhD thesis and seeing how you explored the voices. They are mystical and magical things that I am only just starting to pay attention to again. I wish I had listened to their call more over the years, but somehow the process of growing up, becoming responsible, and becoming an adult got in the way of hearing them.

I remember being an elementary aged child and walking to and from school full of mystery and wonder. On the route, I traveled through a large green space upon a hill. I remember three large trees in a triangle that used to call for me to come and sit with them, to listen to their voices, and to think about magic. It seems like only yesterday I sat within my triangle of towering trees with my back leaning firmly against my chosen one. I can feel the power of the bark pressing into my small back and hear the cascade of voices that chattered to me about all sorts of magical things. I called them my magic trees, as nestled in with them I truly belonged in another world, a type of Narnia where the daughters of Eve and Adam held a powerful reign.

As I grew older, junior high and beyond, I stopped visiting my trio of trees. I stopped spending my afternoons soaking in the sun and listening the rustle of their leaves. I became busy with friends, concerned about my social life, and focused on the important work of "growing up." Little did I realize how much my mind was growing and evolving as I sat silently with my forest of friends. My quiet reflection space became a memory of the past, the magic that I believed my trees performed for me no longer worked, and the branches of alchemy that protected my childhood became shadows that moved only in the moonlight where I no longer payed attention to them.

As a middle-aged adult, I crave the sanctuary of my trees. I long to lean my tired back against their solid bark and listen to the wind as it rustles along the leaves and whispers messages to me. I long to feel their security and strength and sink my spirit deep within their roots embodied with the earth soaking up the nourishment that I so desperately need. I seek to find the magic, the alchemy that bound me to my childhood dreams, my innocence, and my voices. I miss the voices terribly. Perhaps I should return to the trio and see if they are still there waiting for me, if the voices are still whispering, and most importantly of all if I can still hear them.

Alchemy

Five six, seven, eight, nine magical steps and I am embraced within the circle

Leafy arms outstretched into the sky calling me to come and whisper my secrets

Dream all the impossible dreams, hope for impossible things, and listen to the voices

As the roots of my childhood embedded in Mother Earth and connected me to all Being

Ten, Eleven, Twelve, Thirteen and the ground begins to shift immensely

Image matters, responsibility begins to settle in, and my own arms reach out to the sky

Swirling out of the circle and into the world I spin and spiral twisting and turning out of control

Racing into the wind breathlessly crushing the leaves beneath my feet in a frenzy to become

Fourteen, Fifteen, Sixteen, Seventeen, Eighteen I am an adult now

The leaves another task that need to be taken care of, something raked from the debris of the garden

That has finished blooming and now waits fallow for something new to seed

As the roots of life slumber silently in the earth waiting for their time to reawaken

Forty-eight, Forty-nine, Fifty, Fifty-one

I listen as the roots rumble restlessly within the Earth calling me to heed them

The voices are once again whispering from the trees, chanting out our interconnected stories

Synthesizing together in spiralling circles reaching outwards to the sun

With longing, Kimberley

On Nov 15, 2018, at 5:26 PM, Leggo, Carl <carl.leggo@ubc.ca> wrote:

Hi, Kimberley,

I love your ruminative remembering about the trio of trees. May we always hold fast to the connections with the places that have sustained us and can sustain us!

"Alchemy" is another memorable and evocative poem! You summarize a lifetime in 4 stanzas that conjure many memories for you and for your readers. I especially love the final 2 lines:

"The voices are once again whispering from the trees, chanting out our interconnected stories

Synthesizing together in spiralling circles reaching outwards to the sun"

Our stories are always interconnected, and we learn about ourselves and one another as we share our stories. The interconnections are always there. We just don't always recognize the interconnections. Your writing and teaching and living are significantly focused on acknowledging and celebrating the interconnections.

In the process of sharing,

Carl

From: Kimberley Holmes <kaholmes@ucalgary.ca>
Date: Friday, November 16, 2018 at 9:54 AM
To: "Leggo, Carl" <carl.leggo@ubc.ca>
Subject: Re: Connecting

Good Morning Carl,

Indeed, our stories are deeply interconnected in so many complex ways. I am currently sitting at the Alberta Children's hospital with Tristan while he receives his monthly IVIG transfusions. It is two days before his 17th birthday and almost 11 years to the day since our "illness story" began with the vicious virus that choked his breath and threatened to destroy his essence. The threats and terrors have continued on since then. Last night in his sleep he suffered a grand mal seizure, which always makes him appear like he is battling some demon threatening to possess his body, his mind, and soul. They are both terrifying and fascinating to observe and I believe have a much deeper complexity than our current medical model acknowledges or recognizes, as "there are more things in heaven and earth Horatio than are dreamt of in your philosophy." There are so many interconnected pieces that glue together the strands of the body, the mind, and the soul. I cannot help but wonder about the timing, about the body's memories and the need to expel all the poisons in some way. Perhaps illness is our way of expelling the things inside of us that make us sick. I wonder how many years, or even lifetimes, it might take for the healing to fully complete its process.

Our illness story is also directly intertwined with our story of school. Tris was in grade 1, not even 6 years old, when this chapter of our lives began. He was so little, so tired, and so overwhelmed at the drill and kill of school. I should have pulled him out, let him stay home or changed his educational setting. The demands of the environment fed the illness, as when the body, mind, and soul are overwhelmed the breeding grounds for illness expand immensely. If I could turn back time, I would do things so differently, perhaps even home school my children in a caring environment where we could sit and think and wonder. School and its intense structure and rules contributed immensely to our illness story.

Tristan sits beside me and is attempting to read *Brave New World*. It is a difficult text far beyond his current cognitive ability. His English teachers have always been weak, void of pedagogical process and unable to support him. He does not ask me for help—I believe due to a stubborn pride he has developed with his ongoing struggles. I cannot help but be struck by the irony as he reads about "the assembly line model" of producing human beings, their conditioning centers and the complete dystopia that Huxley presents for us. The dysfunctional dystopia that I fear is rapidly becoming our contemporary world. "Oh, Brave New World that has such people in it!"

I try to seek hope, but hospitals are difficult places to find light. Although the Children's hospital is painted brightly, it still reeks of pain and suffering. In spite of our illusions of magic, the reality is that this is a place where people come who are sick. This is a place of sadness, terror, and rage. This is not a place of healing—the healing must occur after one leaves this space and returns home to the love of family and friends. The healing can only begin once the injury is purged, and that process is indeed a type of purgatory that sometimes seems never ending.

I hope your body is beginning its healing process. Stay close to your family and engaged in life. This will allow you to be stronger when more purging is required. My mother is on her last five sessions of chemo. Her armpit is raw, red, and angry. The fire is consuming the illness, and the body is blistering and battered yet continues to fight with a passion that never stops amazing me. In a week she will be finished, and we will continue to prepare for Christmas in her traditional elaborate fashion. It is her favorite time of the year. I am grateful that although we have long and cold winters there is always that sign of light.

In the beginning

In the beginning there were rainbows, mystical creatures, and alchemy
We never ran out of time and the days were filled with pancakes in pajamas
Bob the builder, coloring, music time, and perhaps a swim
Life was slow and easy and wonderful as it should be

Then the system called to send us to the conditioning center
Where we were sorted one by one—Alpha, Beta, Gamma, Delta, Epsilon
Regurgitate your lesson as this is on the test—the longest river in Africa is...
In the end learning nothing and losing everything of who you are

Inflammation, rashes, headaches, and violent seizures of the body
As the spirit screams to return to the world of alchemy and find Santa in the snow
Chemistry, physics, math, and other complex calculations and conundrums
Drummed daily into the head as the pounding rhythm of recitation reverberates

Oh, Brave new world that has such people in it can you not heed the warning
Can you not see that Huxley claimed the darkness and eliminated all the life?
Books, religion, families, and all the stories carefully hidden to be forever banished
Dropping all into a deep and dark never-ending numbness of nothingness

Only the poets fight the process as they rage against the powerful machine

I can only wish to be banished to the island where I can write my "poetry in peace"

Let me see the crashing waves as they dance out of the sea in interconnected patterns

Stop this incessant assembly line of nothingness and give me time to breathe

Breathing deeply,

K

From: Leggo, Carl <carl.leggo@ubc.ca>
Sent: November 17, 2018 2:50:07 PM
To: Kimberley Holmes; Leggo, Carl
Subject: Re: Connecting

Thank you, Kimberley, for your heart-sustaining rumination on Tristan's "illness story." It is a sad, hard story, but ultimately also a story about resilience and love and hope. I met a woman yesterday who told me that she had recently gone to Squamish to sprinkle the ashes of her husband in a favorite place. After a time with ALS, he chose assisted suicide. He was 54 years old. And I met a woman today who told me about how her son was killed in a car accident a few years ago. He was 23 years old. There is so much sadness everywhere, in everyone. But, like Tristan, your mother, you, your whole family, we continue to seek the light, and we continue to celebrate, and we continue to hold fast to the rhythms of seasons and rituals and memories.

"In the beginning" is a moving and activist response to Huxley's *Brave New World*. May the poets always sing out in alternative voices that remind us there are always more possibilities within and beyond the stories that shape and inform our lives. May we always live poetically!

With love,

Carl

From: Kimberley Holmes <kaholmes@ucalgary.ca>
Date: Sunday, November 18, 2018 at 2:05 PM
To: "Leggo, Carl" <carl.leggo@ubc.ca>
Subject: Re: Connecting

Dear Carl,

Yes, our human stories are sad, heart-wrenchingly tragic and filled with sorrow. Such are the cycles of our complex lives, which much be filled with resiliency, love, and hope. Without the ability to face pain and challenge, we fade into a type of empty nothingness that is but thin vapor in the frosty airs of adversity. We need to breathe deeply and powerfully to move forward as our Spirits strive, move forward, change and morph shapes and identities, and eventually come to a place of peace.

It is Tristan's 17th birthday today. After an evening of celebrations and a morning of "race car challenge" at the local track, he is peacefully napping in his bedroom. My wish for him this birthday is a life full of joy and resiliency. I used to wish for all the adversity to end, but I have come to realize that the challenge is part of the story and builds the fibers strong for what is to come. There will be joy, there will be sorrow, and there will be the essence of life itself in a multiplex of complex conundrums and interconnected intimacies.

We did receive the promise of possibility while at the hospital on Friday. Tris's seizures are connected to elevated cytokines in the cerebral spinal fluid. This also causes rashes, skin infections, and other signs of the ongoing inflammation. The fire continues to burn in his body, so we must find some way to stop its consumption. The neurologist has recommended a trial of anakinra. Anakinra is a biopharmaceutical drug used to treat rheumatoid arthritis. It is a recombinant and slightly modified version of the human interleukin 1 receptor antagonist protein so again based in the knowledge of our own human body. Interleukin 1 is a general name for two distinct proteins that are considered the first of a small family of regulatory and inflammatory cytokines. They play important roles in the regulation of acute inflammation. Cytokines are any number of substances that are secreted by certain cells of the immune system and have an effect on other cells. When I look at the word immune the first thing that comes up is this idea of protection. This is an idea of preventing someone from suffering harm and injury. Of course, we cannot be immune to everything, as life causes us pain and suffering, but could we somehow improve our immune response so that our systems do not rage out of control, into a burning inferno that will eventually consume us? Could we have smaller, healing fires that make us stronger instead of breaking us down? Can we change our relationship with conflict so that it becomes something that eventually brings us to a stronger space and place?

For many years I have been insistent that the root problem of inflammation be addressed. It seemed so logical that we seek the root, the interconnected experiences, and the correlation between the body, mind, and spirit. Until Friday, my mother's voice and wisdom were ignored. Finally, the medical professionals have agreed to try to address the root of the problem instead of the ongoing symptoms. For this I am hopeful. I will continue to address the interconnections as well. The work is deep and complex, but it is work I must do as it has become part of my purpose, and the strands of my story.

I wonder if we will finally reach a point in human wellness where we work in prevention instead of reaction? Could this 11-year cycle of hell have been avoided if the physicians had just listened when I told them repeatedly that the cycle of inflammation needed to be addressed? When we wait to treat the symptoms, the fire is already raging violently and difficult to control. If we changed the "illness story" to seek for root causes and sought solutions, would it be illness at all or simply a question of healing and recovery? Would it be a wellness story?

I have so many questions and considerations for both health care and education. I believe the two are intricately interconnected, and the vines of the two disciplines wind around one another tightly. Can we learn to be well, to find root causes, and to allow the human to bloom and actualize regardless of adversity? Can we stop the battles and fights against illness and join hearts in wellness and healing? I believe that we can if we connect the pieces of our own stories, braid those stories with others, and seek the common patterns. Again, the world of story and myth is calling to me to override my faith in science and seek other ways of knowing and being in the world. The voices around me continue to speak and offer their ancient wisdom....

With inquiry and wonder, OX K

On Nov 19, 2018, at 11:45 AM, Leggo, Carl <carl.leggo@ubc.ca> wrote:

I admire your wisdom and spirit, Kimberley!

Your commitment to understanding the root problem is precisely what we need in medicine and health, and education, too. Continue to advocate for your son. Your mother's knowledge will always be very important, especially when informed by your scholarship. You combine a remarkable store of knowledge with a keen heart.

I saw the oncologist this morning, and I will begin a new round of chemotherapy, beginning on Friday.

Enjoying the blue sky on this November morning,

Carl

From: Kimberley Holmes <kaholmes@ucalgary.ca>
Date: Tuesday, November 20, 2018 at 8:59 PM
To: "Leggo, Carl" <carl.leggo@ubc.ca>
Subject: Re: Connecting

Dear Carl,

I was locked out of my email so unable to respond. Funny how communication can be shut down when one needs to change a password. I hope your next round of chemotherapy goes well. My mother is in her final round this week. She is sore and red but remaining positive and optimistic. I suppose this is all we can do when faced with the obstacles.

Tris will be starting his new therapy this week. I am very intrigued to see what a drug for arthritis does to combat seizures. Inflammation is a terrible thing, but I am focusing on the Latin word *inflammare*, meaning "to set on fire with passion." I realize this is often thought of as suffering, but after the suffering comes the renewal. We are seeking renewal.

This world is filled with much suffering, many fires that burn viciously, and nasty aftereffects. Passion can be defined as a strong and barely controllable emotion. This could be a suffering, but it could also be a love. Love has so many forms encompassing a variety of positive emotional and mental states. Love is healing.

Tonight, I am thinking about healing love to help us become well.

Contemplations

As I look out my window into the dark inky clouds of the night
Thoughts of the spirals of life cycles twist and turn through my mind
Splintering, fragmenting, fracturing, and turning into patterns of being
Juxtapositions of wellness and illness, sorrow and joy, passion and pleasure
Intermixed into the alchemy of chromosomes we call life

A lone wolf howls in the darkness screaming in solitude of starvation
His call reverberating across the night and bouncing into hidden spaces
Echoing, sounding, seeking, joining into the symphony of the universe
As the cycle of life ends for the rabbit and feeds the howling frenzy
The flesh of one creature sustains the life of another

Our time on Earth is not guaranteed or unlimited as each day falls to dark
The cycle spins and the passions perpetually drive us forward or back
We seek, we understand, we question, we inquire and connect into something greater
The patterns and themes that run deeply through mythology of time and being
Stories of pain, of passion, of poetry, and of everlasting love that sustain me
(Holmes & Leggo, 2019).   With love, K

On Nov 22, 2018, at 2:53 PM, Leggo, Carl <carl.leggo@ubc.ca> wrote:

Strong wisdom, Kimberley! May all our living and teaching and writing be enthused with passion!

Another beautiful poem full of philosophy and hope!

As you note, "Love is healing."

Living with/in poetry.

Carl

From: Kimberley Holmes <kaholmes@ucalgary.ca>
Date: Friday, November 23, 2018 at 7:04 AM
To: "Leggo, Carl" <carl.leggo@ubc.ca>
Subject: Re: Connecting

Good Morning Carl,

I have a bit of time this morning as it is a PD day which, somehow, I managed to be responsible for. I am working with the English teachers across the system focusing on "why we study the humanities" and what that means in terms of curriculum, teaching, and learning. The timing is ironic as I just had a large conflict with Tris's teachers about the series of questions and answers they are going through in *Brave New World*. I have no concerns with seminar work as long it is connected to the bigger, more meaningful picture of what it means to live a human life and what it means to live it well. Huxley opens so many portals for authentic exploration that need to be wandered through mindfully and with care. It is far too complex a piece to work at such a superficial level.

My writing voices have been silent this week as my own inner voice is struggling to be heard. I must admit I have been in "duck and cover" mode, staying safely within my classroom and my own reflections. I have ignored the things happening around me, the ineffective pedagogy and the lack of connection in my building. I have ignored practices I know are harmful and did not try to help move the work forward. It was simply easier, or so I thought. On the full moon this week I realized that I cannot be silent anymore, that I need to speak up not only for my children but all children. I need to use my voice so they can develop their own. I need to teach others; I need to write, and I need to speak up about what I know to be true and right. This is the teacher's way.

The work is deep and complicated, and I desperately need my mentors. I think of you and the others as I walk to work today. You are all so strong and passionate and with that passion aided me in finding my own voice. Now I need to use it to bring this work forward.

My mother finished her chemo round yesterday. She is sore and blistered but hopeful and ready to renew. I hope the process is much the same for you as the Phoenix rises slowly out of the ashes. I think of the Phoenix often as well as the powerful and poetic voice of Maya Angelou, specifically, "still I rise."

With hope of transcendence,

Kimberley

From: "Leggo, Carl" <carl.leggo@ubc.ca>
Date: November 23, 2018 at 5:10:23 PM MST
To: Kimberley Holmes <kaholmes@ucalgary.ca>, "Leggo, Carl" <carl.leggo@ubc.ca>
Subject: Re: Connecting

Hi, Kimberley,

May we always speak/live/be forthright and brave in our relationships with students, colleagues, administrators, and parents. We need to live truthfully and passionately, always, all ways. Education is so important for our well-being together, and we must promote the best practices of education in every context.

My granddaughter, Mirabelle, lives with apraxia of speech, and her life has been colored by that challenge/gift. She has had very good teachers, but this year she has a remarkable teacher, full of love and experience, a teacher who understands her special needs and is eager to respond to them. What a difference this teacher is already nurturing in Mirabelle's life!

May your mother's health be restored and sustained.

With hope and love,
Carl

From: Kimberley Holmes <kaholmes@ucalgary.ca>
Date: Saturday, November 24, 2018 at 7:14 PM
To: "Leggo, Carl" <carl.leggo@ubc.ca>
Subject: Re: Connecting

Dear Carl,

The pull of the full moon has been strong this week, and I have spoken up many times. I have made people angry, become angry myself, and finally now have come to a place of reflective contemplation. I am saddened to hear that Mirabelle lives with apraxia. I have only recently learned of this and how it impacts speech and language development. I cannot help but be struck by the irony that you and I find words to be our Muse while your granddaughter and my son both struggle with the articulation of language due to complex neurological manifestations. I am happy however that your Mirabelle has a wonderful and talented teacher. Teachers have the power to change not only the spirit of the child but the actual neuropathways of the brain. This is such critical work, and I wish all professionals would understand the significance of our immensely powerful and transformational work.

My first challenge this week was a conflict with Tris's English teacher, who refuses to modify her program to meet his learning needs. She currently feels I am a case for the ATA as I questioned her practice, which I fully admit I did. It perplexes me greatly that our union does not allow us to question one another—if we as experts don't question pedagogy then who can? Hence, I am happy to be brought forth on trial and defend my voice as both a mother and an educator! My principal has pulled the special education act and his individual personalized program plan states he needs modifications, so it won't be much of a battle, but nevertheless a battle that must be fought on public ground for Tristan and for Mirabelle too. As teachers, we need to speak to other teachers who do not rise to meet the needs of our complex learners, who do not understand diversity, personalization, and the power of neuroplasticity. We must speak for those who struggle to find voice.

My second challenge is somewhat ridiculous and evolves around my younger one's soccer team. The team is of mixed level and great frustration is being felt by all the players and parents. As the current manager I have to deal with it. The strong players are being asked to step down a level so the weaker ones can grow. I struggle with this as well. Why do we hold our talented kids back? Our gifted learners struggle equally. Boredom overtakes them, and they experience immense frustration, yet they are to "deal with it" and learn to work at lower levels. Although I am very much a believer in inclusion, I think this is a community level, not a competitive one. One must have a space where one can compete and try to rise to the top. This place is sports. Growing up, the thrill of competition filled a much-needed space in my life and taught me how to work hard to succeed. It is okay to push a little sometimes and see where we can rise, and we don't need to make ourselves small.

I am trying very hard to be mindful, but my patience is minimal this weekend. I must admit I feel like I am surrounded by idiots and simply want to enjoy my life and the process. Sometimes I get very tired of constantly fighting the battles and want to walk away. Is it wrong to walk away? Am I selfish for not wanting to solve the problems? Am I obligated to work through these things?

Huxley's Alphas suffer immensely with the responsibility for others. I feel this passion as well and today feel like simply distancing myself from all the drama. Today I just want to embrace the joy of life.

My mother's arm is healing and her spirits lifting. Tristan shall be starting his new medication next week, and we are hopeful for seizure-free moments. The snow was a brilliant sparkly white today, and the sky glittered a majestic blue. If I did not have to deal with the insignificant details of our day-to-day existence, today would certainly be described as magnificent.

Tomorrow I strive to rise above the idiocy and marvel at the line between the snow and the sky.

Still I rise,

K

From: Leggo, Carl <carl.leggo@ubc.ca>
Sent: November 25, 2018 9:43:40 AM
To: Kimberley Holmes; Leggo, Carl
Subject: Re: Connecting

Good-morning, Kimberley.

I certainly understand your concerns, especially regarding the challenges that teachers face when they need to critique one another. Nevertheless, we sometimes need to speak up; we must sometimes speak up! So, as long as we speak with heart, we can trust our words.

Regarding sports and competition, we need to support our best athletes to become the best they can become. Athleticism is a gift that some people have in exemplary ways, and they need support to excel.

My new round of chemotherapy now begins on Tuesday. I have been told that this new round will likely involve my being tired and nauseous, but I am looking forward to moving forward.

In recent years I have learned that I cannot solve most problems. Instead I need to live with care and patience and courage.

I have attached a new poem about seeking A's in school.

Hold fast to the good news of your mother's treatments and Tris's new medication. And always hold fast to the loveliness of each day—filled with light and dark, but another day to continue growing as a character in lively stories.

Love,

Carl

<u>Scarlet A</u>

the Canadian Carcass Poultry Grading Program
offers three grades:

> **Canada A grade**
> **Canada Utility grade**
> **Canada C grade**

I have been in school more than
sixty years, as a student or a teacher

I learned in the beginning how to be
a good student, and now close

to retirement after a lifetime
of being a student and a teacher

I am still learning to be good
I am on medical leave while
I receive extensive treatment for cancer,
I miss teaching, I miss the classroom

I miss talking with colleagues
about the joys and challenges of teaching

I might never return to teaching
I might need to retire, or I might

simply wave good-bye to the whole
complex, jumbled experience of being

human, and pass on to whatever lies
beyond this—always hoping

I have spent my life seeking A's—why?
why is A prioritized? as a Christian

I anticipate heaven, and really whether
or not there is a heaven, all that matters

to me right now is the idea that I might
soon wake up in a consciousness

THE SPACES IN BETWEEN

or place or livelihood or existence
where I will know that the old life

is done and a new life has begun
or I might not wake up at all

assuming there is a heaven, an after life,
an eternal life, a life with God,

then what will be the value of all
the A's on all the report cards

I have received? should I get
my CV tattooed on my body

so I might somehow carry it with me,
will God want to see my CV?

will I want to show it to anybody?
how do I live in this world as

a hopeful testimony to life after this world?
what is my value? Canada A grade chicken?

From: Kimberley Holmes <kaholmes@ucalgary.ca>
Date: Tuesday, November 27, 2018 at 10:17 AM
To: "Leggo, Carl" <carl.leggo@ubc.ca>
Subject: Re: Connecting

Good Morning Carl,

Today I am home in my sweatpants taking some quiet and reflective space. I read "Scarlet A" a few days ago and have been thinking very deeply about it. The scarlet right away speaks to me of a type of bleeding and/or branding, and the irony of our "grading program" speaks deeply to me on so many levels. It has required deep reflection and consideration, and I appreciate you sharing it with me. It is timely and aids me in my learning.

This past week has been very challenging yet thought-provoking at the same time. It began with a challenge to my colleague regarding my son's learning. She was wrong but took offense at my inquiry. The battle needed to be fought, and it was not pleasant. Then I was charged with mentoring English teachers in the district, and this was an engaging and inspiring experience. The two experiences sharply juxtaposed each other and reminded me that in spite of challenge there are people who still desire to do the work in authentic and meaningful ways. There is still hope, love, and commitment in our educational praxis. When people approach tasks with creativity and open minds, movement begins to occur.

Finally, I created fracture on my son's soccer team. The ideology of what sports are for needed to be challenged. For us, it is an escape to another world where competition and the desire to be number 1 drive all. For others, it is something different. I respect both perspectives but need to allow my son to become big. I believe we need to be big first before we make ourselves smaller for others. We need to let our own light shine and empower others to shine as brightly. We only grow through increased levels of challenge or our "proximal zone of development." It is okay to seek greatness when greatness calls to you. Hence, we are moving to a more competitive team, and some are angry at me for not being a "team player" and remaining with the team that is growing at its own rate. However, sometimes when the team is dragging you down you need to find another space and place that allows you to grow. Sometimes you need to strive for the A because your body, mind, and soul craves that level of stimulation; it is what feeds your energy and makes you face each day with enthusiasm. We need to be challenged where we are at in all avenues of our lives.

My English team at my current high school drags me down. I believe this might be why I feel so sick and tired, as their energy exhausts me and I seek higher challenges to thrive. However, the group of English teachers that I worked with in the system inspired me, so I know there is still a place for me in Education and work that I can do. However, it may require me moving to a different space and place. I think for wellness we need to surround ourselves with those who inspire us not defeat us. I believe this to be true in academia, teaching, and on the soccer pitch. Sometimes we need to cut ourselves loose from negative spaces and places, regardless of what others think of our actions. We need to strive for the A because it is good for us as human beings. It is not about being the best, but perhaps about being who we are. You don't get to pick some things in life; some of our skills and talents are just a part of our Essence required for the work that the world needs us to do.

School teaches us "to be a good student" and to take care of others. I have been taught to do the right thing, and because I am smart, essentially Huxley's Alpha, I have the responsibility to care for others. I love caring for others but am tired of the constant challenge from those who perceive the world in different ways than I do. Although I respect and honor diversity of thought, I am driven to defend what I know is right. These are the challenges and joys of teaching, and I seek strong teachers and mentors to join me on this journey. I seek the voices who are not afraid to sing loudly, write poetically, and challenge things that bring our world to darker places.

I think the value of an A on a report card is not the scarlet letter but what that letter represents. Ideally, if education were fulfilling its mandate an A would signify the ability to lead and be responsible for Others but also the knowledge of how to care for oneself and be well. It would signify wisdom and a life well lived.

Your CV does not need to be tattooed on your body as it is embedded through the fibers of your soul. The grade signifies nothing but the work, and your contribution to the world signifies everything. I believe that God sees all, and we live on "in everything we touch." In the end, it is not my honors status or my PhD that will be judged but how I contributed to the work of the world and how I lived my life. The value of that is invaluable as our Essence continues to live on in everything we have been a part of. Through our students and our impact, we live forever....

Who knows what exists after this life? We will only know when it is our time to cross that threshold. I like to believe this is an intermediate step, and the next one is where we find Nirvana. I like to believe that the "next life" is connected to the work that we do in this life, and our striving for A's is a reflection of our desire to do good in this world.

I would like to share "Scarlet A" with my English 30-1 with your permission. We are studying *Hamlet* and exploring the big existential questions of life. Your poetry would add great depth to the discussion and learning. It would make a difference to how they understand the world, the grade, and the ideology of "to be or not to be" for "in this sleep of death what dreams may come."

I hope your chemotherapy is not too vicious today and that your spirit withstands the storm. I am sending love and caring energy your way today and always. You are my teacher, and my life would not have been as rich without your mentorship.

<u>For Carl</u>

As we measure the worth of a man or woman, do we focus on the transcripts of academia

Or do we look at the meaningful impact a life has had with regards to the complexity of our Universe

Our world teaches us to compete in all aspects of our lives, not just on the sporting field

And although the battle on the pitch is powerful when one completes in life the toil is high

Sometimes we should save our battles for the soccer field and walk away from all the drama of life

To preserve our sanity, find ourselves sanctuary, and save our human wellness in spite of the obstacles

When one earns the sacred status of an A and rises to the ranks of Alpha

Sometimes our own happiness is sacrificed by the magnitude of responsibility we are then charged to care for

The magnitude of responsibility that comes with the brilliant CV that is connected to our wisdom and our very being

When we stand before those pearly gates of judgment it is our role and commitment to life that will be viewed

Our contribution to the world of work, of play, of joy and being all that there is to be in this space

Which sometimes drains both the emotional and physical body of all its energy and leaves us exhausted

Requiring quiet and reflective time to grow, to heal, and to move forward into other spaces and places

I believe that God values our contributions not as a grade but as a sign of commitment to a powerful way of life

Of living a full and vibrant existence committed to learning, to being, and to becoming something powerful

Something that rises above the here and now, the day-to-day existence of being human

Something close to God himself in all his external brilliance for his word is filled with sacrifice

Sacrifice that is followed with a hopeful testimony of what lies beyond the here and now

What could be, what will be, and all that ever was a part of what is and what lies beyond

All is but a reflection of the experiences which compose the story of our complex human lives

With love and reflection,

Kimberley

On Nov 27, 2018, at 11:33 AM, Leggo, Carl <carl.leggo@ubc.ca> wrote:

Wonderful wisdom, Kimberley!! The poem "For Carl" is an evocative response to my poem and a testimony to your vocation as a poet, teacher, and scholar.

Your spirit sings both loudly and melodiously! Always sing the truth!

Please, share my poem with your students. In some little ways, I feel like I know your students.

I hope you can make the plans you need to make about where to teach. Creative and gifted teachers will often need to move.

I will leave for the BC Cancer Agency outpatients' clinic soon. I begin the chemo at 2:30. I look forward to beginning this new round of treatment.

With sturdy love,

From: Kimberley Holmes <kaholmes@ucalgary.ca>
Date: Tuesday, November 27, 2018 at 12:12 PM
To: "Leggo, Carl" <carl.leggo@ubc.ca>
Subject: Re: Connecting

Dear Carl,

I have just returned from a short cross-country ski in the park. The park was silent with no signs of human life. The snow sparkled like diamonds juxtaposed sharply with the bright blue sky. My skis slid along in a graceful glide and the silence allowed for reflection and peace. At one point, in a daydreaming state, I took a small tumble and landed on the ground. The crows laughed out in glee and the echo of their voices vibrated around the trees. I lay there for a few moments looking up at the sky, listening to the crows and waiting for the trees to speak. Their answer was a simple silence which reminded me of the need to just be. We need to be who the Universe has called us to be to allow us to do the work that we need to do.

I look forward to sharing your poem with my grade 12s. I speak of you often to them, so I would speculate they also feel like they know you. My poets especially hear of your work as I remind them, "poets call to one another and we always answer."

I shall call to the poets, the teachers, and the mentors and see where the path leads me. I am a teacher but what exactly that looks like is always changing. Without change and transformation, we get stagnant, stuck in the snow drift, unable to hear the laughter of the crows or the voices of the trees.

My ears are keen to hear the callings of the universe and heed direction I need to take.

May the chemo cause the fire to rage safely through the body and allow the whole to heal. Hold fast to your spirit and your power—your voice is still needed in this space and place.

With gratitude and grace,

Kimberley

THE SPACES IN BETWEEN

On Nov 28, 2018, at 1:21 PM, Leggo, Carl <carl.leggo@ubc.ca> wrote:

Lovely, Kimberley!

You are flowing with poetry.

May we hold fast to gratitude and grace.

Carl

From: Kimberley Holmes <kaholmes@ucalgary.ca>
Date: Wednesday, November 28, 2018 at 7:49 PM
To: "Leggo, Carl" <carl.leggo@ubc.ca>
Subject: Re: Connecting

Dear Carl,

Today I am challenged to hold on to gratitude. This afternoon Tris had a small seizure in math class. He was tired afterward, and I took him home for a nap. I am grateful to my student teacher who managed my responsibilities so I could care for my son.

Tonight was our school grade 9 open house, and Tris was planning on being a tour guide and participating in our first "board game café." He wanted to go back to the school, to participate in the small pleasures of life, so we returned about 5 pm. He was keen to participate, and I watched him giggle, laugh, and be just like the other teenagers. For this small thing I was grateful, for my kid to be happy and enjoying his life.

While participating in "board game café," a few moments into his favorite game, monopoly, he suffered a second seizure. This one took his language, embarrassed him, and left him with a terrible headache. It frightened the other children and shattered the magic. We retreated to the "zen den" to await pick up. His disappointment was evident and heart-wrenching. He so desires just to be like everyone else, to lead the grade 9 tours, to play monopoly, and to just be a kid. His illness has robbed him of his childhood, and I struggle with this immensely. I find it difficult to be grateful as I bear witness to the struggle of my child. This struggle has been ongoing for 11 years, and I want to be done with it, I want to move on, I want to practice gratitude, but at this moment I cannot. I hate the virus that has consumed him, that causes inflammation and destroys his happiness. I hate the seizures, the side effects, and the cognitive challenge. I hate this demon that has entered our lives and refuses to retreat into the darkness no matter how hard I kick at it or strike it with light. In spite of my repeated attempts to banish this creature, it rears its ugly head again and again. I desire to decapitate it, to choke it of its strength, and force it to release its vicious hold on my child. I desire to destroy it with a rage that fills me in darkness and threatens to consume me. It leaves me gasping in panic and choking back a deep and dark frustration that threatens to erode the essence of my soul.

I also hate with all the power of my being the cancer that rages through the essence of you and my mother. I am angry that this disease has hurt my mentors, my dreamers, and my guides on this complex journey. I am furious that illness threatens to choke out the laughter, the love, and life itself. I wish I could strike out at it, rip it away from the physical body, and stomp it violently and viciously into limpid puddles of nothingness. I wish I could change things; I wish I could fight this; I wish I had more answers; I wish I was smarter; I wish I could stop this from happening. I wish I had more power than wishing and could actually do something to prevent this all from happening.

But I cannot.

So instead I allow the tears to flow down my face, my frustration to consume me, and my anger to rage in fiery ways. I allow it to seep through my body, burning and hissing as I struggle to manage my rage and grief. I allow it all to rage through my body, the fire burning rapidly and destroying all essence of gratitude, all positive thoughts and emotions. I allow the burn to continue, consuming all that I am until only the dusty flecks of ashes remain flickering in the deep darkness.

Then the tears begin to slow, and a calmness slowly and silently engulfs me. My sobbing subsides, and although my body feels tired, there is a remnant of energy vibrating deep within me. There is something struggling to rise out of the burning remnants of ash and face the world again. There is a force calling me to not give up, to believe in magic, and to hope when hope seems futile. It whispers to me to breathe, to stand tall, and to face the obstacles. It whispers to me to continue to fight against the darkness that threatens to consume those I love and overwhelm me with its suffocating grasp. I struggle and gasp for air, my breathing intense then slowing to a slow and steady pattern. My heart continues to bleed and rage, but my mind begins to steady. It stabilizes and calls for me to find a way to walk through the darkness seeking this light.

Seeking,

Kimberley

THE SPACES IN BETWEEN

From: Leggo, Carl <carl.leggo@ubc.ca>
Sent: November 29, 2018 10:34:28 AM
To: Kimberley Holmes; Leggo, Carl
Subject: Re: Connecting

Oh, Kimberley! I know your pain. I lived for at least 20 years with my son Aaron who suffered with terrible challenges of migraine headaches, asthma, allergies, and other ailments. It was always unbelievable to Lana and me that he suffered so much. He still suffers with medical challenges, but he is a strong, loving, patient, generous man, now in his later 30s. My response to Aaron has always been to love him dearly. And, in turn, he has always loved me.

Embrace the darkness and anger when you need to, but also know, as I know you know, that there is light, abiding light.

I have attached a recent poem that I hope I haven't already sent.

With love,

Carl

<u>Lunatic Scholars</u>

education research and practice
should always charge us with insights
(in legal electrical business military ways)

living with the flux, listening to ducks
laughing on the dike, an encouragement
not to duck the flux, to laugh too

dance a highland jig, even if we don't
know how, right in the middle of
the flowing, furling, flashing flux

leave the models and wall charts
and kits and formulas to others
who wear suits or pretend they do
we become masters like Ted T. Aoki
is a master, always pushing boundaries
we have not yet seen or been

to inscribe our own insights
we do not need to repeat
everything others have done

our hang-ups are the stories
we seldom tell, the handicaps
that trip up our successes

the hang-ups are our humanity,
at least as integrally who we are
and are becoming, as any gifts

perhaps the classroom needs
to be a place where human beings
hang out with their hang-ups

instigating a revolution,
a twisting turning, to and fro,
in the heart of pedagogy

why do scholars speak so quietly?

why do scholars mumble rumble stumble?

why do scholars amble in their preambles?

if you are going to be witty, ironic, comical,

be prepared (in the best Boy Scout ethic) to be

misunderstood, misinterpreted, misrepresented

write with a kind of reckless, ruthless,

ruminative, reveling resolve

to defer solution and resolution

From: Kimberley Holmes <kaholmes@ucalgary.ca>
Date: Thursday, November 29, 2018 at 3:07 PM
To: "Leggo, Carl" <carl.leggo@ubc.ca>
Subject: Re: Connecting

Dear Carl,

As I stare out my classroom window at the setting sun I am thinking again about all the interconnected braids of the story. So many struggles, so much passion, and so much to contemplate and consider with regards to this complex human condition we call life.

I am so sorry that we share this story of suffering children. I believe it is the worst possible thing in the world. I personally can struggle with incredible adversity, but to watch my children struggle absolutely destroys me. It is the powerless feeling that I detest the most, the inability to stop things from happening, to fix things, and to create a better situation. This lack of power drives me to the brink of insanity, and I am left to my poetry to help me sort out solutions amongst the jumbled mass of overwrought thought and excessive emotion.

Tris also suffers with migraines, asthma, and allergies. The root of all these things is the inflammation in his central nervous system. It is a root I always identified but the medical professionals denied. They were intent on treating the symptoms, not finding the manifestation of the problem. I have intense anger towards the "professionals" who did not look at the big picture, did not connect the dots, and did not understand the whole of the child. Although I would like to find peace in this process, my anger continues to simmer. Yet that anger fuels my passion to create better spaces and places for children to learn, to live, and to thrive.

Tris currently attends grade 11 at the school I teach at. He is the reason I am in this building at this moment. For years I watched him struggle with school, with teachers, and with friendships. I knew deep in my heart that a kind and caring teacher could change all this for him, but that person did not appear in his life. Hence, I knew in grade 10 not only did I need to be his mother, but I also needed to be that teacher. Daily he spends noon hours in my room playing board games or just connecting with others in a safe space. He often does not talk but sits in the room and eats his lunch. I still remember volunteering many years back at his elementary school. At noon, he was sitting quietly by himself. I now realize this was the pattern for many years. This child who struggled with illness was often left isolated and alone. I do not blame the children, for they are children. I blame his teachers for not paying attention, for not caring, and for not being present to this little boy who struggled. The lost high school student that I see today is a direct reflection of their negligence. I have intense anger towards these "teaching professionals," not for what they did but what they did not do to help my son and many others like him. Daily 30 or more students claim noon hour sanctuary in my room. Some are socially challenged, some have cognitive struggles, and others are just seeking human connection. All crave the sanctuary and the community. In my mind, this is what schools are for—to create safe and caring communities where all can thrive.

I am hopeful Tris will become a strong man like Aaron. I love him dearly with all my heart, sometimes so much it feels like my heart will burst and shatter into a bloody pulpy mess. But it never does—daily it continues to beat on with increased intensity and passion. Daily it demands that I pay attention and do the work that needs to be done, regardless of how unpleasant the task. As an educator, and as a human, I am called to engage in these battles to help children. I am sometimes incredibly frustrated that I spend significant time supporting the children of others when no one helped mine. It makes me want to walk away from it all, but I never do. Tristan has me as his mother to support him. Some of these other children have no one so I must fill that role. However, some days it is really complex and difficult, and I struggle to keep my panic and breath in check. Inhale, exhale, repeat....

"Lunatic Scholars" speaks strongly to me today. I am indeed a lunatic most days "ducking the flux" and trying to present models for change. I still need to act on my integral teaching model, as it does make so much sense regarding how we teach and live in the world. I need to trust my insights and my professional knowledge and figure out how to bring this work forward. I also need to "hang out with my hang ups" because I have my own baggage, my own anger with the professionals within the system. To do this work authentically, I need to move beyond my anger and work towards a reconciliation and a healing.

Academic Angst

When I was blessed with my PhD I thought the world would begin to unfold

My wisdom would flow from my pores and my colorful robes would be recognized

As a voice of reason

When I returned to my classroom the rules of the game had not changed

My award-winning thesis considered an "academic exercise"

Signifying nothing

Do you think my knowledge was all gathered from books in a short study?

Do you believe what I know was a short-term event for the thrill of the ride?

Or have you considered that I care

I care about children trying to find their way in the world amidst challenge and struggle

My heart bleeds for those struggling with physical, emotional, or social demands

I seek to find a solution

The PhD and the honors status, my parade of A's does not determine the human

It is the paths that I have chosen, the experiences that I have, and the tears that I have shed

That build the foundation of my wisdom

My books, my stories, my heartaches, my experiences, my loves, and my life
Drip onto the pages of my poetry, seeking understanding through the metaphor
The roots reaching deeply into the Earth

The small seedlings that are planted and cared for under our tutelage
Will only ground deeply, grow strongly, and blossom
If we teach them to reach for the light

Roots and wings, dreams and desires the endless clichés of the journey
Are but the seeds of possibilities that each soul may shelter within
Awaiting the awakening

With angst and love,

Kimberley

On Nov 30, 2018, at 9:41 AM, Leggo, Carl <carl.leggo@ubc.ca> wrote:

Thank you, Kimberley, for writing so passionately from the wholeness of your living experience, for crying out in ways that we must learn to hear, for practicing daily all the understanding and insight and love that generates your heart. Tristan is blessed to have you for his mother!

Always continue to write and speak and live with forthright courage and care!

"Academic Angst" is quintessential Kimberley!! Everything you live and believe is evoked in this poignant poem that holds so much angst but also so much conviction!

May we always live with hope for the possibilities of transformation.

With love,

Carl

From: Kimberley Holmes <kaholmes@ucalgary.ca>
Date: Saturday, December 1, 2018 at 6:27 PM
To: "Leggo, Carl" <carl.leggo@ubc.ca>
Subject: Re: Connecting

Dear Carl,

I am currently in Fernie, having spent the day wandering about the mountains with the snowflakes gently falling amidst the whisperings of Christmas. This little ski town seems to hold a mystic wonder that transcends the gray reality of Calgary city life. Life is slow here, no one is rushing, homemade trinkets fill the stores, and artists abound. Underneath the freshly fallen snow the grass is still green, still holding on to the vibrancy of life. We will be staying here until Monday in hope of rest and rejuvenation to prepare for the final three weeks of frenzy we call "school." I teach until the 21st and then come back for one short week in January prior to the semester's end. It is a crazy cycle that is not mindful of the Earth's natural patterns calling us to slow down and rest. Instead we ramp up in a rush to get to the finish line. Combine that with the pressure of "commercial Christmas" and overconsumption, providing a perfect recipe for disaster and burn out. This year I am opting out of the frenzy. We shall stay in our mountain sanctuary for a few days and avoid the chaos. We shall try to avoid the sugar crash, the overconsumption, and the consumerism and seek true meaning of family connection around a scrabble game. We shall try to hold onto our mindfulness.

On Friday I juxtaposed "Scarlet A" with Shakespeare's "To be or not to be" in my English 30 class. My students were moved by your work in deep and powerful ways. Many had tears in their eyes and commented on your "CV tattooed on your body." It was a timely moment to undertake this work as the senior class is faced with finishing the term and preparing for diploma exams. Much of their "Christmas break" will be spent studying and worrying on a frantic and desperate quest for A's and the coveted entrance into the Academy, which they currently believe will ensure their success and happiness in life. Your poem connected your story to theirs and built a common understanding of this big question of being and living in our world. I am hopeful your words may have struck a chord with them and perhaps grant them permission to walk away from their books and take some time for self-care and reflection. I hope that they take some time to enjoy the moments, laugh with friends, and participate fully in their lives. We have robbed this generation of something very precious while we encouraged them to strive for perfection in a never-ending series of evaluations and rankings. We have robbed them of imagination, of dreaming, and of the joys of childhood itself and given them standardized tests in return. Their worth is often measured by the number of bubbles filled in correctly, or at least what is deemed by the "experts" to be the correct answer. It makes me very sad, and I wonder how long this model of education will reign before the students tumble down in exhausted fragments, the lead of the HB pencils broken along with their spirits. I hope this generation might be the one to fight back, to reclaim time, and return to a world where one could practice the artistry of cursive writing, get lost in a book, or spend hours with the alchemy of poetry. A world where one could spend time listening to trees and hearing their voices. I try to inspire them towards this vision, but they are drawn towards their scarlet A's and their drive to perfection. This is what we have taught them, that their worth in life is determined by standardized measurements that really mean very little in terms of authentic academic learning. They could learn so much more from wandering the mountains and listening to the whispering of the trees.

With hope and love,

Kimberley

From: Leggo, Carl <carl.leggo@ubc.ca>
Sent: December 3, 2018 9:36:51 AM
To: Kimberley Holmes; Leggo, Carl
Subject: Re: Connecting

Hi, Kimberley,

The past weekend has been especially difficult, and today I am feeling worn out!

I am very glad for your eloquent ruminations on place and living and imagination. May Fernie always provide you with this kind of poetic dwelling!

I am delighted to read about your children's experiences, which remind me of so many of my own childhood experiences in Corner Brook, Newfoundland.

And thank you for sharing my poem with your students. May they know how there are always different ways of being in the world!

I wish you well in these next few busy weeks of school. Lean into the possibilities of quieter, more family-focused ways of being together.

With heart,

Carl

From: Kimberley Holmes <kaholmes@ucalgary.ca>
Date: Monday, December 3, 2018 at 2:24 PM
To: "Leggo, Carl" <carl.leggo@ubc.ca>
Subject: Re: Connecting

Dear Carl,

I am sorry that the trials you are undertaking are wearing on your energy. It is time to cocoon, to take rest and allow your body to heal. My mother is also having some challenges. We thought all was well as she completed the last round of radiation but were blissfully unaware that the radiation continues to course through the body, wreaking havoc, creating blisters and throbbing pain. It is easy for me to remind her that it is healing since my skin is not blistering. I feel her wounds in other ways, deep embodied ways that rumble around my gut, twisting and turning in compassion and suffering. We are so tightly connected to our parents and our children; our hearts seem to be in sync and our souls bleed together.

I would be interested in hearing the stories about your own childhood in Corner Brook. I greatly regret not gathering the stories of my grandparents when I had the opportunity. I lost both my grandmothers in the past year and find myself deeply missing them and wishing I could pick up a phone and ask them questions or just tell them how my day has been. Having both lived through a war and times of incredible stress and difficulty, they had a wonderful way of framing current reality and helping me build and maintain my own strength. They had many stories which I wish I had gathered and savored. I wish I had taken the time to listen to their stories.

Yesterday we put up a bit of a Christmas "shrine" with handicrafts made both by my mother and my mother-in-law. The boys cherish these family keepsakes, and they are what grounds our traditions. I try to remind them to spend time with their grandparents, to gather the stories, play board games, or just pop in for a quick cup of tea. As teenagers, their lives are busy and the demands high; however, they are diligent about phone calls, conversations, and connections. If my mother is well enough, they plan to do traditional Christmas baking with her. As I do not have daughters, my boys have taken on this role. It is quite a beautiful thing to see my teenage sons baking cookies with their grandmother.

My students now inquire about your well-being. You have become a powerful voice for them in understanding the complex ways that the world works. I have many budding poets, their words and images hiding deep within their Essence, and I am hoping I can help them find their voice just as you helped me find mine. I am trying to find ways to build the braid strong, to continue to weave the stories together in a powerful strand that has the strength and vibrancy to bind us all together in an interconnected web of community.

May you find strength as you work through this part of your human journey. I am sure the challenges will be difficult and your energy a challenge. Turn inwards to your Essence and remember, although now it is winter, Christmas is coming. There is always hope glimmering softly in the darkness.

With love,

Kimberley

On Dec 3, 2018, at 8:19 PM, Leggo, Carl <carl.leggo@ubc.ca> wrote:

Thank you, Kimberley!

I admire your spirit/heart/essence!

May we always seek the stories of others and may we always share our stories with others!

Love,

Carl

From: Kimberley Holmes <kaholmes@ucalgary.ca>
Date: Monday, December 3, 2018 at 8:39 PM
To: "Leggo, Carl" <carl.leggo@ubc.ca>
Subject: Re: Connecting

As I admire yours. Without our stories, our traditions, and our ways of understanding, we would be lonely and isolated. We need to hold to our stories of wonder, of loss, and most importantly of our shared humanity.

We decorated our tree in Calgary tonight. Although it is artificial, we strove to find one that would simulate nature as close as possible. It is adorned with white vibrant light to guide us through the dark and long nights. It is a beacon to symbolize the everlasting life and the hope. It is finished with silver and gold to symbolize the gifts and the power and strength of a community.

I often wonder if Christmas found its time and meaning as a result of the dark nights. As we near winter solstice on the 21st the days will once again become longer. However, for now the sun sets outside my classroom almost immediately following the school day, and the world feels cold and drafty. I find I retreat home at the end of the day and seek the sparkling lights of the Christmas tree. Nature (although imitation) and pure brilliant white light— to help us navigate our ways through the dark days.

Winter Magic

Snowflakes fall softly from the sky dancing on the cheeks of children

Scrambling in the drifts, kicking piles in the air, and making a game out of life

The evergreen tree stands tall and majestic holding fast to its power

Sparking lights adorning its branches in a celebration of all that is light

The child curls up by the fireplace snuggled up by the evergreen

The ornaments sparkling the glitter of all interconnected things that are gold

As the alchemy unfolds around things that were once average

The magic of the season sparkles and takes hold

In this season of darkness hold on to the light and the magic

Let the stories of time and celebration spin and braid through your mind

In spite of our obstacles, our broken dreams, and our fanatical illusions

Snowflakes fall softly and the magic is seen in the children

Hold fast to the magic and seek out the light. For in the end, our stories are all that we are, all that we were, and all that will ever be.

With alchemy and love,

Kimberley

From: Leggo, Carl <carl.leggo@ubc.ca>
Sent: December 4, 2018 9:26:49 AM
To: Kimberley Holmes; Leggo, Carl
Subject: Re: Connecting

The poem is gorgeous, Kimberley!!

You evoke the wonder of Christmas beautifully in each vivid image of the poem, in each heartful hope, in each clear testimony to wonder! I especially love the line: "In this season of darkness hold on to the light and the magic."

I have attached a recent poem I wrote for Mirabelle, my second granddaughter.

May we always breathe with the spirit of Christmas!

Love,

Carl

<u>Santa Claus</u>

(for Mirabelle)

when I was a child, long ago, I sneaked
into my parents' bedroom and found
a store of Christmas toys on top

of a shelf in a closet, dark and hidden,
tucked behind extra bed clothes
and towels from Duz detergent

faced with a crisis of faith, I knew
my parents were either Santa's elves
or, worse, there was no Santa at all

when Mirabelle was ten months old
she first met Santa at the Richmond Mall,
luxuriant, laughing beard, a Coca-Cola ad

but Mirabelle refused to sit in Santa's lap
and the next Christmas sat in her mother's lap
beside Santa but wouldn't smile for the camera
by the third Christmas Mirabelle still
refused Santa's invitations with a stern
unwillingness to play the game, but while
I held her in the long line, Santa dropped
over, here and there, to say hi, and when
he invited her again, Mirabelle finally

cuddled him with smiles, and Santa sidled
over and gave me a high five as we remembered
past Christmases, how belief is rooted in experience

Santa Claus was omniscient, loving, patient,
and with Mirabelle I believed in magic
steeped in myth and infectious possibility

From: Kimberley Holmes <<u>kaholmes@ucalgary.ca</u>>
Date: Wednesday, December 5, 2018 at 10:51 AM
To: "Leggo, Carl" <<u>carl.leggo@ubc.ca</u>>
Subject: Re: Connecting

Good Morning Carl,

I have felt compelled to reflect on Christmas as it appears all our traditions are somewhat under attack. I heard on the news that the carol "Baby, It's Cold Outside" has now been banned. My leadership kids were frustrated as we were required to take down our Christmas tree for the grade 9 tours. The reason given was that it might offend someone. As the tree is a symbol of everlasting life and hope, I struggle immensely with this. In the name of political correctness, we are losing many of our traditions and culture, which leaves gaping voids in our existence. If we take away myth and story we will only be left with science. Huxley warns us of this fate, but we are not heeding the message. It frightens me as we move closer and closer to the dystopian world where books, religion, and art are completely banished and forbidden.

It speaks strongly to the need for a comprehensive and detailed study of the liberal arts. We need to understand our symbols, the themes and the patterns of human life and history, recognizing the commonalities instead of expressing offense. Why can we not, as human beings, celebrate our humanity, in all the diverse and respectful ways that tradition and myth have to offer us? Why can we not be open to the possibilities in spite of our differences? Why are we trying to silence our diverse stories?

Your poem, "Santa Claus," invokes powerful memories for me. As a child, Christmas Eve was sacred. We would gather as cousins at my grandparents' home and sing carols under the tree in hopes of Santa hearing us. As we were singing joyfully and with all our hearts' passion, Santa would ride by on his sleight and candy would rain down from the sky. We squealed in glee and gathered the chocolates, blissfully unaware of my uncle in the corner performing the magic.

As we got older and became more sceptical, we would rush outside the house to find evidence. My grandfather had left large boot prints and often "reindeer hoof" marks in the snow. Our disbelief was denied as the physical evidence of Santa's presence was clearly marked in the snow. After my grandfather passed, I had a dream where I was walking with him. In my dream, I asked him what Heaven was like, and my dream rapidly shifted to Christmas Eve.

As the oldest, I was the first to realize the game but continued to play and helped to create the illusion. It was the start of my Santa schooling, and my understanding of the need to always hold on to the magic. It is the way that we keep our souls inspired and hold on to our childhood. There is such a brief window to believe in the magic, but a very long time to create it. This is our work as parents and grandparents, to hold on to the magic of the dream.

This Christmas will be different for us as our family was badly broken following the death of my grandmother and an uncle this past year. It was not the death that broke the bond but the bitter battle that ensued over the estate. Greed and anger turned the family into enemies. It breaks my heart, but I have come to recognize that this is a common story. Although we honored the will, and did exactly as stated, people felt angry and left out. I now understand that underneath the tinsel and the magic of childhood often brews family conflict, anger, and resentment. This was probably present in my childhood, but the magic protected me from the reality of the situation. My childhood illusion of family was truly my bliss.

I am trying to think about what we can do this Christmas Eve as we will not be visiting my aunt's house and joining my cousins. They are bitter and angry over the estate. It is my children and theirs who shall be punished by that anger. I am sure my grandparents are frothing in heaven over their misfit family, but perhaps they knew this might be the eventual result. Eventually old magic fades, and we need to find a way to create something new to sustain us. This year I shall be seeking a new type of magic for my immediate family. We leave for Mexico late Christmas Day to join friends for the new year. We will still have magic, but the way that it materializes will be different.

Reflections on Santa

Christmas Eve at Grandma's house with all the family gathered round the tree

Wonder and magic everywhere as long as we believed

Underneath the tinsel wrap the tempers simmered slowly

Yet smiles lined the frozen faces and candy reigned down from the sky

As my cousins and I screamed out in glee and happiness

Christmas Day and presents overflowing everywhere in attempts to buy happiness

Santa had arrived and everything on the list was there in abundance

The wrapping paper scattered around the room then burnt in the fireplace

Satisfied by materialistic consumption, the toys brought temporary happiness

But the culmination was the large family dinner and watching

Miracle on 34th Street over and over again seeking the true meaning

Santa is the magical myth but really symbolizes the joy of giving not receiving

Giving what we have in abundance to those in need and sharing wealth and happiness

He also is a way to control those nasty and defiant children through the dark season

Who will receive nothing if they rebel against the adults and misbehave.

And the Elf on the Shelf, well he is just a dirty little spy for Santa

Waiting to rat the children out to the big Boss and seeking the Sugar Plum fairy

Our perception is our illusion and what we choose to believe is what we see

We can choose the anger simmering underneath the tinsel strands and be offended

Or we can take a deep breath and seek the lost and hidden magic of the past

Make friends with the Elf and recognize Santa as a type of Robin Hood

And with our positive perceptions of reality create new type of magic

Seeking new and powerful magic,

Kimberley

From: Leggo, Carl <carl.leggo@ubc.ca>
Sent: December 5, 2018 2:24:17 PM
To: Kimberley Holmes; Leggo, Carl
Subject: Re: Connecting

There are many stories in your last message, Kimberley!

I am glad to hear about family celebrations, and I am sad to hear about family divisions! So often, that is the way! Nothing seems to break up an extended family like the death of the parents/grandparents and the decisions about the estate. Sad, but familiar! Family is always familiar—unfortunately, we don't always hold fast to the familiar as magical. Instead, we let "family" dictate stories of loss and waste and resentment.

A week in Mexico sounds wonderful! I love Mexico!

Like your poem, may we continue to create "a new type of magic."

Always with poetic anticipation for new possibilities!

Carl

From: Kimberley Holmes <kaholmes@ucalgary.ca>
Date: Wednesday, December 5, 2018 at 2:33 PM
To: "Leggo, Carl" <carl.leggo@ubc.ca>
Subject: Re: Connecting

Dear Carl,

Yes, there are so many stories that swirl around our experiences and shape who we are and how we walk in the world. The break of the "family" is certainly a common theme, and although I am saddened by it, I am not at all surprised. Families are frail and fraught with human fallibility. Human nature is often competitive, and oppositional forces between family members seem even more intense. It is what it is, and we can only move forward and shape what can be possible.

My grade 12 class is working their way through "The Yellow Wallpaper." Mental health is also an old story. We speak today as if we have a mental health crisis, but I think the crisis has always been there. The literature is full of the questions of existence, breakdowns and disconnects. In the past, we represented our struggle metaphorically, and now we document it with science and feed it with antidepressants. In the end, regardless of how we measure it, when mental health is in peril the "rest is silence."

I often reflect on how I can model wellness amidst complex circumstances, relationships, and emotions. How I can hold my own sanity in check while surrounded with elements of insanity? My yoga practice is sparse these days, and I have neglected myself, as the business of the days and the early arrival of night tend to leave me with little energy. I am awaiting the winter solstice, where the days begin to get longer, and light slowly returns to the earth. I am anticipating the warmth of the Mexican sun and the loving embrace of their culture. I too love Mexico and their commitment to enjoying life. Perhaps that comes from living in close proximity to both the sun and the water. Although we do get sunny days in Calgary, the bitter chill tempers the effects of the sun. It is best observed through a window, sitting close to a brightly burning fire, which at least creates the illusion of warmth.

I feel like I need to seek something during this period, to reflect on something and perhaps find a way to move forward. However, I don't know exactly what that is. I feel restless and somewhat bored with the day-to-day routine. It is indeed time for the seasons to begin to shift again. The new moon is arriving on Friday. The new moon corresponds to the energy of exhalation when the force of *apana* is the greatest. *Apana* is the contracting downward moving force that makes us feel calm and grounded, but dense and disinclined towards physical exertion. My body needs to remain still and grounded so I can listen to the voice of my spirit to see where we need to go now.

Awaiting new moon,

K

From: Leggo, Carl <carl.leggo@ubc.ca>
Sent: December 6, 2018 9:48:49 AM
To: Kimberley Holmes; Leggo, Carl
Subject: Re: Connecting

Good-morning, Kimberley!

Reading your thoughts about your everyday living right now, I am reminded how much my life has changed in the past half dozen months. I was once robust, busy, active, enthusiastic—full of plans and commitments and goals! These days, I just cling to whatever life and liveliness I can hold. There is much sadness in this new life of illness, but I am still glad for whatever I have and might have. Yesterday I picked up 2 granddaughters at school so their parents would be less busy than usual. I have been providing this kind of care for a decade. Unfortunately, yesterday I had to take a nap while they visited! Until my recent illness, I have almost never napped in my whole life. Now I sleep a lot! The challenge each of us faces every day is how to live well with wellness in the midst of each day's demands and challenges and opportunities.

I am having trouble with e-mail this morning. The system collapses. This, too, is a part of each day's odd experience. I wish I could learn to embrace all the oddities!

Listen carefully to your body! It will always guide you clearly if you are willing to honor its language.

With love,

Carl

Here is a recent poem that I hope I haven't already sent you:

<u>A Poem Is</u>

a heart beat   a light breath

a dream hanging on the line

stretched between poles we cannot see

falling in love with the alphabet

growing intimate with grammar and syntax

a game of peek-a-boo   scribbles in snow

a call, filled with hope somebody will hear

a message in a bottle dropped in the sea

attending to the familiar with unfamiliar words

a love note sent to creatures light years away

words infused with the heart's rhythms

words, efficacious, capacious, effervescent words

enjoying the sunlight through the study blinds

learning to live attentively in tentative times

cedars dancing in my neighbor's backyard

From: Kimberley Holmes <kaholmes@ucalgary.ca>
Date: Thursday, December 6, 2018 at 1:41 PM
To: "Leggo, Carl" <carl.leggo@ubc.ca>
Subject: Re: Connecting

Good Afternoon Carl,

I am considering how quickly things can transform from everyday life to adversity and illness. I am also thinking about how that shapes the patterns of our experiences and our perceptions. It makes me think of Tris's "illness story" which began in grade 1. For 11 years this has plagued us and shaped our lives, and I often wonder what life would be like for us if that virus had not struck him down. My mother's cancer also appeared at a young age for her. This is her third round of battles, and her life and mine have been shaped by these challenges and these experiences.

I wonder if I would have pursued my PhD, studied the neuroscience, or engaged in my writing explorations if life had been "normal and everyday." Would I have stayed cocooned in my normalcy, a suburban soccer mom touched by very little? Was this catalyst a spark to put both myself and Tristan on a path for something we were destined to do or to become? Do I need to learn something in this lifetime for my spirit to go forth to what may be next? My thoughts run deep on this and I wonder. In my yoga studies we unpacked the concept of the Sanskrit word *dharma*. This is behavior considered to be in accord with the divine order that makes life and Universe possible. It is a type of "cosmic law and order." The root is *dhri*, which means to support or hold or bear. Hence, my teachings state *dharma* is universal order and being able to bear what life has in store for you to prepare you for what is to come. Perhaps, this is the reason behind all our life and experiences: to simply prepare us for what is to come.

My grade 12s studied the graveyard scene of *Hamlet* today and reflected on the problem that, regardless of whether one is a king or a beggar, in the end we may all fall to the same demise. In Shakespeare we also learn of the divine order and what happens when we disrupt the pre-determined patterns of the Universe and fate. The theme of interconnectedness is predominant. The cycle of life goes on long past our physical existence, and although poor Yorick is but a dusty skull, Hamlet remembers his jokes, his laughter, and being carried on his back in fits of happiness and glee.

Your granddaughters are so blessed that for decades you have picked them up from school. Those memories will sustain them for a lifetime. I still recall my grandfather carrying a young precocious me around with him. I remember, much to my grandmother's dismay, spending time at the Legion with him eating potato chips and learning how to count cards, ironically a skill which served me well in life! I remember his laughter and his joy at life and hold on to this memory. My grandfather passed to spirit when I was 15 and in grade 10. It was my first experience with death, and it rocked me to my core. I was old enough to understand but not old enough to accept that it is what it is. Are we ever really old enough to accept it?

Our human life is filled with oddities. I think the ability to embrace the oddities is what keeps us sane or at least reminds us that we are human. I like to believe that his human stage is part of a much larger journey, that this is an age or a step that we travel through. Our body knows this process and tries to guide us along the way with subtle and not-so-subtle signs and symptoms. It tries to speak. One way I allow my body to speak is through my poetry. It comes from a deep embodied place that I know not of, nor understand its root. It speaks from some independent place deep within me that understands the "scribbles in the snow" and a "love note sent to creatures light years away."

With deep thought,

K

From: Leggo, Carl <carl.leggo@ubc.ca>
Sent: December 7, 2018 9:27:28 AM
To: Kimberley Holmes; Leggo, Carl
Subject: Re: Connecting

Thank you again, Kimberley, for your strong wisdom, fired in the crucible of living experiences.

May we always hold fast to the understanding of life as an emerging process with a beginning and an ending we might never understand definitively. We are often coached to perceive living stories as chronological with a beginning and an ending, but perhaps our living experiences are far more mysterious than any single story that can be plotted on a graph or a storyboard, or in a book or film. Perhaps our lives are pixelated fragments that can be organized and composed in countless ways.

Much to consider!

Carl

From: Kimberley Holmes <kaholmes@ucalgary.ca>
Date: Saturday, December 8, 2018 at 7:20 PM
To: "Leggo, Carl" <carl.leggo@ubc.ca>
Subject: Re: Connecting

Dear Carl,

As I watch the sparkling white lights of the Christmas tree glitter in the darkness, I imagine we are but stardust spiraling around in different patterns, synthesizing in different formations for temporary status and then returning to particles swirling through the sky. Our living experiences are indeed mysterious and complex and sometimes defy completely any sense of logic, justice, or reason. They are filled with passion and pain but also love and joy. It is a continuum that swings just like the cycle of the seasons, and every season has some type of reason.

I have a group of 14-year-old boys in my basement currently making a gingerbread house. Although they appear to desire "grown up" status, they are still seeking the sanctuary of childhood. They hold regular "poker parties" at our house where they play cards and pool. However, tonight they arrived with a gingerbread kit and are happily decorating cookies. It is a call back to a younger age, a less complex time when life was more magical and less serious. Although they are teens and appear almost adult on the outside, they are just little boys on the inside. It is interesting to observe.

These are the fragments of a lifetime. From an infant, to a child, to a teen, and then adulthood which spins by so rapidly one loses track of the time and the years. Life goes by in patterns, sometimes forward and sometimes back but always moving and changing. It is a type of perpetual metamorphism where one might eventually emerge Enlightened or simply cocoon into a perpetual darkness. Who knows what the eventual transformation will result in? I am not sure where the past 20 years have gone as they seem but a wrinkle in time, indeed a pixel of something much larger. Sometimes life seems to be just dots on a vast landscape, a tiny part of something much larger that beckons to us to go forward.

One wonders what a human lifetime symbolizes in the big scheme of the Universe. Our history goes back so many years, so many lifetimes, so many stories. Perhaps it is just a never-ending spiral that keeps rounding upon itself, a series of circles and connections that keeps spinning around us, enveloping us in a warmth that protects us from the element of dark.

My grandfather played poker and pool with his friends every Saturday night. It was his tradition, his favorite night of the week, and something he enjoyed immensely. He passed to spirit long before Jayden was born so they did not cross paths on this part of the journey. They did not know each other, nor has my son heard many stories of how my Nono lived his life or spent his time. Yet my son joins his friend every Saturday night in our basement for poker and pool just like his great-grandfather did so many years ago. It makes one wonder....

With reflections on the spirals of existence,

Kimberley

From: Leggo, Carl <carl.leggo@ubc.ca>
Sent: December 8, 2018 8:41:27 PM
To: Kimberley Holmes; Leggo, Carl
Subject: Re: Connecting

Wonderful, Kimberley!!

May the boys always play!

In poetry,

Carl

THE SPACES IN BETWEEN

Here is a poem that focuses on some of my questions about life and poetry:

<u>Fragments or Fractals</u>

… as always, we are deceived
by words, for language
imposes on us more logic
than often exists in life.
(André Gide)

+

like a line of poetry
seeking its apt shape
on the page, may you
follow the light
of poetry calling you

+

does everything have a voice,
singing a song we need to hear?

+

semantic   semiotic   symbolic   somatic

+

like you can't put new wine
in old wine skins, new ways of
knowing need new kinds of writing

+

what is the con in context?

+

is the glamor in grammar
a magical evocation
of hopeful possibilities?

+

what is the etymology of nincompoop?

+

beginning a new cliché:
it was a dark and stormy morning

+

found poem
(did it know it was lost?)

+

a poem is porous
but not poor

+

what is the syn in syntax?

+

he lost his story
and with it, his way

+

since my life is a collection
of short stories I will
begin a new draft

+

the root of truth is play

+

what is the middle of a muddle?

+

fund (past tense of fun)

+

love is indefinable, and hence poets
are always seeking to define it

+

what do you hear when

you listen to a flower?

(Leggo, 2016, p.10)

From: Kimberley Holmes <kaholmes@ucalgary.ca>
Date: Monday, December 10, 2018 at 1:12 PM
To: "Leggo, Carl" <carl.leggo@ubc.ca>
Subject: Re: Connecting

Dear Carl,

Yes, may children always play and find ways of being joyful in our world. As I sit in my English classroom today, I cannot help but think deeply about our educational "system" and how we often suck the joy out of learning. "Fragments or Fractals" spins a strong story for me, a story of teaching and learning through the process of joy. I wish daily for myself and my students to "follow the light of poetry calling me." Poetry speaks to us in strange and mysterious ways and requires a deep place of contemplation and consideration. We are so "busy being busy" in our day-to-day life that we forget to seek these hidden poetry portals that take us to spaces and places beyond the current moment. I desire deeply to find my way to the poetry portal, to hear the voices singing all the songs that we need to hear. There are so many things that we need to listen to, to simply pay attention to. We need to pay attention to the silence and the joy so it can burst forth in a special type of creative alchemy we call learning.

Words are playful, joyful, and a special type of mystical magic. What indeed is the con in context and where on earth did nincompoop originate? These thoughts bring a smile to my face and laugher to my students. How often have I had a "dark and stormy morning" and what a brilliant writing prompt on those ever so stressful days. What does it mean to storm deeply inside our being, and can we take the violent wails of the storm and turn them into art? How can we hear the flower or define love other than through our art, our poetry, and our voices?

I was hoping to attend a workshop at the University last Friday on creativity in teaching and learning. Alas, the Chinook rolled in, and I was sidelined with a throbbing headache and missed the day. I hope another workshop will present itself as my need for creativity and play is high. I need to feel joy and allow the poetry to pass through my Essence and land on the paper in new patterns and ways of knowing the world.

On Sunday I visited the Louise Dean school in Calgary. This is a school for unwed mothers and their babes. Some of the girls are as young as 13.... However, the sense of creativity and joy was evident in the building. Currently there are 100 moms or expecting moms and about 60 babies in the school. The walls are covered with art and inspirational messages. School is flexible and mindful of the context and situation. While they are there, the girls learn what they need to do to be well and take care of themselves and their families. This small model speaks to the essence of what all schools could be. Can we not create safe and caring spaces that meet all students where they are and take them where they can go? Can we not let go, once and for all, of this silly factory model where children are pushed through and then assigned a market value? I wish for a world where "the root of truth is play" and we can seek together the bigger picture of teaching, of curriculum, and the interconnectedness of human life. I wish....

<u>Wish</u>

Once upon a time the world was filled with magic and lazy decadent days

Pancakes for breakfast and a purple dinosaur followed by a walk in the park

Picking dandelions and blowing the fragments into the wind watching spirals

Of fluff float through the skies onto the next cycle of life

Then we had to send the children away early in the morning

THE SPACES IN BETWEEN

The tears fell from their faces as exhaustion overtook their small bodies

And the desire to snuggle deep under the covers ran deep

Illness raged and wracking coughs took hold as time rushed rapidly by

In a mad rush to nowhere

I still send my children to this strange place where exhaustion and frustration reign

Where words are turned to vocabulary lists and the magic of the story is lost

Numbers are no longer games but a nemesis to struggle with and conquer

Life something to be endured and days of dandelions are long diminished from memory

I wish to seek the spirals of flowers blowing gently in the wind and watch the patterns

Of the earth as she unfolds her magical messages all around in majestic beauty and wonder

Play with words, find the root, and seek the alchemy deep within the perplexity of pattern

Remember when learning was filled with joy and pancakes and a purple dinosaur

Singing I love you...

Wishing,

K

From: Leggo, Carl <carl.leggo@ubc.ca>
Sent: December 10, 2018 2:55:56 PM
To: Kimberley Holmes; Leggo, Carl
Subject: Re: Connecting

Wonderful, Kimberley!

I love the concept/practice of the Louise Dean school—may all schools be focused on serving the specific needs of children and young people!

You understand clearly how words are dynamic with imaginative possibilities for "mystical magic." May we always hold fast to the vitality of words for communing and communicating the stories that enliven our hearts. And may we always wish with vibrant enthusiasm for the experiences of wonder and love.

Alive in poetry,

Carl

Here is a poem I wrote recently. (I don't think I have sent it to you.)

Almost

for five hours Mona Rose bobbed in the Strait
of Georgia, exhausted with life and survival

saw the spotlights of BC ferries, Coast Guard Zodiacs,
and a Cormorant helicopter, all searching for her

though she did not want to be found on the eve
of Halloween after jumping in slow motion

from the Queen of Cowichan halfway
between Horseshoe Bay and Departure Bay

THE SPACES IN BETWEEN

six months after going to a doctor who told her
with definitive authority she was dying with cancer

announced on Facebook a plan to die skinny dipping
in the Pacific Ocean she loved with all its creatures

but when Mona Rose stripped, left a suicide note
on top of her clothes, and jumped, somebody

triggered the alarm while she swam away
now full of guilt so many were trying to find her

felt love everywhere and prayed, and an orange
life ring floated to her, so she clung to life

till a coast guard crew retrieved the ring and found
her inside like she was ready to jump out of a cake

hypothermic with danger etched in her face, still
breathing, Mona Rose knew she didn't want to die

and soon learned the diagnosis of cancer was an error,
glad the obituary won't be needed any time soon

From: Kimberley Holmes <kaholmes@ucalgary.ca>
Date: Monday, December 10, 2018 at 2:55 PM
To: "Leggo, Carl" <carl.leggo@ubc.ca>
Subject: Re: Connecting

Dear Carl,

"Almost" is a chilling and thought-provoking piece in so many complex ways. How often are we "exhausted with life and survival"? Sometimes it seems more energy to "bear the whips and scorns of time" and easier "by opposing end them." Hamlet's reflections are still so powerful today and the deeper questions of human existence remain the same. To be or not to be—a complex question that can only be answered by the seeker.

I cannot speak to what it would be like to be diagnosed to be dying with terminal cancer. I can only observe how you and my mother have responded to the challenge, and it strikes awe into me. I think I would be weaker, more afraid, and less resilient, but I might manage to pretend for my children that all was well. Perhaps it may even be well regardless of the dire predictions of the medical professionals. They could be wrong, and the story may not end as they tell us it shall. I do not trust them, nor believe them, as my experiences with Tristan have proven otherwise.

We do not know how our stories will unfold, so why do we assume that the medical professionals know so much? Miracles do happen, the physical body morphs, and significant errors are made in diagnosis. We are only human and cannot profess to understand the deep complexities of our Universe. There is much more to our essence than can be encompassed by our science. The spirit is a powerful enigma that guides much of the journey in ways I can only begin to understand. Indeed, "there are more things in heaven and earth than are dreamt of in your philosophy."

Having spent many days on the ferries traveling between the islands, I can visual Mona Rose in the cold and dark water and also hear the cries of the community seeking to find her. I admire her plan to die skinny dipping, returning to the water of the ocean much like she emerged from the waters of her mother. Water is such a sacred space. It has the power to give life and to take it away by blocking the passage of air. Too bad we could not return to our pre-natal state and simply submerge ourselves under the water and experience a rebirth into a new form. Mona Rose seems to be seeking that return to water.

It seems in the face of death or illness we do cling to life. Perhaps it is fear of the unknown or perhaps we are simply not done living yet. I think of the words of Robert Ross when the nurse offers his tortured body and soul a quick release. His simple response, "not yet...."

Not yet

The skin burns and blisters as it fights to expel the disease
That rages and flames through the body, racking the soul in deep convulsions
The spirit hides deep within the battered shell and waits for a portal
An opening to find new and sacred spaces to float and to be

The body is but a shell which harbors our inner Essence and protects the light
That flickers daily through the obstacles of being, breathing, and becoming
Sometimes the prognosis is heart-breaking and we seek an escape from it all
A return to the deep and mysterious waters from which we came

Yet the spirit flutters within us seeking the sanctuary of the orange life raft
That can help us float to the surface into the awaiting arms of the rescue team
And although the body screams of torture and fantasizes of relief
The soul whispers not yet......

With deep reflections on life,

k

On Dec 11, 2018, at 9:54 AM, Leggo, Carl <carl.leggo@ubc.ca> wrote:

Hi, Kimberley,

Your ruminations on life and dying are full of strong, tempered wisdom! Living and dying are the essence of human experience, and we need to attend to what it means to live and to die.

"Not Yet" is an evocatively titled understanding of the liminal space we occupy between life and the end of life as we know it. You call forth the tension between the body and the spirit. It is likely the body and the spirit are one. We just don't have the language to understand the integrity.

I hope the final couple weeks of school before the holiday are filled with resonances of hopefulness.

Always with joy,

Carl

Here is a recent poem that I wrote in response to this and that:

<u>Black Holes</u>

(April 2017)

on my way to El Dorado Royale

an adults-only paradise
in the airport in Cancun a man hands me
a card promises to debunk Black Holes

Revolutionary new ideas in plain and simple language.

I am always suspicious when offered plain and simple
language since language is never plain and simple

he is hawking an anti-Hawking view
of the universe none will ever know

Astro-physicists imagine non-existent Dark Matter & Dark Energy
to justify the incorrect Big Bang Theory. Galaxies actually form
slowly from Inside to Outside. WhiteHoleTheory.com explains
galaxy formation, the 3 major galaxy types, early galaxies,

THE SPACES IN BETWEEN

Great Walls, central bars, and high linear & rotational velocities.

on the Mayan Riviera I don't give much
thought to Black Holes or White Holes

seaweed spills along the beach
like an endless gold ribbon

all day young Mexican men shovel
seaweed into barrows and cart it away

occasionally a tractor like a Zamboni
roars by and scoops up seaweed too

a girl in a bikini lies on the edge
of the sea, photos with a selfie stick
an old man in a bright 1980s Speedo
hair watches the girl with the selfie stick

Lana in her Victoria's Secret bikini
is the best looking Nana on the beach

I am watching everybody falling asleep
waiting for another piña colada

Claudia the concierge worked hard
to convince us to go to the timeshare update

but I fended her off, not even sympathetic
for her concern she will lose her job

if I don't go, went once, never
again, so many people sucked into

the light hole of promises, buying
into unimagined luxury

I have mostly stayed away from e-mail
    John died
    Haim will retire
    Bart is in trouble again
e-mail fills my imagination
with fictions like Facebook

I read an armful of novels
wrote a few scraps in my journal

as stories wash ashore like seaweed
to be buried in holes at the back of the resort

black holes or white holes don't really matter
on a day, perfect or imperfect, on the Mayan Riviera

From: Kimberley Holmes <kaholmes@ucalgary.ca>
Date: Tuesday, December 11, 2018 at 6:09 PM
To: "Leggo, Carl" <carl.leggo@ubc.ca>
Subject: Re: Connecting

Dear Carl,

Your poem "Black Holes" was just what my struggling soul needed this evening. In 14 days, I shall be in El Tigre, Paradise Village, designed specifically to help me slow down, relax, and savor every moment. It is indeed a plain and simple concept where we can simply daydream and listen to the crashing sounds of the waves and feel the warmth of sand squishing between my toes. It is a place where I will not check my email (except perhaps to write to you) and hope to read armfuls of novels and write in my journal, gathering all the dusty and dark thoughts and tossing them into the waves to be swept away by a sunbeam.

Today has been a particularly grueling day. I spent most of it in meetings with administrators, strategists, and specialists regarding educational programming for our at-risk learners. I don't understand why it is so difficult to comprehend that all children learn differently and that the standardized model does not work. I also struggle to understand why I cannot question a process without wounded feelings, insecurity, and harsh denial. Is it not our jobs to reflect mindfully on our praxis, be open to questions, and engage both students and parents as part of the greater learning community? The work goes far beyond an academic grade, as our work deals with the mind, the body, and the very soul of a child. This work requires deep and careful reflection, a willingness to be open to possibilities, and a recognition of other ways of doing things.

During the meeting I listened silently for the most part, nodding my head in agreement as the specialists confirmed what I know to be true. Inside my guts twisted and turned, and I could feel my body physically quivering inside. There is something deep within me that needs to come forth, but I am tied by the rules of the system, bound by protocol and unions that forbid the flow of authentic thought, deep feelings, and serious questioning. The system is oppressive, and protective of protocol. It hates questions and interlopers who lurk in the shadows of knowledge and seek to bring in the light. It is Plato's cave where the shadows are preferred to the sunlight, and within its confines I find myself withering inside, and almost dying of something bright and sparkly that once filled my Essence. I find myself trembling and shaking within yet unsure how to uproot this disturbance and bring me to a place of balance.

I am starting to realize that my son's story of school and our illness story is deeply intertwined with my academic work. It is personal and a place of deep consideration. It is something that has significantly addressed me and seeks my understanding. Somehow, I need to find a way to bring this work forward to a larger context, beyond the box of the classroom and into a deeper realm of understanding, being, and becoming.

As I write this, tears currently threaten to overflow from my eyes and then freeze in their path. My face remains somber and serious. I have been trained to defend my ideas, and my emotions will not overrule me. However, my gut rumbles and gurgles, reminding me in ancient ways that trouble is stirring, and I need to be aware and pay attention. I worry about my own physical stress as I swallow the conflict. I want to simply walk away but recognize it is my role to advocate for those who cannot advocate for themselves. This was a role I took upon myself when I chose to be a scholar. The more one learns, the closer to Enlightenment one walks, the greater the responsibility to care for others. This responsibility makes me struggle to breathe; it speeds up my heart rate and twists my intestines in knots. It makes me want to run to my own teachers, hide behind their scholarly robes, and beg ignorance from all responsibility and knowledge.

Hence, at the end of this day, instead of reviewing my lessons and checking on my students, I retreated to the small shop across the street and had my fingernails done. I sat quietly and watched whatever current show flickered on the TV. I listened to the hum of Christmas carols in the background and tried to steady my breath while my intestines continued to moan their distress. Yet, I continued to sit and listen and admire how pretty my fingernails are. Answers did not come, but I am waiting for the voices to speak, for the path to become clearer, and for some understanding of my role and purpose in life to emerge. I am listening to my body, but all it allows at this moment is to address the distress. It is not allowing me to move forward, and somehow, I need to find ways to address this. Although I have been trained to defend against and manage conflict, it is not a space where my spirit is happy. It is not a space that is conducive to wellness. Perhaps it is not my space to be, yet if I don't speak up who will? How will we ever move forward if we all wait passively for change to occur while the wheels of the factory continue to turn?

I have a pedicure booked in a few days and am considering what color pink I shall paint my toes. Perhaps I will add a reindeer or some sparkly glitter that I can admire while sitting in my beach chair. I look forward to not giving much thought to the problems of the world, or the problems of my job, or even the problems of my family because all will cease to exist. My family will be with me and full of joy as we bounce in the waves and dance in the moonlight under the warmth of the sun and the celebration of the season. I realize this will be temporary, and I may be dragged back to the cave kicking

THE SPACES IN BETWEEN

and screaming and fighting. I may not have a choice but to fight these demons, to whatever end may come or whatever greater purpose must be served. I only hope that they will not kill me within their darkness and that I find a way to find the sunlight again. Perhaps it will be reflected off my pretty pink toenails as the sun shimmers out on the Mexican beach....

With dreams of simplicity and peace,

K

From: Leggo, Carl <carl.leggo@ubc.ca>
Sent: December 11, 2018 8:42:00 PM
To: Kimberley Holmes; Leggo, Carl
Subject: Re: Connecting

Dear Kimberley,

Always dream the possibilities! No day will likely ever be what we most want, but each day is filled with possibilities. Your vacation will rejuvenate your whole family. May you enjoy many hours of lingering in the sun with one another!

Glad to hear about the manicure and pedicure! We need those kinds of experiences, especially in the midst of all the busyness that fills our lives.

Teaching and parenting are always emotional enterprises. We must always live with our hearts.

With care,

Carl

Here is a new poem titled "One Line" where I remember a school principal I once worked with for 6 (long, tough) years. There is a little swearing in the poem. I almost never swear anymore, but the poem called for it!

One Line

just read a joke in Esquire

I first heard the joke in 1982 in Newfoundland
told by Hank, the principal, at a school staff party
I'd never heard Hank tell a joke before
couldn't even remember his ever laughing

staunchly Pentecostal he almost certainly
said heck, maybe hell, definitely not fuck

but I laughed hard and I'm still laughing even if
Hank is still the monster in many of my stories

more than 30 years since I left Hank's world
I remember how he could not negotiate conflict

liked to tinker with locks CB radios computers planes
liked to administer by stipulation suspicion stupidity

but while writing this poem remembering Hank
I hear that Billy Graham has died, for 99 years

he refused to shape Christ and Christianity
like a fundamentalist fiction, even if

he played golf with presidents who were glad
to shine with a little sacred sanctimony

and I read his books about angels, death, hell
and the need to devote more time to study

his Christianity was a counterweight to the harsh
theology of Hank's Jubilee Pentecostal Temple

and I wonder what Billy Graham would say
if he knew I am still rehearsing my one line

HARK! THE CANNONS ROAR!

From: Kimberley Holmes <kaholmes@ucalgary.ca>
Date: Thursday, December 13, 2018 at 10:36 AM
To: "Leggo, Carl" <carl.leggo@ubc.ca>
Subject: Re: Connecting

Good Morning Carl,

Yes, we must always dream of the possibilities and anticipate a life with joy. When we live with a feeling of dread that is what we actualize, and the world appears dark and oppressive. This is my focus and my mantra as I move forward past the obstacles in my life that currently drain my energy and leave me void of creativity. I cannot help but think of the voice of Maya Angelou and the refrain, "still I rise." May we always rise to meet the challenge of what threatens our light. May we always see the ribbons of sunlight through the clouds and find better spaces and places to learn, to live, and to grow.

Teaching and parenting are indeed emotional enterprises that swirl my energy in strange patterns, bouncing from joy, to rage, to fear, and then back to wonder. I had no idea when I had children what it might feel like to have your own heart walk around in another body. I now understand, and the impact is astounding. I now truly understand the "mother bear." The ruling passions of parenting and teaching are not for the faint of heart and remind me of the significance of a mindful lifestyle where one takes time to observe emotions, honor them for what they are, and then allow them to move outwards where their impact is not so violently felt. Inhale, exhale, move forward, repeat ....

"One Line" made me laugh out loud. Sometimes our experiences do call for swearing; it is the only type of word that seems to express the experiences. Sometimes, we need to add power to our words—many of my slam poems have colorful vocabulary and descriptors, but this seems somehow needed to capture the voice in a way that was true to that state of being!

The irony of the rote memorization of the line, independent of context and circumstance, is not lost on me. It reminds me of Brave New World where they use sleep hypnopedia to memorize the facts. However, when the wording of the "fact" is changed in even a minor way, the children are unable to express their learning. Learning was not present and understanding of context void, leaving children often wondering, "What the fuck was that?"

There are many "monsters" in my story of education. We are all still rehearsing our line in so many ways!

<u>To be</u>

Life is but a lonely player that dances and struts upon the stage

Causing a ruckus, breaking hearts, bleeding passionately on the hardwood

Of the theater of life itself while the players take their roles and wander

Through the portals to the wardrobe where our dreams and nightmares merge

The sludge, the garbage, the anger, and the vicious barbs in forms of words

Are hurtled in the competition to determine who is right and who is wrong

Who will be and who will not be upon the stage of life when it is time for victory

And who will be wandering through the forest seeking other voices and patterns

By opposing do we end this sea of troubles that we are blindly bobbing within

Or do we drown a thousand deaths, sputtering and choking in the murky depths

Do we spew the water from our lungs and scream victoriously not yet
Or do we swallow inwards and allow the sea to slowly consume our soul

To be or not to be that is indeed the question of our human journey
Slay the monsters, tame the dragon, bring the white witch to her knees
Then bow your head in deep and reflective prayer and gratitude
That you have been blessed with the power to undertake this quantum quest
To be

With hopes of possibility and growth.

OX

K

On Dec 13, 2018, at 8:16 PM, Leggo, Carl <carl.leggo@ubc.ca> wrote:

Thank you, Kimberley, for all this sturdy wisdom!

"To be" is a compelling response to Hamlet's life-searching questions, as well as a compelling testimony to a life that is lived with the heart on fire.

I had another MRI early this morning. I see the oncologist on Monday morning. I wonder what news she will give me—always wondering about the news!

May we continue to rehearse our line(s).

With heart,

Carl

Here is an old poem—actually included in my first collection of poetry titled *Growing Up Perpendicular on the Side of a Hill*—poems about growing up in Newfoundland. I am sending it today because a friend in Kingston phoned me yesterday and told me he wanted to read a poem for me. He read the following poem:

A COFFIN AND A CHEVY

*My father bought the '58 Chevy,
maroon and new, drove my brother and me
out of the city along the Trans Canada Highway
to cut a Christmas tree, parked on the shoulder,
left my brother and me, sank into the snow
like quicksand, my brother, only four, laughing,
and I was laughing at my brother laughing
as my father waved a hand, his mouth a tight line,
just before he was swallowed by snow and dark trees
and my brother jumped up and down in the back seat
while I pretended to drive away for help
but went nowhere, and my father didn't come back,
my brother full of fear, no longer laughing,
and the air was thick with chewy toffee,
my father gone, my brother going crazy,
so I grabbed the ice scraper and jabbed holes
in the maroon velvet over me like the inside
of a coffin, no escape, and my father returned,
creature from the snow lagoon, bearing a tree,
a wide grin where the line had been,
and the car was a car, not a coffin,
my father was alive, my brother was laughing,
and my father looked at the neat triangular flags
hanging from the ceiling of his new Chevy,
said nothing, drove back to the city
in a Chevy once more a coffin.*

From: Kimberley Holmes <kaholmes@ucalgary.ca>
Date: Friday, December 14, 2018 at 8:54 AM
To: "Leggo, Carl" <carl.leggo@ubc.ca>
Subject: Re: Connecting

Good Morning Carl,

We too are always wondering about the "news." Tris and I are at the Alberta Children's hospital this morning for his monthly IVIG. As we arrived this morning the juxtaposition between light and dark was startling. The trees outside the building are adorned with bright Christmas lights, and mini "streetlights" at the front entrance sparkle to announce your arrival. The sun in its brilliant colors of orange and pink was rising, creating a candy cane sky of wonder. Inside the building a majestic Christmas tree stands at the center, glittering and sparkling with hope. At the Children's hospital political correctness around Christmas is not a concern as evidence of the season is everywhere. It appears to be a place of joy, the illusion of happiness reflected in the shiny decorations decked in the branches of the trees. It offers parents and children an escape from the reality, a promise of magic, and hopes of a rebirth.

Yet we all recognize that children only come here if they are sick. They walk through these doors only if they are battling physical or mental demons that refuse to leave them, that haunt their childhood and take away the magic of youth. It was 11 years ago that I was sitting in the ICU unit watching my small child struggle to breath. Today, I sit beside him while the blood plasma of others offers him the gift of life. The contrast between the "Chevy and the coffin" is evident. Today we are in the Chevy, although "the neat triangular flags hanging down" still threaten to darken our days and return us to the coffin. Today the "thin line on my face" is replaced with a wide grin as I practice gratitude. Today I hope that one day this illness may be but a memory that I ruminate about in my poetic prose.

My blood still runs cold as I return to my memories. In retrospect, I am not sure how I survived mentally as I watched my child struggle to breathe. I don't think I ever consciously registered that he could die at any moment for I believe if I had I would have crumbled into empty nothingness. I believe I lived in a state of denial, an illusion grounded in mythology of magic that helped me cope and be strong. Perhaps this world of illusion has been my reality for the past 11 years as I struggled to cope with the obstacles. I wonder if I just removed myself to another space and place, pretending that this was not really happening to us, that the reality was not real at all, and that tomorrow we would wake up in our own home and have pancakes for breakfast and none of what is currently real will be reality. I used my books, my learning, and my literature to protect me, to transport me somewhere else where perhaps I had some semblance of control, some way of stopping the rapidly spinning cycles of our lives. My writing and my words allowed me to process and to remove the anxiety for my life. For as the words fell on the page, I somehow managed to make at least a temporary sense of the world. The words performed a type of magic as the story was shared with others and the strands of the web of life were strung tightly together.

I think perhaps this is how we survive the uncertainty of life. We live out our stories. Last night my parents were over for dinner and to trim the tree. My mother's body is blistered with burns from her chemo, her skin red and angry, yet she insisted on having her arms deep in the dish water to clean up the remnants of dinner. My reprimand of "take it easy" was ignored with a dirty look, and she continued to help take care of the needs of the family, just as she had done every day of her life. She takes no time for pity, for sorrow, or for sadness; she simply moves forward and does what needs to be done. This is the legacy of the woman who raised me. Don't waste your time in sorrow but move on, move forward, and enjoy whatever time we may have left.

Time

The rapidly marching hands of the clock demand that we focus on progress

That we continue to improve, be efficient, and make the most of our days on earth

Make sure you are the smartest, the strongest, the best, and the brightest

As you scamper and clamber and stumble and fall, clawing your way to the top

The winds swirl violently at the top of the mountain as the elements howl around you

It is lonely, as not many venture this far or seek to look down upon the others

The cold air swirls around you and sharpens your breath making it difficult to inhale

The icy swirls in your lungs painfully expressing the body's need to breathe

Out out brief candle that struts and frets upon the stage singing the song of the idiot

For in the end, regardless how high the pinnacle all that remains is the silence

Enjoy the view, recognize the significance of the breath and inhale deeply all that life

Might offer you be it pain, be it sorrow, be it lessons of what might be or what may become

All that is, all that every was, all that can ever que sera sera

Is painted through the portraits of our human history and our human hearts

As the drumbeat carries on, in the pounding rhythm of the blood surging through the heart

Dancing the patterns of human life admits the sorrow of the days

With dreams of dancing, K

On Dec 15, 2018, at 11:01 AM, Leggo, Carl <carl.leggo@ubc.ca> wrote:

Dear Kimberley,

You are blessed by many gifts, including the wonder of your mother!

I love the thoughtful ways you describe the hospital, and the sense of peace you hold fast to as you sit again with Tris in the hospital that is so familiar, so startling.

May the drumbeat continue, and may we dance the stories we can dance to the beat of the drum!

With love,

Carl

Here is a "somewhat grim" poem, but a poem that evokes much of my spirit these days:

If I Knew I Was Dying

if I knew I was dying, I would write a poem
for Lana and tell her she is beautiful

if I knew I was dying, I would write poems for Anna and Aaron
and for Madeleine and Mirabelle and Gwenoviere and Alexandria

if I knew I was dying, I would not read any more books
and focus instead on remembering all the books I have not read

if I knew I was dying, I would watch Doctor Zhivago again,
no movie has ever captivated me like Doctor Zhivago

if I knew I was dying, I would hike a favorite trail

in Newfoundland or British Columbia

if I knew I was dying, I would eat a jumbo fries
at New York Fries (with gravy and malt vinegar and salt)

if I knew I was dying, I would clean out my office at UBC
and hope the next occupant will enjoy it as I have enjoyed it

if I knew I was dying, I would send notes to a circle of friends
and colleagues to wish them well in their life journeys

if I knew I was dying, I would sit quietly
and let God fill my imagination with prayers

if I knew I was dying, I wouldn't watch much TV
or read internet stories about Donald Trump

if I knew I was dying, I would drink
pinot noir and gin martinis, every evening

if I knew I was dying, I would listen to a lot of music,
especially Leonard Cohen and Willie Nelson

if I knew I was dying, I would go to bed early
and wake up late

if I knew I was dying, I would go to the Cactus Club
and order the Rob Feenie-inspired barbequed duck club sandwich

if I knew I was dying, I would enjoy
a bath every day with Avon Skin So Soft

if I knew I was dying, I would look forward to life
after death, the eternal journey, the heavenly life

if I knew I was dying, I would sit on the patio
with Lana and hold her hand and tell her I love her

if I knew I was dying, I would stop

writing this poem

(Holmes & Leggo, 2019)

From: Kimberley Holmes <kaholmes@ucalgary.ca>
Date: Saturday, December 15, 2018 at 5:01 PM
To: "Leggo, Carl" <carl.leggo@ubc.ca>
Subject: Re: Connecting

Dear Carl,

"If I Knew I Was Dying" brought tears to my eyes. Your relationship with Lana is so beautiful as your first thought was to write her a poem and tell her how beautiful she is. This is the type of relationship that I have always sought but never found. My family has always been dysfunctional, including my current one. Various social challenges and neurocognitive difference make communication strange and inhibited, strangely stifled, and I often find myself deeply craving that intense human connection that is so lacking in my life. Although I am connected to my boys, as they grow older that connection is less. I realize this is normal and that they are preparing to have families of their own. My grandmother always said a son is a son until he takes a wife, a daughter a daughter for the rest of her life. I have no daughter, no sisters, no nieces. I am surrounded by boys, although I am not sure biological sex is the defining factor, and sometimes this makes me feel so alone and disconnected. Perhaps, I am simply a poet in a world of engineers and geologists. Perhaps I am an artist struggling to survive in a world that honors science and technology. I miss my Nana immensely as she was the one family member who was like me. Without her, I often feel like an abandoned orphan trying to find roots. I feel like I am seeking something, or someone that is missing. I am seeking that someone that I could write poetry to....

Is it only when we are faced with death that we realize what it means to live? What does it mean to live? I know we are to "follow our bliss" and "gather ye rosebuds while ye may," yet how often are we granted permission to do that? My first job was at age 13. I realized young that if I wanted to move forward in my life, I would have to work at it. I spun cotton candy at the local amusement park, the pink strands of sugar covering my hair and resting on my eyelashes. Then I cleaned up garbage at the stampede, worked as a bus girl, learned the rules of customer service in retail and restaurants, and carefully picked my way up the latter via my experiences. There was no easy way up, no trips to Europe to find myself or Ivy League education. Just me putting in time to seek what I perceived might be success only to learn that "life goes on—long after the thrill of living is gone."

I don't enjoy jumbo fries as the salt makes me sick and my stomach swells up. A good glass of red wine often gives me a headache and causes my face to flush. Hence, food does not offer the portal to happiness. A luxurious bath works temporarily but the warmth often washes down the drain with the remaining soap suds leaving me chilled and shivering. These things are but temporary fixes for a much deeper-rooted problem of disconnection.

Huxley's Alpha characters are portrayed as unhappy and miserable, seeking to "write their poetry in peace" and find spaces and places where "we wish we could find something more." In this world poetry, literature, religion, and relationships have been forbidden, leaving a gaping void where emotions were once felt. I often wonder if I live in this emotional world now, where I crave to write poetry, share ideas, and engage in debate. I reality, I live in Calgary where the market reigns and competition is fierce. A place where ideas are threatening to the status quo and conversations evolve around oil and production. It is a place that lacks beauty and wonder, and I struggle as I seek deeper meaning, greater purpose, and ultimately a means to find happiness.

Hence, I use my illusions of peace and my poetry to protect me in a world that I don't really belong in or fit into very well. Although I do have many blessings, I also have many obstacles. I cannot defeat these obstacles, only honor their existence and the impact they have had on my life. In many ways, we don't get to choose our destiny but simply accept it. Life is not always grand and sometimes it is downright shitty. Children seize, mothers get cancer, treasured mentors may be lost. Tears run freely but their power is limited to the release of the cortisol that surges through my body. In the end, I am virtually powerless regardless of my knowledge, my experience, or my Ph.D. In the end, I should have spent my life doing other things, but the pressures of society pushed me to do what I thought I was supposed to. The paradox of our time, higher "lifestyles" but less life.

My apologies on my own "grimness," but I also find myself in this space and place, and sometimes I need to dwell in it, listen to it, and honor it for all its darkness. When I am done dwelling in the dark, I shall try to hear the drumbeat and find ways to convince my feet to dance and not drag.

Seeking meaning and love,

Kimberley

From: Leggo, Carl <carl.leggo@ubc.ca>
Sent: December 17, 2018 2:19 PM
To: Kimberley Holmes; Leggo, Carl
Subject: Re: Connecting

Dear Kimberley,

Thank you for writing with the kind of frank and confessional truth that can singe eyebrows! I appreciate your commitment to your heart, and your unrelenting devotion to writing what you need to write. Never surrender your commitments!

I have had a few busy days, and this morning I had a tough meeting with my oncologist. She informed me that the brain tumor has returned—fast and furious! She will call me later today to let me know about plans for radiation—probably the only treatment that is left. So, I live with this difficult news, and Lana lives with it, too. The cancer journey just grows more challenging with each day! Nevertheless, I will live the story with faith, hope, and love, and I will live the story for as long as I can.

Sending love to you and yours,

Carl

Here is a poem I wrote for Lana a while ago (I hope I haven't sent it already):

Algebra

(for Lana)

love is the unpredictable predicate
no calculator can measure

love is enough heartbreak to fill
a season of Coronation Street

love is fictions fragments figments fractures
fired in the heart's foundry

love is Madeleine in her Oscar costume
wearing the dress you wore on our honeymoon

love is knowing the creation is always creating
with the creator's collaboration

love is leaning into the wind, hauling hard
on the line that does not break

love is the geometry of the Steveston winter sky
trusting in a fundamental theorem

THE SPACES IN BETWEEN

love is Mirabelle on roller skates
remembering our first date

love is saying good-bye to family and friends
moving from one ocean to another, new stories

love is getting it wrong much of the time
but still shaping a right angle in complements

love is seeking the divine and ineffable amidst
the distinctly human, even in the inevitable wounds

love is Gwenoviere, arms stretched out
for the whole world like we knew long ago

love is Yahtzee Monopoly Scrabble where
so much depends on who gets X

love is caressing a scar, a reminder
of what was and might have been

love is living on borrowed money and hope
remembering heartbreak with forgiveness

love is Alexandria, wearing wigs and costumes
like her father always wore, filled with make-believe

love is learning to live alongside the stranger
the inscrutable and intimate other

love is inerrable irritable inimitable illimitable
inhabitable irresistible irascible inflamed

love is algebra (Arabic, al-jabr), like our story
the reunion of broken parts

From: Kimberley Holmes <kaholmes@ucalgary.ca>
Date: Monday, December 17, 2018 at 8:44 PM
To: "Leggo, Carl" <carl.leggo@ubc.ca>
Subject: Re: Connecting

Dear Carl,

Thank you for understanding my "confessional truth." I have the unfortunate habit of speaking (or writing) what I think and feel without much regard to potential outcome or impact. Sometimes this offends people immensely, and at other points it earns me great respect for authenticity and honesty. At this age and stage, I am okay if people are offended. It means it is probably not someone I can be honest and authentic with. Those who accept me in my "rawness" are the people I need to be around. Those are the ones that allow me to burn and seethe so that I can eventually shine bright again. The process of melting down is needed to allow growth. In the end, some people will find me offensive and some enduring. Thank you for being one of the people who accept my voice for what it is.

I am sorry to hear about your meeting with the oncologist and that the nemesis has returned to taunt your well-being. It is difficult news and makes me want to rage about what garbage cancer is and how we really need to find a way to deal with this demon that threatens so many. I wish cancer was a thing that I could kick and punch and physically destroy, but it is a strange enigma which we are unsure how to battle. The inability to fight back feeds my frustration and my anger, and I rage inside over the injustice of this disease. I feel deeply for you, although I cannot begin to comprehend what you must be feeling or experiencing. I would assume you feel sorrow or perhaps rage. I would also assume you are worried about Lana and how she will cope. Illness is not an individual thing but something that strikes a whole family.

I love the poem "Algebra" as it speaks powerfully to the alchemy and intersecting levels of this elusive concept we call love. It is indeed an "unpredictable predicate" that is not measurable, as it defies the data collection and sifts the pieces together like a soft perfume on a hot summer day. The pieces are fragments of memories, a scent of something intoxicating and the interwoven strands of the family. The images of Madeline wearing the honeymoon dress and Gwenoviere, her arms stretched out, breathing of innocence and joy and life itself, are touching and powerful tributes to the cycle and patterns of love and life: It is "the reunion of broken parts" a process within which we become whole and also become fragmented. Love is having your heart a part of another's heart and increasing your probability that both hearts might break, shattering into broken splinters that cause painful bleeding deep into the soul.

Love is part of life and part of death. When someone we love leaves us, we bleed deeply, and part of our heart is broken. We must heal that part with more love, different kinds of love that weave gold threads over the broken part, leaving the beautiful memories bound carefully among the strands of gold. Memories of love are what sustain us through the dark, what helps us battle the obstacles, and what binds the broken pieces of the human heart.

Lamentations of a Wannabe Artist

I am seeking a portal to the truth

Yet deep inside my heart is blocked and the life does not wish to flow there

My spirit is frightened and wants to be left alone to my illusions of strength

Because the truth hurts every part of my Being and makes me want to vomit

Bits of held-in thoughts and words that I have swallowed inside me and hidden deep

The truth cuts deeply into my flesh leaving seeping bleeding wounds

Rich, red, flowing blood that saps the energy out of the various portals of my body

Threatening to destroy my very being driving me to the brink of insanity

A screaming, seething mess of nothingness incapable of functioning in the day to day world

I get why van Gogh cut off his ear and mailed it to his lover

He wanted to be heard and what a brilliant bloody metaphor to send

A seeping bleeding, bloodied ear to the desire of his intentions

I get why Atwood, Hemingway and Findley all seem like they are completely crazy

Because when you go deeply into the realm of human emotions and feelings

Demons bubble up and threaten to block your throat and stop your breath

The darkness of the world seems so overwhelming that there is really not a glimmer of hope

And then you curl up lonely and afraid upon the floor and die a slow and painful death

So frankly I really do want to go there and maybe I don't want to be an Artist after all

But if I really want to speak the truth, I asked for something to push me, I asked for this

I asked the Universe to send me a teacher so I could understand this wild swirl

Of emotions, of worlds, of confusion, of tears that find a home deep within me

That impedes my voice, traps my words, and impedes my ability to go forth

That threatens to overwhelm me, to snap me, to drop me to my knees into darkness

From which I may never emerge again

The seething insects in my head gorge themselves on the vicious lamentations of my mind

On a feeding frenzy of memory that should best be buried deep inside

But I know things buried deep will rot and fester, seethe and scream their rage

And I will get physically sick from a variety of interconnected diseases, and then I will die

So, I shall speak the truth because otherwise the burning will never slow

Nothing will ever arise from the ash

THE SPACES IN BETWEEN

I have a son who has a brain through which electrical currents rage causing him to seize

The doctors call it epilepsy, but I believe it is a memory from a childhood of illness

A memory of needles, and fear, and terror, and an inability to breath

That he needs to expel from his body somehow so his entire being seizes in fits of rage

When he falls to the floor, his mouth contorted, his body jerking and froth spewing forth from his lips

I maintain a demeanor of calmness, hold his hand and tell him to breathe

While inside my own body and mind a thousand demons scream that this is my fault and somehow, I caused this to fall upon us because of my negligence.

They remind me that I must be present, I must pay attention, and I must not ever relax

I live in terror that one day I will not be there to stop the threat

That one day I will not make the 911 call and place the oxygen mask upon his face

And that one day he really will die with a twisted face and gasping screams in front of my eyes

While I stand there helplessly holding his hand and trying to make him breathe

Mumbling ancient chants and holding on to a power which I really do not have

Because the truth be told, there is not a thing that I can do about any of this

Helpless

I pretend this is okay and I deal with my terror wrapped behind high fashion

My clothing and my jewelry protect me, build an armor around my soul

But then my brain explodes in pain and beams of light pierce through my eyes

Striking me to the ground with its intensity and I retreat to a dark room

I vomit violently and expel all those things that need to be said into the toilet bowl

And with a flush, send them away from me, try to make them all go away

I vomit again, and again and again each time with more violence and rage
But the vile taste does not leave my mouth, so I brush my teeth and disguise it
I put on fresh make-up and look good, and strong, and powerful
I am superwoman and I can do everything. The image is complete
So perhaps I am an artist as I paint myself a new face while I disguise the truth

I am the teacher, I am the wise one, I am the protector of others
Amongst the path of the hero's quest, the ultimate journey which I teach to others
I fall and stumble along the way picking up the bloodied pieces
And wrapping them in a Burberry scarf adding a touch of bright red lip stick
And a Prada handbag so the image is complete
The outside perfection while the inside threatens to implode the walls of the fortress that I have so carefully constructed around the walls of my heart

Consciously pretending that my reality doesn't bother me, and I am happy
And finally realize that Disney princesses don't live happily ever after
But they curl their hair, reset their makeup, and vomit the reality of their lives into the toilet bowl

Head throbs, cancer grows, and our bodies become vicious, raging agents of destruction holding in all
That needed to be expelled out into the Universe and away from my heart
The truth that needed to be faced and explored and recognized for what it is
The truth is that the truth is not really very pretty after all

I have no control over these things that swirl and twist around me
Threatening to choke my breath out of my body and drop me into internal hell
If I let the demons rage within me, they will become me, so I need to

SURRENDER
And recognize the truth but not let the truth consume me
For if I allow it to embed its tentacles within the flesh of my tender soul
Then I will die

And I am not really finished living yet....

(Holmes & Leggo, 2019)

Sending love to you and to all those who love you,

Kimberley

From: Leggo, Carl <carl.leggo@ubc.ca>
Sent: December 18, 2018 1:09 PM
To: Kimberley Holmes; Leggo, Carl
Subject: Re: Connecting

Beautifully expressed, Kimberley!

I don't think I feel any rage. Unlike Dylan Thomas, whom I typically admire a great deal:

"Do not go gentle into that good night,
Old age should burn and rave at close of day;
Rage, rage against the dying of the light."

Instead, I think I am surprised by the sudden turn in my health. The brain tumor is very quick and aggressive! I am certainly sad, too. But as a spiritual person, I trust that I will continue to receive the news about health with a poetic imagination.

"Lamentations of a Wannabe Artist" is a loud, earnest cry of love! Always hold fast to love!

I will see the radiation specialist tomorrow at noon. I am glad for the quick medical support!

Sending love,

Carl

From: Kimberley Holmes <kaholmes@ucalgary.ca>
Date: Tuesday, December 18, 2018 at 6:00 PM
To: "Leggo, Carl" <carl.leggo@ubc.ca>
Subject: Re: Connecting

Dear Carl,

The reference to Dylan Thomas reminds me of a young man I taught a few years back. Madis was in grade 10 when I met him and non-communicative. His learner profile stated he was gifted but he had stopped writing and talking with others. Daily he would arrive at my class, pull his hoodie over his head and promptly fall asleep in the back row. He was an enigma to me, a challenge that I needed to unlock and understand. I would often walk slowly by his desk contemplating how to reach him. Slowly, as time passed, he began to come to my classroom over the noon hours, often with a book in his hand. We would make small attempts at conversation, but he did not have much to say and preferred just to sit quietly in my room and share the space. As I began to understand his story, I learned his father had passed away suddenly in the last year. According to his mother, Madis had been very close to his father as he was one of the few people he felt he connected with. When his father passed, Madis simply stopped speaking to anyone and retreated quietly into himself. When I met him, he was a soul lost in sorrow, deeply immersed in his own thoughts and terrified to connect with anyone.

During our noon hour "visits" I would give him things to read and consider. I was attempting to try to get him to write but was rather unsuccessful. However, he did read, specifically the poetry books that I left lying on his desk. One day, he came in quite animated, a far cry from the downcast loner that I usually met with. In his hand was a book that contained the poem, "Do not Go Gentle into that Good Night." This poem spoke to Madis and his lived experience with his father. He was very angry with his father for dying, and he felt betrayed. As he discussed the poem, his emotions flowed out of him. His rage, his anger, his guilt, and his sorrow poured out. He demanded to know why his father did not fight, why he left him, and why people had to die. He recognized that Thomas was writing this ode to his dying father for within the poet's words he recognized his own voice. He recognized his own need to survive, and Madis not only began to read more poetry but began to write. The portals to healing were opened, and although I do not know the final outcome, I am hopeful he found his way out of the darkness through the poetic verse and learned to "rage, rage against the dying of the light."

Life and death are the two certainties that we face. What happens in between is an enigma of sorts depending on a great deal of interconnected variables. We know not to ask, "for whom the bell tolls"(Donne), for as humans our stories are all interconnected. Our celebrations of life and death are always a part of the greater whole, as "any man's death diminishes me, because I am involved in mankind." We each contribute a verse to this grand poetic anthology we call life. Our stories and our poetry bind us, connect us, and help us deal with our adversity. Together we heed the call and seek the deeper messages.

<u>So, You Want to Be a Poet</u>

You claim that you want to write poetry

But before we step further to the edge, I need to understand your desire to do so

Do you understand the claim this will make on your heart, your soul, your body?

And if you open the portals of your skin to poetry, allowing it to fuse through the spaces

Your life, your world, your Being will tingle with the anticipation of the next poem

The next chance to let the life words slip through your fingertips falling softly on the page

Allowing your life to be felt in dynamic notes of pulsating pattern and beat

That vibrate through the blood of your living breathing body

Are you willing to let the words of your life slip through your fingers onto the paper?

The memories of your story etched forever in the written word as it swirls in patterns

Spiraling in a desperate attempt to make meaning out of nothing and nothing out of meaning

Are you willing to sit for hours while your fingers cramp and your ass aches?

While your body screams to move but you know you must wait patiently for the moment that

The flood gates are open, and the words rush rapidly into the river to be consumed in all that is

Can you hold in the moment and wait for the memories to expel themselves?

In a flurry of roller coaster thrills that leave you breathless and wanting to vomit

But at the same moment still craving another ride, seeking another moment to feel so alive

To reach the peak of the loop, hang for a moment in the air, then rapidly descend again

Are you ready to hit the highs and the lows at a speed so rapid the tears bubble unbidden to your eyes?

And fall softly down your cheeks as they wash away the remnants of the memory?

Are you really ready and willfully wanting to go there?

Can you face your fears, your heart's desires, tell the truth?

Or will you hide behind the fairy tales, the pretty words, and the secrets better left untold?

The gut churns and cramps fill the abdomen as words trapped expel through the orifices

The heart sings at the release and begs for more, seeks the higher understanding

As the body speaks its own poetic verse through the steady beating of the heart

And the slow rhythm of the breath

And the gentle waves of human consciousness as they transcend through the obstacles

Are you willing to face the pain, the power, the struggle to slow the rapid patterns of the mind?

Can you sit silently and wait for messages to appear or will you run away in fear?

THE SPACES IN BETWEEN

Can you gaze silently into the eyes of the inner teacher, who calls to you to remain silent and listen

Or will you close your eyes and pretend that all of this is just mumbo jumbo poetry shit

Stuff that hippies do, people who don't have real jobs and live in the real world

Stupid things you had to do in school that never really made any sense to you anyway?

Because poetry is one of those funny things that cannot be taught

But needs to drip out of your Essence as the soul begins to speak

(Holmes & Leggo, 2019)

With poetry and passion,

K

From: Leggo, Carl <carl.leggo@ubc.ca>
Sent: December 18, 2018 8:41:29 PM
To: Kimberley Holmes; Leggo, Carl
Subject: Re: Connecting

Dear Kimberley,

The story of Madis is poignant and powerful and pedagogic! You could write a series of snapshots of students you have known. You help me understand Dylan Thomas by locating his words in the story of Madis. Thank you!

You understand the potency of poetry: "as the soul begins to speak"—beautifully expressed!

Sending love in these shortest days of December,

Carl

Here is a new poem, still raw, still in need of more revising perhaps, but for now I like the sad raw energy of the poem based on the phone call I had with my mother yesterday after I met with the oncologist, who gave me the bad news about the resurgence of the brain tumor.

A Mother's Lament

I had three good men, the best,
cancer is taking all of you

It's not fair, just not fair,
I don't know what to make of it

It's too much, I've got nobody
to talk to about any of it

My heart broke with Bud's death
but after a long time, I got over it
I can't get over Rick's death,
too young, too soon, too unfair

Now your struggles with cancer
that just go on and on, why?

I just don't understand any
of it, none of it makes any sense

I had three good men, the best,
cancer is taking all of you

From: Kimberley Holmes <kaholmes@ucalgary.ca>
Date: Tuesday, December 18, 2018 at 8:36 PM
To: "Leggo, Carl" <carl.leggo@ubc.ca>
Subject: Re: Connecting

Dear Carl,

Your poem is raw but speaks of the struggle one feels when trying to understand the nature of illness. There is no reason to the invasion, and it is indeed unfair. It does not make any sense and words do not seem capable of addressing the magnitude of emotions. Yet poetry seems to find the power to transmit what is needed, to allow frustrated feelings to expel in strange and mysterious ways which somehow seem to aid us in attempting to understand what is not understandable.

This is a poem I wrote when my mother was going through her chemo. It does not make a lot of sense, nor it is written well. However, it captured what it needed to at that moment and allowed me a way to process.

<u>*A Prayer to the Divine Mother*</u>

Seeking the poets, seeking the spirits, seeking the swirling interconnected spirals of the circle of life

Of the breath of the Universe as it pulsates the rhythms and songs of our interconnected Being

Dancing gracefully around the magical fairy ring celebrate and let your story sing

Crown your head with a daisy of purest white

As you bravely face the power and vibrancy of the light

Follow the yellow brick road

Follow the yellow brick road

Follow follow follow

Call not the dark, dense rotting stench of disease

Seek the goddess divinely dancing in the moonlight

Allow your spirit to soar gracefully above the clouds, and then return again

Release the fermenting memories that are trapped within your breast

Manifested by the dormant desires of your heart

ILLUMINATION!

A light that soothes, that heals, that protects the Goddess within

The Goddess who is preparing to dance through the darkness rejuvenating the cells

That have manifested this disease that now hides deep within the tender flesh

Do not let your luscious life slowly slip away as blood seeps from your wounds

DRIP, DRIP, DRIP

Reclaim your divine goddess and seek stories of the past while recognizing

The stories that still need to be lived and shared around the campfire ring

Be gone culture of dank and rotting disease and darkness

Putrid bits of flesh explode into benign fragments of nothingness

Swimming through the portals of the body and out into the Universe

No more poking, prodding, bleeding, seething

DRIP, DRIP, DRIP, DROP

NO!

You will not bleed my life away today or evermore

Loving touch to the pain to provide a soothing balm

And stop the bleeding of the Goddess heart

That holds all the joy and pain of life itself

With stories left untold

With words seeking voice, seeking to be written, seeking to be heard

What stories are locked within the tender tissue of a woman's breast

The loving flesh that feeds a child and fuels the emotional vibration of a Universe

Through which the milk of human kindness deeply flows

Within which a dark and angry lump has demanded to manifest to express its outrage

For stories that are not yet written

Seek solace, seek the story and then let it slowly slide away
Surrender to the Divine Goddess within you
Do not let your life slowly drip into a fine and fragile thread
DRIP, DRIP, DRIP, DONE!

Crown your head with a daisy ring and within the circles strongly sing
Follow, follow, follow, follow
DRIP, DRIP, DRIP, drop, STOP
Be gone oh vile and cruel illness and let the Goddess reign

This is my prayer to you all
The wounded women who walk the Earth
Who hold pain and suffering within the tender tissues of the breast
Seeking courage, seeking a heart, seeking a brain to find a mindful space
And trying to find their way home

May we all find our way home....

With deep contemplation and love on the dark days prior to the solstice,
K

From: Leggo, Carl <carl.leggo@ubc.ca>
Sent: December 19, 2018 6:06 PM
To: Kimberley Holmes; Leggo, Carl
Subject: Re: Connecting

Dear Kimberley,

You write with a woman's keen perspective on the heart and emotions. Yours is a poetic voice that is uniquely yours—like nobody else. Your students return to you because they heard (and they remember hearing) a kind of wisdom that they need, a kind of wisdom that they do not often hear. Always be the teacher who speaks, writes, and lives wisdom.

May we always seek "a heart"!

Carl

Here is a poem (a sad regretful poem) that I wrote for my brother when he was diagnosed with cancer:

<u>Did We Forget to Speak?</u>

as boys we were light and shadow
we swung on wild lines of ludic resolve

always shape shifting, we dangled tangled
with limits, pushed and poked one another
the language we spoke did not include
I love you, verbosity verboten

even though you and I knew our love
sprung from winter's wild wanting

now the shadows are faintly etched
the light grows dim with regret

a spring breeze stirs the heart
with a soft percussion, resonant

but trembling with the haunting song
of a hole, more hollow than holy

From: Kimberley Holmes <kaholmes@ucalgary.ca>
Date: Wednesday, December 19, 2018 at 8:07 PM
To: "Leggo, Carl" <carl.leggo@ubc.ca>
Subject: Re: Connecting

Dear Carl,

Your poem makes me think of my own boys, interconnected brothers who often "poke and prod" at one another in the strange way that boys show their love. I cannot imagine them as anything other than a pair. We have been through so much as a family it has sealed the bond of blood tightly. Time has gone by so quickly and they have moved from babies, to running toddlers, to young men who are striving to find out who they are and what their place in the world is. I am not sure if they will continue to walk together or at some point take individual paths. My memories of their childhood spin and merge like the fragmented colors of the kaleidoscope, interconnected yet unique patterns of joy, of sorrow, and of love.

I am not sure I have wisdom as I don't feel particularly wise. In fact, as I age, I feel less confident, less knowledgeable and somewhat dated in my learning. Somehow, I still manage to make an impact with my young charges, and I suppose perhaps that is the root of teaching. Being able to touch another and cause them to reflect, to wonder, and to grow in some capacity. I do on most days still feel like an imposter, lacking the skills and wisdom to do the work I am called here to do. One would think with the granting of my degrees and the years of experience this feeling would pass but alas it has not. I still question most things and I think will forever. I know so little yet seek to understand so much.

I am attaching a poem I wrote prior to my candidacy exam reflecting on this process of becoming a scholar. I have simply realized that there is so much more that you need to learn and so much that we will never really know at all.

<u>*Musings of a Doctoral Candidate*</u>

We seek to find out the answers of the Universe, or at least our research question

And I seek to understand how I can survive in a world that demands so much of us

As my fingers ache and my head is filled with heaviness that I cannot clear

As the world begins to bloom outside my window and robins dance on my roof

I consider carefully the chirping of the birds and the patterns of time, space, and fifth dimensions

As exhaustion threatens to overtake me and render me into a pile of empty nothingness

Do your homework, get good grades, and this will ensure your success and happiness in life

This is the fable of the American dream that has been scientifically unproven to this day

In fact, have we not proved exactly the opposite effect?

A basic law of physics states for every action there is an equal but opposite reaction

Everything we do has a consequence, and the outcome of the pressure is yet to be determined

Have we not learned from Willy Loman that the quest for the American dream is all in vain?

Plant the bloody garden, claim some space, and get out of the goddam boxes that we have built

That threaten to suffocate our life spirit and keep us forever trapped

Indebted to the demon of anxiety and stress that we worship as our deity to ensure our success

Will it take blood dripping slowly though our fingertips to recognize the futility of this game?

The tiny buds of nature stand in anticipation outside of my window whispering secrets of life

Mother Nature may blast them with another shrieking bout of winter madness any moment

But still they present their tiny buds hoping for the new life, a new beginning, to spring forth

Tentative, yet hopeful of a future soon to emerge

A research question soon to be answered, a new paradigm of thinking to emerge

Children trudging to school dragging their feet as they attempt to escape their fate

Books weighing down their backs, knowledge to be memorized and synthesized

Then vomited back for evaluation and assessment of their worth as a human being

Young buds on the trees hoping to bloom but aware of the cold winter wrath

Children seeking open space to spread their wings but struggling in a system

We seek to find the answers, the solutions, the real reasons behind black holes

Parallel universes, quantum physics, poetry, and love

Love, love, love

We seek like the tentative buds on the tree knowing the winter's cruel punishments

May be just around the corner to freeze us to death.

From: Leggo, Carl <carl.leggo@ubc.ca>
Sent: December 20, 2018 3:04:32 PM
To: Kimberley Holmes; Leggo, Carl
Subject: Re: Connecting

Hi, Kimberley,

We will never know all we would like to know, think we might need to know, hope we can know! We just keep on moving in the living process, learning as we lean into the next moment, always interconnected with all the moments just left behind or imagined or dreamed.

I especially like the following part of your poem: "We seek like the tentative buds on the tree knowing…"

I just enjoyed a coffee with a former doctoral student—a brilliant scholar who is in the process of transitioning from a woman to a man, who is a Christian minister, who is an actor—a wonderful friendship! He and I have been engaging in conversations for many years, and the conversations grow richer and richer! I am glad for those conversations.

May the last couple days of school unfold with joyful anticipation of Christmas rest and fun.

Carl

Here is a recent poem about hair. I have an appointment for Saturday at 2pm to get my head shaved. The hair is now falling out fast and furious!

Hair

almost all my adult life I have had
long hair, a long time I have been my hair

I have had long hair for so long, I don't
know who I am without long hair

now diagnosed with cancer, I am assured
my hair will fall out with chemotherapy

I am quite startled by how quickly old age
crept up and whacked me in the head

a woman shampooed my hair once, massaged
my scalp so perfectly I fell in love with her

my four granddaughters all have long
flowing hair, they all like my hair, too

Samson, Absalom, Willie Nelson,
Tony Little, Karl Lagerfeld, Tarzan

Howie Mandell on the cover of Zoomer
happily looks good with a bald head

last summer a boy asked, are you a boy
or a girl? I said, I haven't decided yet

the Apostle Paul thinks long hair
on a man is a disgrace to him

Ujjal Dev Singh Dosanjh, Steven Tyler,
Wang Deshun, Randy Savage

occasionally in places like restaurants women
my age will caress my hair, I like your hair

in a world where I feel invisible most
of the time, I am always glad to be seen

in life one thing leads to another, so eventually
we see our lives plotted like lines on a graph

what will the future hold? always
hopeful there is some future

(Holmes & Leggo, 2019)

On Dec 20, 2018, at 6:21 PM, Kimberley Holmes <kaholmes@ucalgary.ca> wrote:

Dear Carl,

Hair is such a significant part of who we are, our identity in the world.

My mother also struggled with the hair loss. She bought some fancy wigs which looked quite fantastic. Perhaps we can find you a long, flowing wig so you can keep your signature hair style. Or maybe you will look fabulous with no hair—many men do, and I have encouraged my husband to try this look. It might present a whole new way of seeing the world or at least a new way of being seen in the world.

Yet, we all fight the loss of our hair. My husband back combs his bald spot, my mother buys wigs, and I on a much lesser scale recently cut my long waves shorter. I currently have a short 1950s bob. Everyone complements me on it, but I do feel like an actor trying on a different costume. Somehow the short sassy look does not match my poetic nature as well as the wild free flowing waves did. Yet, we must remind ourselves that the hair is just part of the costume, and our costumes, much like our lives, change and flow with the varying circumstances of our lives. It might be time for me to be "short and sassy" to be able to transcend this strange age and stage.

I cannot imagine you ever "feeling invisible." Your vibrancy is so much a part of your Essence, your way of walking in the world. It comes from a much deeper place, as I recognized it in our email conversations long before I had any concept of your physical presence. Your words and wisdom illuminate the world in deep and powerful ways. I do believe our beauty comes from deep within us, and although it can be enhanced by our outside appearance, the deep glow of authenticity radiates out in vibrant energy circles which shape our daily existence. Although you shall miss your hair, it will in no way fade your brilliance.

We are watching Rise of the Guardians in English 30. My fellow teachers are slamming the students with tests and unit finals, and we are retreating to the world of myth with hot chocolate and popcorn. It is a wonderful story rich with literary motifs, powerful lessons, and a call to find out who you are. We will connect it to all the literature we have studied this term as I remind them to believe that light always triumphs over dark if children believe. I highly recommend snuggling up with your grandchildren and watching this lovely little tale of Jack Frost. It does have some very sad moments, though, as life always does. It is through the sadness that often, under the gaze of the light of the moon, we find our purpose for being.

Tomorrow we shall finish the movie and engage in conversation about believing in the guardians' power to always overcome the nightmares. I shall send them away for the break with thoughts of hope and love. This is our work as teachers, for we are also the guardians....

<u>Possibilities for Pedagogy and Human Recovery</u>

I ask my adult students what does it mean to be a teacher of the humanities

And they respond they need to teach grammar and history and get the facts

Into the minds of the learners who will clamor around them in anticipation

Of new learning and share their love of their subject discipline eagerly

As they write their essays, answer the questions, and go through the process of doing school

And I smile as I know this is what they believe teaching to be

A delivery system between the teacher and the student where knowledge

Is imported from one to another in a logical and simple fashion that meets the requirements

Of the factory model they experienced themselves as students in school

And now is the time to unlearn the efficient habits of the past and shape the future

Where imagination, creativity, and discovery reign over rote memory and regurgitation

Where poetry is not meant to be broken down into disconnected elements

while seeking figurative language, structure, and form void of holistic meaning

But savored with the body searching for an embodied essence that embraces the harmony of life itself

Shakespeare did not mean for us to fret over the meaning of every fragment of thought

But sought to share the stories he saw unfolding around him every day as humans struggled to survive

A world not quite perfect and full of obstacles that forced complex and often frenzied human emotion

Complicating the story even further bringing passions to a bloody boil resulting in tragedy

A novel is just a beautiful version of carefully chosen words encapsulating a soul's simple story

Brought to life by the alchemy of worlds dancing around to create visions in our head

And sometimes brought to film so we can see the story represented in a different way

As scenes and images flash before sharing the raw human essence of who we are

Much like a play bringing the human story to our senses stimulating our awareness so

We can understand the deeper meaning of this thing we call life and carefully contemplate

This complex interwoven and interconnected process of becoming fully human

Breathing, being, and becoming through the days of our lives

Tomorrow and tomorrow and tomorrow, creeps in this petty pace from day to day

Gather ye rosebuds while ye may, Old Time is still a-flying;

Willy Loman dies chasing the fallacy of the American dream

And our Brave New World has gone astray

Charlotte is still spinning her beautiful web and new life shall soon be born

And the human mind is capable of just about anything

Look you can see their breath! And you really can.

What does it mean to be a teacher of the humanities and the guardian of the dream?

What does it mean to hold the keys to the future of humanity as daunting as it might seem?

To be or not to be that is the question we all must ask

Is it better to step bravely forwards or battle the demons of the past?

THE SPACES IN BETWEEN

On the Rainy River Tim struggled with indecision and was forced to make a choice

And many years later he finally found his voice

What does it mean to be a coward and what does it take to fight a war?

While you lie nodding nearly napping what will come rapping at your door

And will you be ready to open the portal and face what is on the other side even if it is only the Self?

Touch the heart, touch the soul, teach the stories seeking the human essence

Slowly slowly horses of the night as the dark demon's destructivity dance through the dream

Seek out Scout and see the world of injustice as only the child perceives

It will make you sick so you might want to pretend that you really don't understand

But only through careful listening of the heart will we ever comprehend

This complex web of humanity that binds us all together linking us forever

As the rest is nothing but the silent echo of what could have been

We live in the flicker....

Out out brief candle for life is short and each day we must do our best

To impact the quality of the day is a higher achievement than the rest

A heart of wisdom is what we seek as each story becomes part of the stand

A mindful brain must answer the call so peace and empathy can reign

This job is not a simple task but a calling you must embrace

If you find this daunting, you may need to find a degree and profession in a different space

I ask my adult students what does it mean this calling they have chosen

And they begin to unlearn the rote lessons of the past slowly and carefully

Unraveling the lived experience that has brought them all together

Into this time, this space, my classroom as we share the complex introspective journey

The facing of the inner teacher we must all do before we truly understand the process of

Building together the stories of the future and embracing the path of the teacher

(Holmes & Leggo, 2019)

On Dec 21, 2018, at 10:23 AM, Leggo, Carl <carl.leggo@ubc.ca> wrote:

Hi, Kimberley,

I am having trouble with e-mail today, so this message is just a quick word to say that I have read your last message with keen attention, especially the discussion about hair!! Thank you!!

I love the ways you incorporate what you are teaching into your poetry, so that there is a kind of tapestry that emerges from the many diverse threads of your typical day's activities.

I will begin radiation on Christmas Eve!

May Christmas bring many joyful moments with family and poetry and sunshine!

Carl

From: Kimberley Holmes <kaholmes@ucalgary.ca>
Date: Saturday, December 22, 2018 at 5:50 PM
To: "Leggo, Carl" <carl.leggo@ubc.ca>
Subject: Re: Connecting

Dear Carl,

It is the first official day of holiday break, and I find myself sitting in the window in a state of complete relaxation or perhaps utter exhaustion! It is amazing how quickly the body and mind slide into holiday mode and discard the need to be busy and productive. Today we had my parents, my brother, and his family over for an early Christmas brunch. We misread our tickets for Mexico and are flying out Christmas Eve, so have moved celebrations to this weekend. We shall arrive in Mexico at 6 am Christmas morning. It shall be a bit strange but a new experience which I am looking forward too.

Today is the full moon, which followed yesterday's winter solstice. I can hear the birds happily chirping in the trees outside my window, almost as if they can feel the magic present in the Universe. Apparently, there are even meteorite showers this weekend. For someone who is auspicious there are a lot of signs swirling around at this moment. I am hopeful they signal change, transformations, healings, and new beginnings for all those I am interconnected with.

<u>Winter Magic</u>

The sky is streaked a brilliant blue and white as the birds chatter in the trees

The green of grass peeps tentatively through the winter snow holding on to life

As the sparkle of the crusted ice and snow is reflected and refracted in the sunlight

The moon rises full and luminous into the evening sky casting a sacred glow

Around the darkness of the night whispering of light and illusion and alchemy

Of the man in the moon, Santa Claus, and little elves dancing in the darkness

Children everywhere and every age wait in anticipation of something special

That they have been taught occurs every year as the days get longer

And the moon shines brightly with the sparkling stars dancing in the sky

It is this special type of winter magic that overrides the cold and darkness

Illuminating our lives, our stories, and the interconnected spirals of humanity

In a special type of alchemy that heightens our awareness of our Being

With love,

Kimberley

On Dec 23, 2018, at 9:45 AM, Leggo, Carl <carl.leggo@ubc.ca> wrote:

There is a lovely tone/voice/quality in this message, Kimberley! You are looking backward and forward as you continue to review and preview. Enjoy your holiday time with family in the sunshine!

The poem is lovely—full of magic!

With love,

Carl

From: Kimberley Holmes <kaholmes@ucalgary.ca>
Date: Sunday, December 23, 2018 at 8:43 PM
To: "Leggo, Carl" <carl.leggo@ubc.ca>
Subject: Re: Connecting

Dear Carl,

We celebrated our gift exchange early today and just finished a walk to the Christmas light display. Although it is only -4 degrees, it feels chilly, and my bones need warming in a hot bath. Tomorrow we shall have dinner with my parents and await our midnight flight to the sunshine. It feels strange doing our "free styling" Christmas as we are in our own little space and place. We have had turkey, Christmas cookies, hot chocolates, and movies, and it is not even Christmas Eve yet. It shall feel strange to leave in the middle of the night and fly to the beach.

I hope your treatment goes well tomorrow and does not take too much of a strain on your wellness. Sending you love and energy.

OX

Kimberley

THE SPACES IN BETWEEN

From: Leggo, Carl <carl.leggo@ubc.ca>
Sent: December 24, 2018 9:57:14 AM
To: Kimberley Holmes; Leggo, Carl
Subject: Re: Connecting

Enjoy all the adventures of family, Kimberley!!

With Christmas hope,

Carl

From: Kimberley Holmes <kaholmes@ucalgary.ca>
Date: Monday, December 24, 2018 at 8:05 PM
To: "Leggo, Carl" <carl.leggo@ubc.ca>
Subject: Re: Connecting

Dear Carl,

'Tis Christmas Eve and I sit watching the sparkling lights of the tree and the flickering candles. My family awaits the taxi that will transport us to the airport and then on to the Mexican sun and sand. It feels somewhat strange and disorienting. I have just realized that this is the first Christmas Eve I have not spent in my own bed and the first time my children have not awoken me Christmas morning with the contents of their stockings. Jayden has spent all the Christmas Eve's of his life in our current house, and Tristan was too young to remember anything but this space and place. I am a bit teary eyed tonight, and I am assuming it is because I am being visited by the ghosts of Christmas past and recognizing that life is changing and shifting around me.

My parents came over for an early turkey dinner tonight. Although we had agreed not to exchange presents, they arrived with a present I assumed was for my sons. It was for me. I have been quite sad this year for a variety of reasons, and my parents were seeking a way to make me laugh. Hence, they bought me a Ms. Beasley doll. As I opened the box, the tears ran freely down my face, and instead of laughter I felt an intense sense of sadness for things that have been lost. My first Ms. Beasley was presented to me when I had my tonsils out. I must have been about 5 or 6 and was tired, cranky, and had a very sore throat. Ms. Beasley arrived at my hospital bed and everything was well. I can remember the feeling of joy as if it was yesterday, how everything changed with the arrival of the doll.

I think my parents were trying to remind me that all can be well again, if only I believe in love and magic and remember to laugh with joy. Tears fall freely down my face as I think back on my childhood, a time when I was protected from the cruel blows of the world and my parents made everything so magical. I was well loved and well cared for, and for this I am eternally grateful. I was sheltered from the harsh realities for many years, and only when I became a parent myself did I begin to understand the responsibility I had to the world and the dragons I would need to slay.

I miss the childhood days of magic and wonder. I wish I could sit with Ms. Beasley and all would be well again. I miss the magic of Christmas past, of cousins gathered at grandparents', of my parents young and spry dancing the swing around the pool table. I miss the laughter, the fun, and all that was taken for granted. I feel a terrible yearning for these things yet recognize that our lives are always subject to change, that life is an interconnected spiral of beginnings and endings, and that we need to find different ways of being in the world at every age and stage. My own children's childhood is also ending, and I hope they have some fond memories. Their experience is so different than mine, but I did my best to make it magical. I never did give them a talking doll that could make them believe everything was going to be okay but tried to find them the magic that sustained me through my childhood. They have iPads and video games but very little magic in their day-to-day competitive lives. This makes me sad and somewhat nostalgic for the ghosts of Christmas past when it seemed so simple to find happiness and joy.

I may not have many years left with my parents. This also makes me cry. My father tired quickly tonight and headed home about 7:30. I watched his energy fade tonight and suddenly realized how much a toll my mother's illness has taken on him and how much he is aging. He has always been our guardian, and his work has been very hard this past year. With my mother's cancer, the death of both his mother and his mother-in-law, and Tristan's ongoing struggle with seizures, he carries a great load very silently. He stays strong for us all. I can see that his responsibilities have worn him down and that he is tired. I am so blessed to have both my parents in my life.

I find it difficult to comprehend that one day my parents may no longer be a part of our Christmas. I am sure your own children are feeling this way as well. It seems only yesterday I was 5 and my father was carrying me into the house Christmas Eve. Life is but an instant, a brief memory, a game of monopoly and some sugary treats. Then it moves forward, and everything changes and suddenly you are not the child but the parent and then the grandparent and then we are at the end. Yet somehow, in spite of the constant change life seems to go on in various ways. Although I would like to hold on to the past, I know I must look to the future. Perhaps one day I shall "regift" Ms. Beasley to a future granddaughter as a present from her great-grandparents. Perhaps one day....

Tomorrow, I will spend Christmas Day at the beach and then join friends for dinner. It will be different and new and wonderful. My toys will warm in the sand, and the saltwater will soothe my soul. The sun will bring me light and joy and a new type of wonder, and we will create a new memory different than the others. Tonight, I will think about the ghosts of Christmas past, the incredible magic my parents created for me, and how grateful I am to have had such an incredible childhood filled with joy. Tonight, I will remember the joy and hope for the future. Tomorrow I shall dance in the sun.

<u>Christmas Eve</u>

Belly filled with shortbread and children tucked in tight awaiting all the magic

Stockings on the end of bed, eyes opened wide to catch the sight of Santa in the night

A morning filled with magic as all the dreams came true

Mystery, magic, happiness, and wonder as a child and a teen too

The perfect gift could do it all, the magical toy beneath the tree

Really symbolizing that someone in my life truly loves me

The safety and security of a family's warm embrace

A merry merry Christmas to all and to all a memorable night

May the ghosts of Christmas past protect your Christmas futures

May the memories bring tears and laughter to your soul

May the cycle of life continue on in different versions

And may we always hear sleigh bells in the snow......

With much love, Kimberley

On Dec 26, 2018, at 10:56 AM, Leggo, Carl <carl.leggo@ubc.ca> wrote:

Dear Kimberley,

I trust that you and your family are enjoying your time in the sand, sun, and sea of Mexico!

Christmas has been delightful! Lots of fun with family and lots of food and lots of love!!

Your ruminations on life and parents and children and aging are all heartfully rendered and true. Our lives are mortal, and we need to embrace them with their limits and possibilities like blank pages where we write our stories with joy and sadness—the light and shadow of our daily complex experiences. Our big task is how to hold the hopefulness of each day while also acknowledging the challenges that break/disrupt our narrative lines.

I love the following lines in your poem:

May the memories bring tears and laughter to your soul

May the cycle of life continue on in different versions

May we always journey with the cycles of living!

With love,

Carl

Here is a fairly recent poem written for my brother:

<u>The Rock</u>

I will return to the backyard where
my brother and I once played

though the house was long ago
demolished and Lynch's Lane erased

a townhouse complex erected on tons
of backfill to gain a harbor view

I am confident I will find the rock
my brother and I sat on like a plinth

sometimes pretended we would scoop
around so we could drop it into the ground

the rock that held five little boys in a row
in souvenir hats after Queen Elizabeth's visit

the gray mottled rock that holds secrets,
our desires and fears beyond grammar

eroded to smooth curves by faithful winters
this rock utters stories from a time more

ancient than my brother's and mine, traces
of mathematical mysteries to be teased out

in conversation with history and eternity,
a procession of signals waiting for translation

From: Kimberley Holmes <kaholmes@ucalgary.ca>
Date: Wednesday, December 26, 2018 at 7:16 PM
To: "Leggo, Carl" <carl.leggo@ubc.ca>
Subject: Re: Connecting

Dear Carl,

"The Rock" is a powerful reflection on the interconnected cycles of life and the changing patterns of living and being. I love the play of words "in conversation with history and eternity." It speaks to the power of life to move forward, to record its lessons, and to forever impact our future. The Universe indeed holds "secrets, fears and desires," and although the physical rock may no longer stand, the memories etched in the human psyche will last forever. Inside each man resides the boy that once was and many memories swirl of times past. It makes me think of the little dolls that hold one smaller one within. The tiniest one is our purest Essence and carries on long after the outside shells deteriorate. Our body is but a costume, a type of armor, that protects the spirit and then is shed as our Essence returns to pure energy.

Today we had a solid buffet breakfast and then spent the day on the beach with the masses seeking the sun and the sand. My boys were keen to sit on the beach and simply play. However, we overdid it in the past few days, and just prior to a late lunch Tristan suffered a small seizure. Hence, even in Paradise Village illness continues to plague us and stalk our happiness. I find it difficult to relax as I am always on edge but have accepted this is just a part of my life. The seizures impact all of us. His younger brother gives up a lot of experiences out of concern for Tris's well-being, and I never seem to be able to fully relax. There is always something hanging over us, threatening to darken the sunshine. We are always watching, ready to leap to action, anticipating emergency procedure, and never ever lacking presence. I am always aware. However, we continue to attempt to seek the light and strive to find ways to live life to the fullest. Perhaps one day, we will find a reason for these seizures and be able to control them. It has been many years of challenge, and I am ready for us all to be able to live our lives without fear. I would like to have a day where I did not have to pay close attention. I miss the days of my childhood and my wishing trees.

Tomorrow will be another bright sunny day in Paradise Village. This is the name of our resort. The word Paradise means "walled enclosure" or "royal park." It is interesting as this is a gated community and we are indeed separated from the outside world. We have a golf course, tennis courts, a fitness center, a beach club, and practically everything that one could possibly dream of for happiness. Yet, not all in this little village appear to be happy, connected, or fully alive. The juxtaposition is not lost on me. I am deep in thought about what might be truly required for paradise to be achieved.

Paradise

Touch down in a shanty town or torn and dirty tents with children living in a dump

Scavenging their way through life seeking food and shelter in a cardboard box

Grateful for everything they may gather and seeking what can be found

THE SPACES IN BETWEEN

Finding joy in a torn sweater discovered underneath a broken vase that once held flowers

Cross the heavy gates and the armed guard allows entrance into the Paradise complex

Food is abundant and often wasted by wealthy tourists seeking instant gratification

Disdainful of anything not worthy of 5 stars and the standard of excellence

That might cause a dust stain to diminish the glow on their shiny white tennis shoes

The water of the mighty ocean swirls around the feet of both the grateful and the disdainful

The sun kisses everyone and the sand massages the weariness out of bones

The definition of paradise a bit of a conundrum of terms dependent on the perceiver

Gratitude and indifference intermixed as the birds swirl in circles in the sky

Seeking gratitude and joy, OX K

On Dec 27, 2018, at 4:31 PM, Leggo, Carl <carl.leggo@ubc.ca> wrote:

Thank you, Kimberley, for sharing a few experiences of your family time in Mexico!

Wherever we are, our lives unfold in much the same ways! We learn to lean into new experiences; we learn to know how all experiences are shaping us in meandering stories that do not run in only one direction. Our stories are diverging, detouring, distracting. We always hope that the stories will find their way to happiness and hope and humility.

I am leaving soon for the Cancer Agency and a second round of radiation. Always with anticipation!

Sending love, Carl

From: Kimberley Holmes <kaholmes@ucalgary.ca>
Date: Thursday, December 27, 2018 at 8:00 PM
To: "Leggo, Carl" <carl.leggo@ubc.ca>
Subject: Re: Connecting

Dear Carl,

I hope the second round of radiation helps to slow the process of the tumor and does not dampen your spirits. We do need to hope our stories find happiness, hope, and humility, regardless of how challenging the chapters are to work our way through. We need to hope there is method to the unfolding of the Universe and that every season has a reason and purpose. We need to try and trust in some type of greater being who guides each day and has a purpose for each of us. Without this trust I believe we might descend into the dark pit of madness.

Today we thought we would start the day at the fitness club and try to reset our systems. Tris is a competitive swimmer, and we know that vigorous exercise calms his mind and stops the inflammation response. While we were all on our respective workout machines, Tris suffered a small seizure. He was on a treadmill and somehow managed to step off the rapidly moving conveyor belt and stand behind the machine. For this, I am eternally grateful. He could have been pitched off the treadmill into the metal weights behind him and suffered serious injury. Two women who were beside him working out rapidly rushed to his aid, as they were concerned he was going to faint. He was having an absent seizure. I ran to his aid and secured him in case he fell to the ground. I am grateful that he did not, and he came out of the event within a few minutes. As we were standing there concerned, many fitness center staff came to our aid, offering cold cloths, water, and any type of aid we may have required. For this I am grateful. Hence, although I hate this illness with all my heart and am angry and frustrated that we cannot manage the seizures today, I am focusing on being grateful for the people who came to our aid. I need to focus on this; I need to remember that people will help when needed, and I do not have to deal with this alone. I need to remember we must continue to try to live our lives and move forward despite the daily obstacles that plague us. I need to focus on light and hope instead of darkness and despair and move forward.

Tomorrow we are booked to go ziplining with our friends. It is a group of 12, but I am currently very unsure if this is a good idea. It is at a nature preserve off the main areas, and I am unsure of accessibility. There is also a large natural water slide that drops into a magnificent pool of water. The question is do we just go forward and take the risk? Tonight, I am unsure what to do. Do I give in to the fear of living with this demon? As a mother, is it my responsibility to avoid such risks, or is it my responsibility to let me son live his life? Tonight, I just don't know. I sit on the sofa of our condo and listen for my voices, listen for guidance from one who may understand the workings of the Universe more than I can.

Out of the mud blooms the lotus....

With deep contemplation,

Kimberley

On Dec 28, 2018, at 10:27 AM, Leggo, Carl <carl.leggo@ubc.ca> wrote:

Dear Kimberley,

May the lotus always bloom!

We have so little control over all the events and exigencies that populate each of our days. We learn to lean into each next step, each new circle, each concentric circle. And we learn to trust!

I hope the zipline action is lots of fun!

With hope and love,

Carl

From: Kimberley Holmes <kaholmes@ucalgary.ca>
Date: Friday, December 28, 2018 at 5:18 PM
To: "Leggo, Carl" <carl.leggo@ubc.ca>
Subject: Re: Connecting

Dear Carl,

We decided to decline on the zipline, much to the boys' dismay. Then I felt guilty for shutting down the party and sent them out parasailing, so they did get to do something adventurous. In the end, Tris was fine today, but Jayden developed a headache from too much sun and Coke. Hence it was his turn in bed. We really do have very little control over the events and experiences of our lives. Basically, life happens, and we need to learn to accept it for what it is. We cannot change what happens to us, only our response to it. I must admit as Tris prepared to launch for his 10-minute parasail I sent silent prayers to all my grandparents who have gone to spirit. Then I focused on the water and counted my breathing until he landed. There was nothing I could do to prevent a seizure from occurring up in the air. Yet I also cannot refuse to let him fly. This is the challenge of parenting. We need to protect them from harm, but we also cannot clip their wings and inhibit their ability to soar with the clouds. We let them launch and hope for the best, hope we made the best choices, and take a deep breath. We learn to control the mind and ignore the rumblings of fear for we cannot control the outside world. We cannot change the experiences that are waiting to happen to us, only our own breathing and our own response. All I can manage is my inner Essence, my own racing heart and the deep and steady pattern of my own breath. Inhale, exhale. The rest simply is.

In retrospect we should have gone on the zipline with friends. Fear won the round but, in the afternoon, we decided to live. This is our challenge to overcome the fear of what if and live for what is. For what is, is all that exists.

The Ride

Buckles tightly strapped standing perched in anticipation on the back of the boat

Feet grounded, face determined and strong as excitement and exhilaration fill the air

Floating dramatically into the sky in a rainbow cloud parachute arms outstretched

Enthusiasm bubbling over in the passengers in the boat as the adventure begins

Seven to ten minutes in the sky soaring with the birds high above the waves

As a mother counts her breaths in the boat and prays to her grandparents to protect

In a feeble and frightened attempt to control what cannot be controlled

In an effort to accept the complex conundrum and challenges of life and move forward

Touch down on the back of the boat eyes shining with excitement and victory

Speaking of the feeling of peace experienced as one is floating in the shining sky

Free as the birds swirling in the air and calling out to one another in a cacophony of song

Celebrating the freedom to choose the exhilaration of life

Life is but a short ride that spins us through the passages of air and wind

Sometimes floating us gracefully but often bringing us crashing to the ground

Dropping to our knees in a burst of energy that often threatens to consume us

But quickly disperses into the wind swirling and whirling with the birds in the sky

Dreaming of the lotus, or perhaps the Phoenix....

With much love, Kimberley

On Dec 29, 2018, at 12:37 PM, Leggo, Carl <carl.leggo@ubc.ca> wrote:

Hi, Kimberley,

The images of parasailing are delightful!

May we always make the decisions we think we need to make, followed by the wisdom to assess the decisions made so we can make "other" decisions, too.

The challenges of parenting are always full and pressing—may we surrender ourselves to the calling. I love the poetic line, "quickly disperses into the wind swirling and whirling with the birds in the sky." May we always swirl and whirl!

Enjoy every adventure!

Carl

From: Kimberley Holmes <kaholmes@ucalgary.ca>
Date: Sunday, December 30, 2018 at 7:16 PM
To: "Leggo, Carl" <carl.leggo@ubc.ca>
Subject: Re: Connecting

Dear Carl,

It was a cool and cloudy day in Mexico, and it reminds me a great deal of Vancouver except for the excessive party mode and chaos. We should know better than to travel between Christmas and New Year's to spaces and places that are known for their beer and tequila. As a non-drinker I sometimes find the excessive celebrations challenging and crave a quiet poolside to read my books in peace.

Today we went to the boardwalk in Puerta Vallarta, a brilliant space with art and culture. It was masses of people swirling down the stormy boardwalk and almost sinister in a strange way. The wind whipped our hair, and waves crashed angrily against the sand sculptures that stood majestically on the beach. We retreated to the comfort of a Starbucks, and poor Tris had a small seizure. Luckily, we were seated at a table and managed to avoid any serious harm, yet all of us were somewhat frightened and perplexed about what we would do if we experience an emergency situation. His spirits are dampened by these daily interruptions, and we have decided to head home on January 2nd so he can be reassessed and treated at the Alberta Children's hospital. Although our desire to live our lives is strong, common sense is even stronger. As the storm brewed around us today, it was almost as if the Universe was giving me a silent warning to take it easy and retreat to safer ground. We are in a third world country that is wired to party, which is a wonderful and festive thing if one is well and strong. It is not what we need, so after celebrating the new year we shall return to our safe and quiet home, close to excellent medical care. Both boys are somewhat hostile but understand the rationale. There will be other days, other holidays and other experiences. For now, we need to cut this one short. It is hard on all of us as we never truly relax when we are haunted by this mysterious enigma that causes Tris's mind to stutter. We must find a solution to this problem so we can proceed with life.

Hence our lives for the next few days will consist of sleep, eat, beach, and repeat. We will ring in the new year with our friends at a small and somewhat quiet restaurant on the beach. Quiet and New Year's in Mexico is a bit of an oxymoron, but we shall do our best. We shall be mindful and present and send up hopeful messages for a bright and healthy new year. We shall focus not on what could have been, but what will be as we move steadily forward and face the obstacles and challenges that lie before us. I am envisioning 2019 to be a year of strength and power. I am envisioning new beginnings, transitions, and transformations for us all.

I have learned this year, through many different messages, never to take the gift of health and wellness for granted. If I could have one wish it would be for health. Happiness would naturally follow I believe.

<u>A Wish</u>

I wish with all my heartfelt love upon the magical stars shining brightly in the sky

THE SPACES IN BETWEEN

A wonderful world not fraught with incurable illness and a place no one would ever die

I realize this is not remotely realistic or a potentially plausible way to dare to dream

However, wishing is meant to be magical mystery to change the way we see

I wish for a world where children played and danced and never were struck ill

A world where harmony and health trumps all the pain and happiness is near

I fill my family with the fruits of the earth and seek the nourishment of the sun

Hoping beyond all hope and dreams that this epic battle can be won

I wish my son could live his life and not suffer with this powerful plague

I wish the cancer that haunts our lives could wither and no longer remain

I dream of a world without these obstacles but realize that would change the journey

Yet as the new year tiptoes closer I cannot help but wish to clear the path

I hope with all my heart that if I wish just hard enough that miracles might happen

That if I am a good enough person and am always kind that karma might pave the way

That just maybe that magical sparkling star really does hold some power

And when I wish upon it

    My dreams may just come true

Wishing upon the star I see overhead,

Kimberley

On Dec 31, 2018, at 10:47 AM, Leggo, Carl <carl.leggo@ubc.ca> wrote:

Dear Kimberley,

I am sorry to hear that your vacation has been punctuated with health challenges. I trust that you are making the best decisions for your family, and I wish you well in your return home. Hopefully, the next couple days will still be fun.

Your poem is a tender testimony to hope: "My dreams may just come true."

With love,

Carl

From: Kimberley Holmes <kaholmes@ucalgary.ca>
Date: Monday, December 31, 2018 at 4:31 PM
To: "Leggo, Carl" <carl.leggo@ubc.ca>
Subject: Re: Connecting

Dear Carl,

Today was a slow and mindful day that started with a leisurely breakfast on the deck watching the "obstacle golfers." We then spent the entire day on the beach. We walked up and down, dashed into the waves, and built castles in the sand. It was slow and mindful and perfect for what we needed. Sometimes being forced to be still and stop moving can be a good thing. It forces you to pause, take breaths, and simply enjoy life for what it is instead of rushing towards what could still be found. So, although we did not accomplish anything, we accomplished everything needed.

I wish you all the best as we head into 2019. My resolution is to live a healthy and good life, and I am sending out to the Universe a wish for good health and happiness in 2019. Tomorrow we shall celebrate the new year in the waves. Although we are "leaving early" to return for Tris's treatment, we have still had 8 days here. In a strange way I am looking forward to a return to my Christmas tree at home, to the snow and perhaps a cross country ski next week. It is quite remarkable one can hit the sand and surf and then ski in the snow with only a few hours in a plane.

Sending you joy and love on the last day of 2018,

Kimberley

THE SPACES IN BETWEEN

New Year's Eve

The kitchen staff is busy and the restaurants all a vibrant buzz
Fireworks poised ready to be fired as the clock chimes midnight
Symbolizing endings of old and the start of something new and fresh
As the baby new year tiptoes in during the wee hours of the morn

The celebrations are a ritual of the passage of time and lives gone by
A celebration of the darkest days slowly returning to the light
New energies bursting as the party rages on in hopes of the possibility
Of tomorrow's January sunrise and what may lie around the corner
Brilliant colors of fire shall soon light the sky as bands blaze out the tune
Cardboard lanterns set out to sea with the dreams of light and hope
As the lanterns rise into the dark night sky and fade slowly from our vision
A new hope for powerful beginnings and new transitions has begun

Let the countdown begin to end the old and welcome in the new
Faces shine in anticipation and the champagne corks begin to pop
Tequila flows for the brave and the rest of us slowly sip the bubbles
All wishing for the magic of the new to embrace us all.

On Dec 31, 2018, at 7:22 PM, Leggo, Carl <carl.leggo@ubc.ca> wrote:

Thank you, Kimberley, for all your wonderful gifts of love and language, of spirit and sensitivity!!

Your plans sound lovely and humane and heartful!

Happy New Year!

Carl

From: Kimberley Holmes <kaholmes@ucalgary.ca>
Date: Tuesday, January 1, 2019 at 5:01 PM
To: "Leggo, Carl" <carl.leggo@ubc.ca>
Subject: Re: Connecting

Dear Carl,

I hope the new year arrived smoothly and all is well today. Our evening consisted of dinner on the beach and a brilliant, although somewhat terrifying, show of fireworks that exploded from various parts of the beach. The safety standards for fireworks are a bit different here, but no one seems to respond to the fact that we could be set off in sparks ourselves at any moment. The paper lanterns were lit and launched to the sky with hopes and dreams of light for 2019.

While walking down the beach, with the fireworks exploding around us, Tris discovered a newly hatched baby turtle working his way towards the water and the dangerous fireworks. There is a turtle sanctuary on the beach, and daily new turtles are released carefully to the sea. This tiny little guy somehow managed to escape his protective home and was working his way to the water right in the middle of the New Year's celebrations. We carefully gathered him up and walked with him to the water's edge, through the crazy crowds and exploding lights. At the shoreline we carefully released him into the water and hope he swam out to his family in the dark currents. I am not sure how Tristan managed to spot him amongst the chaos, but at the strike of the new year he was on "turtle rescue." Turtles are very sacred and live a very long time, so we are hopeful we started him on a 100-year journey. Finding a turtle is said to be good luck. Turtles are representative of longevity, endurance, persistence, and the continuation of life (sometimes against incredible odds). We found it quite appropriate and reaffirming to find this little guy crossing Tristan's path as the baby new year tiptoed in, symbolizing fresh starts and new beginnings. We shall take this as a sign for what lies ahead of us.

With love, Kimberley

On Jan 2, 2019, at 9:58 AM, Leggo, Carl <carl.leggo@ubc.ca> wrote:

Hi, Kimberley,

Your account of Tris and the turtle is filled with lovely wonder! You have enjoyed some big adventures in Mexico.

May your flight home go smoothly!

I am leaning into the New Year with anticipation for whatever unfolds!

With joy,

Carl

From: Kimberley Holmes <kaholmes@ucalgary.ca>
Date: Thursday, January 3, 2019 at 7:20 PM
To: "Leggo, Carl" <carl.leggo@ubc.ca>
Subject: Re: Connecting

Dear Carl,

We are home safe and sound, although my personal trip was quite perilous. I managed to get a migraine headache while waiting in the complete chaos of the airport. It proceeded to worsen and by the time we boarded the plane I felt as if a thousand hammers were pounding in my brain. Nausea followed, and I spent 5 1/2 hours vomiting into the paper bags. Add some nasty turbulence and it was about as close to hell as I desire to get. Although I did not vomit on anyone directly, I managed to dump my vomit bag on my husband. My children calmly played their video games through all this process, which tells you how used they are to my getting ill. Sigh....at some point in the future I am sure I shall find the story of dumping my vomit bag on my husband quite amusing, but at this point, while my headache still lingers, the unpleasantness of the process overrides any potential humor!

Today I was grateful for my warm bathtub, my clean and quiet house, and the access to health care if needed. I am off to an early sleep tonight with hopes of a better day tomorrow.

Tris will be at the hospital in the morning tomorrow to get training for his Kineret injection in hopes of combatting the seizure disorder. Once trained he gets to practice injecting oranges!

Out of the mud blooms the lotus! Muddy and tired, Kimberley

On Jan 3, 2019, at 9:14 PM, Leggo, Carl <carl.leggo@ubc.ca> wrote:

Oh, Kimberley!

Sounds horrible!!

I wish you well/ness in your return home.

Always with hope for the lotus, even in the mud, Carl

From: Kimberley Holmes <kaholmes@ucalgary.ca>
Date: Friday, January 4, 2019 at 6:49 PM
To: "Leggo, Carl" <carl.leggo@ubc.ca>
Subject: Re: Connecting

Dear Carl,

It was horrible! It is a good thing that memories fade and eventually we are ready to go forward again. I am now amused at the fact that I dropped my vomit bag on my husband, and it sends the boys into hysterical laughter when Dad complains of Mom dumping her puke bag on him. He is lucky he did not get directly vomited upon! It is a very strange feeling to be violently ill in a small confined space breathing into a paper bag you have recently expelled vomit into. You feel very self-conscious but unable to do much about it. I suppose the fact that there are vomit bags in every seat back speaks to the fact it may be more common than I thought. It was a new experience for me and certainly not one I am keen to repeat. Yet another one of life's obstacles leading me to the lotus. When the flower finally blooms it should be spectacular!

Tris had training for his Kineret injections today. We are on a 6-week trial, and if this works, we shall begin weaning him off the epilepsy medication. I will be joyful too for this as I am not sure the epilepsy medication did anything for us. We were treating the symptoms instead of seeing the root of the problem. I find this an unfortunate characteristic of Western medicine. We always try to mask the pain and suffering without really considering what is causing the body to speak. We need to learn to listen to the body, to recognize its calls for help, and provide intervention at the root. If this treatment works, he will make medical history and change the way things are done. I am hopeful our experiences will lead to change and ensure that no one else will suffer through this experience

I also will be taking more wellness days, to sit silently and contemplate the moment and listen for my voices. Otherwise my voices are replaced by sledgehammers that pound viciously at my temples and threaten to destroy me. I need to take time for me to think, to be silent, and to heal. The mother of a sick child carries the pain and suffering, yet she swallows it deep within her own being in an attempt to protect the child. Eventually it bursts forth and bubbles everywhere.

When my body speaks, it screams quite loudly. I need to pay attention to the softer, subtler messages because the screaming and expelling is not desirable and will eventually consume me. Lesson learned.

The Body Speaks

It begins in my gut a small whisper of dissatisfaction gurgling and swirling

A slight twinge that something is out of order but easy to ignore and disregard

A deep breath and I continue on with my day overriding the primitive warning

It moves throughout my body making me feel tired and disengaged within a deep haze

Often anger simmering on the back burner threatening to boil and violently overflow

Into a simmering lava of bitterness and rage that burns and blisters all in its path

Then the sledgehammers begin their relentless powerful pounding and throbbing

A thousand lashes to the head and the nausea begins to rise as the room begins to spin

Hot and cold flashes the temperature fluctuating as the waves of nausea crescendo

Darkness and despair overrides everything and I curl into a ball of pathetic helplessness

The pain and the nausea overriding everything that is and the struggle to breath

Is the only thing that can be focused on as I try to move through the angry assault?

Time merges into a staccato of hammers that relentlessly pound and torture

The body expels all that it is holding in as it attempts to find balance and release the pain

The body screams out the message that began as an ancient gurgling left unheeded

The body whispers its messages beginning in the gut as a twinge and a rumbling

Surging through the body in a stronger current as the mind does not heed the message

Ending in a vicious assault that demands attention must be paid to the messages

With consideration of the gurgling,

Kimberley

On Jan 5, 2019, at 3:46 PM, Leggo, Carl <carl.leggo@ubc.ca> wrote:

You are brave, Kimberley! Very brave!!

Continue to live with courage in each moment's purposefulness, always aware of how the moment co-ordinates with other moments to create a sense of meaning and meandering!

Your poem is superb!!

With love,

Carl

From: Kimberley Holmes <kaholmes@ucalgary.ca>
Date: Saturday, January 5, 2019 at 8:06 PM
To: "Leggo, Carl" <carl.leggo@ubc.ca>
Subject: Re: Connecting

Dear Carl,

I am not sure if I am brave, but I just don't really have the option not to deal with things. These things just happen in my life and the life that occurs around me. I do not have a choice to wage battle, for the battle is part of the process. I am within the battle, and it engulfs me within its frenzy. It is either work things through or pitifully perish. I suppose one could just yield to the pain and the onslaught of suffering, but that does not stop the relentless banter. The mind continues to chatter, to fight, and the physical body continues to throb as it expresses its concern at the nemesis that swirls around it.

THE SPACES IN BETWEEN

The motif of breathing is a powerful one today. I have just returned from my younger son's soccer game. During the game his teammate hyperventilated on the pitch. He was in the middle of playing when he suddenly crumpled over and struggled to breath. No one seemed to notice this child gasping for breath in the middle of the competitive match. I saw him begin to shake and was worried that he was going to seize. Without thinking I rushed down to the pitch yelling at the ref and coaches to pay attention. I then went through the scorekeeper's box and onto the bench and helped this child to breath. I placed my hand instinctively on his stomach and my arm around his shoulder and calmly asked him to inhale and exhale. Eventually he calmed, stopped shaking violently, and reclaimed his ability to speak.

Being able to breathe through the pain, breathe through the crisis and find our way through life is such a difficult yet essential skill. If we can calm the breath, we can calm the furious fluctuations of the manic swings of the mind. If we lose control of the mind, we lose everything. As a yogi, I have been taught to surrender. The surrender is what is difficult, the ability to accept what happens for what it is and just let go of all attachment and emotional response. This concept is such an oxymoron to our Western philosophy of fighting our way to the top. Tonight, I am contemplating this juxtaposition between striving and fighting to get ahead and simply surrendering to what may be. If we surrender to what might come, will the Universe align us to fulfil our purpose, or will it simply pass us by as a missed opportunity? I am contemplating this conundrum and trying to decide what it might mean to my life and my purpose.

I am going to pay careful attention to how each moment co-ordinates with others to create meaning. I am going to pay attention to the meandering of life and see if I can find the meaning.

Just Breathe

The world spins and swirls as the cycles of life morph in a kaleidoscope of colors

Merging, synthesizing, connecting, and then splintering into a thousand tiny fragments

Sharp and jagged, they threaten to cut deeply into permanent festering wounds

That blister and bleed deeply as our spirit swirls around us in raging rivers of red

Red the color of reckless rage, the color of perpetual passion, and the color of love

Swirling portals of emotion that embody our Essence and transport our perspective

Imagining worlds and images beyond the here and now that are no longer recognizable

To the naked eye that cannot perceive the depth of the interconnected spiraling systems

The heart beats rapidly, the body sweats and shakes as it begins to descend into darkness

Emotions and pain overriding the physical stamina bringing the human to their knees

In a surrender to all that is and all that will ever be that is so far beyond our conscious control

We pull the air deeply into our lungs in deep and mindful ways of being and becoming

The mind slows, the body begins to unwind, and the oxygen flows through the bloodstream

The sweating stops and the shaking of the body begins to settle into a peaceful calm

The heartbeat slows to the natural pattern of the drumbeat of human time

As the breathing soothes the Spirit and returns us to the place of sweet surrender

Just breathe

(Holmes & Leggo, 2019)

On Jan 6, 2019, at 10:14 AM, Leggo, Carl <carl.leggo@ubc.ca> wrote:

Eloquently expressed, Kimberley!

Your understanding of breath and breathing is profound!

Above all, you know that we must attend to the other, and that we will know how to attend to the other when we pay attention!

The last line of your poem, "As the breathing soothes the Spirit and returns us to the place of sweet surrender," is a beautifully evoked call to breathe.

With love,

Carl

From: Kimberley Holmes <kaholmes@ucalgary.ca>
Date: Sunday, January 6, 2019 at 7:09 PM
To: "Leggo, Carl" <carl.leggo@ubc.ca>
Subject: Re: Connecting

Dear Carl,

It is the eve of back to school, and I already feel the pangs of panic at the thought of early mornings and scheduled routines which previously drained my energy and crushed the enthusiasm of my soul. Although our break was far from perfect, it was a break from the day-to-day drill we call education. Tomorrow we are back to schedule with a diploma exam to write in one short week. My goal will be to remember to eat, to drink a cup of tea, and to breathe as I teach my students to approach life in mindful ways that care for our Essence.

Our rhythm of high school is such a juxtaposition to the natural patterns of life. We gear up for exams and finals in a time of darkness when one should be resting. We burn the midnight oil in the dark of night in a quest for the sacred A grade that in theory guarantees our success in life.

Hence my thoughts tonight are punctuated with concerns of breakfast prep, what to pack for lunch, and what activities need to be attended to. I am not even sure I have a lesson prepped for tomorrow as the remnants of my migraine still cloud my brain and make my thoughts somewhat hazy. When the alarms go off in the wee hours of morning, I cannot imagine there will be a great deal of joy here as we have not seen signs of teenage life prior to 10 am over the holidays. I am going to attempt to arise an hour earlier and attend a yoga practice. I resolve to start my day breathing mindfully amongst others who also crave peace of mind and wellness. Hopefully I can maintain a pattern before I begin to burn out again. Second semester is kinder to everyone, so I am hopeful it will be more palatable. There are more breaks in the routine, lighter days and the promise of graduation and summer vacation. These are things that sustain us through this process of "educating the young."

Doing School

The lazy days of summer and the setting sun have not yet ended
But the standard setting committee is busy at work
Getting ready to sort, organize, and classify
The unsuspecting souls who are hoping for an authentic education

The grade 10 students do not do well on the standardized assessment
So, we need more tests so that they can jump the hoops
Like a well-trained monkey executing his tricks and receiving the grade
On the diploma exam which we all bow down to with great reverence

Class sizes are bursting with impossible numbers with the cry to personalize
Each and every learner should be given a chance to learn in a way that they can
As the classroom teacher balances limited time between 115 learners a term
Doing the best that she can to help each soul find the way through the stress
Pushing them through the recommended graduation date on time
As they walk through the doors, they are given a scarf reminding them of
Their date of maturation when they need to walk across the stage with wisdom
Regardless of knowledge whether they are ready or not

This is the game that we play with our children that is called
Doing school
Or perhaps it should be called
Doing time

On Jan 7, 2019, at 9:31 AM, Leggo, Carl <carl.leggo@ubc.ca> wrote:

Brilliantly expressed, Kimberley!

Continue to write/say what needs to be written/said!

"Getting ready to sort, organize, and classify" is a splendid line in a strong poem!

With hope,

Carl

From: Kimberley Holmes <kaholmes@ucalgary.ca>
Date: Monday, January 7, 2019 at 7:28 PM
To: "Leggo, Carl" <carl.leggo@ubc.ca>
Subject: Re: Connecting

Dear Carl,

We all survived re-entry, though I must admit I am already in my pajamas and will be in bed early tonight. My energy is already low, but I am hopeful it will just be getting used to the routine of school again. One day back and the stress level is already rising as some of my students have 3-unit finals this week prior to writing diploma exams. This is such a strange and unsound system that we have created. We spend so much time testing in sharp contrast to taking the time to learn, to reflect, and to grow. Although as a system we are attempting to rethink our structure, our "high achieving" high schools hold true to the intense testing and stress-filled environment. It is all about the number and how we score on the standardized tests. At least in my own classroom I can impact learning in meaningful ways, and I shall endeavor to speak and write about what needs to be said. It is not always received well, but I suppose that was Plato's warning to those who return to the cave. It never stops amazing me how so many still cling to the shadows although the sunlight brightly glimmers just outside the doorway.

Tris has started his new treatment tonight. He will now have an evening injection of Kineret, which will stop the inflammation that plagues his central nervous system. The challenge is finding spots on his body to inject the treatment as he is a lean swimming machine with zero body fat. Our instructions are to inject into fatty tissue, which he is seriously lacking. I am hopeful this treatment might work. If it does, we will wean him off the epilepsy medication, which impacts his cognition and daily functioning. I am hopeful perhaps my child can have his life back. I am hopeful for health.

It seems our life has been a series of obstacles via either health care or education. I believe both are deeply interconnected, and we need to be keenly aware of the cognitive, emotional, social, and physical components of our Beings. We are interconnected in so many ways and need to find ways to live our lives mindfully and with joy.

I hope the new year has crept in gently and your treatments are helping your body to heal. I think of you often, and my students asked how you were today. Your story and theirs have become interwoven as we explore the complexities of this complex journey of humanities.

With love,

Kimberley

On Jan 8, 2019, at 9:47 AM, Leggo, Carl <carl.leggo@ubc.ca> wrote:

Thank you, Kimberley, for your words, full of hope and purpose!

May we always continue to seek solutions/remedies/possibilities!

I hope that you, Tris, and your students will find the ways to healthy success in each day's lived experiences.

With love,
Carl

From: Kimberley Holmes <kaholmes@ucalgary.ca>
Date: Tuesday, January 8, 2019 at 8:56 PM
To: "Leggo, Carl" <carl.leggo@ubc.ca>
Subject: Re: Connecting

Dear Carl,

Second day back with only 3 days left in the semester, and emotions are raging in the halls of the high school. I dealt with various meltdowns, rage attacks, and tears today. The exams are endless, the sleep deprivation obvious, and the ridiculousness of "doing school" is almost surreal. My student teacher has stayed this week to volunteer with the classes she is teaching. She is shocked by the pressure and the meltdowns that occur in our high achieving high schools. It is certainly not normal or something we should aspire to, yet when the Fraser report results roll in, that seems to be all that matters to anyone.

We have a temporary adventure in the works. My husband is being considered for a 6-month contract in Germany. At this moment, the idea of running away to Europe sounds quite appealing. Tris's medical details will need to be worked out, and I will have to secure a leave from the school board. We will need to acquire a "German pet passport" if we are going to travel with our dog, but my mother has also offered to keep her if things work out. Hence, we shall see if the lotus shall indeed bloom out of this mucky mess and a new opportunity glistens right around the corner.

I am watching the flames of the fireplace dance in brilliant patterns of blue and orange flickering swirls of light. The colors merge and dance in a captivating pattern, calling for me to reflect on its beauty. Beauty can be found in almost anything if we simply pause and pay attention. Our interconnected patterns of life often consume us in fire but leave us with the possibilities of magical experiences arising from the ashes.

With reflections on the flames,

OX

Kimberley

On Jan 9, 2019, at 9:44 AM, Leggo, Carl <carl.leggo@ubc.ca> wrote:

Fascinating possibilities, Kimberley! Six months in Germany sounds like an adventure!

May you and your family find the way that will serve all of you with success and joy!

With hope,

Carl

From: Kimberley Holmes <kaholmes@ucalgary.ca>
Date: Wednesday, January 9, 2019 at 7:02 PM
To: "Leggo, Carl" <carl.leggo@ubc.ca>
Subject: Re: Connecting

Dear Carl,

The possibilities of spending some time in Berlin are looking bright. However, both my boys are somewhat opposed to the idea! I am hoping they will be able to see it as an adventure.

The timing of this escape is quite perfect as my colleague, who is currently teaching Tris, has lodged a complaint against me for questioning her practice. Hence, I am due to be punished by the ATA, or at least put on trial. I cannot help but think of the witch trials and how people who are threatened by wisdom feel the need to prosecute. I will not ever stop speaking up for my child. I will not ever stop speaking up for effective and mindful pedagogy. They can punish me if they wish, although I really have not done anything wrong, but they will not silence me, especially when it comes to speaking up for my son.

It concerns me immensely that due to a union we cannot question the professional practice. If we do not question, who will? It sets a very dangerous tone for public education. Hence my desire to return to the University burns even stronger. It is so difficult to go back to the cave when you have seen the light. The next few weeks or months may be quite challenging. If the Germany experience actualizes my husband will leave soon, and I will be left to the details. I will also need to attend to the details of my "trial" and deal with a colleague who clearly has insecurity issues and is unable to reflect on the process. I shall need to keep reminding myself that out of the mud blooms the lotus.

My words are somewhat stuck today. Part of my heart is hopeful for new opportunities and experiences. The other part is dark due to the negativity and toxic environment of the school I spend my days in. I shall feed the hopeful and try to pass through the dark and muddy sludge.

In need of a pep talk,

Kimberley

From: Leggo, Carl <carl.leggo@ubc.ca>
Sent: January 10, 2019 9:43:31 AM
To: Kimberley Holmes; Leggo, Carl
Subject: Re: Connecting

Dear Kimberley,

I am very sorry to hear about the trouble with your colleague and the ATA. Be brave! You must speak up for Tris! Always!

Trust that this story will unfold as it ought to—with support for Tris and for all students who need support.

Sending love, Carl

From: Kimberley Holmes <kaholmes@ucalgary.ca>
Date: Thursday, January 10, 2019 at 10:38 AM
To: "Leggo, Carl" <carl.leggo@ubc.ca>
Subject: Re: Connecting

Dearest Carl,

I shall continue to speak regardless of the witch hunt. It is not the first time and will not be the last. The system of school has been trying to silence my voice for a very long time. I wrote about it in my thesis, and I live this oppressive story daily. I shall not be silenced, and I shall never allow a child to be silenced.

I am reviewing the Alberta Learning Standards for Special Education (June 2004) based on the recommendation of a wise and trusted mentor. It is terribly dated and may no longer be relevant. I am also going to look at Human Rights Legislation and the new school Act. The Standards for special education state:

"Parents have the right and responsibility to work with boards to ensure their children's special education needs are met, subject to limitations based on the reasonableness in each circumstances" (pg. 1)

Why do we, as educators, not take an oath? We are responsible for the holistic wellness of children. Is there any other task as daunting? Do we not need to question all the time, finding ways to improve and grow so all may flourish?

Thank you for being my teacher and my trusted colleague. I am not sure I would have the courage to speak if I had to stand alone.

With gratitude, grace, and love

Kimberley

From: Leggo, Carl <carl.leggo@ubc.ca>
Sent: January 10, 2019 6:04:43 PM
To: Kimberley Holmes; Leggo, Carl
Subject: Re: Connecting

Eloquently expressed, Kimberley!!

You understand what you must do. So, do it, and rest confidently in the assurance that there is always an ethical principle that transcends the "letter of the law" and opens up the real, actual experience of teaching and learning so that nothing supersedes the rights and values of the child.

Tris is very fortunate to have you as his mother. That is a big part of your being both a mother and a teacher. Live your convictions with confidence! Live your convictions with heart!

Sending love,

Carl

From: Kimberley Holmes <kaholmes@ucalgary.ca>
Date: Saturday, January 12, 2019 at 1:15 PM
To: "Leggo, Carl" <carl.leggo@ubc.ca>
Subject: Re: Connecting

Dear Carl,

My life seems somewhat surreal these days. It has been confirmed that we will temporarily be residing in Germany. With the current conflict at the school it will be good to be far away. It shall give me some time to think, some space, and I am hopeful more time to read, to write, and to reflect.

Our plans are vague at best. We don't know what we will do for school other than registering for German Language and Culture 10 online. We have all downloaded the Duolingo app and are making our first attempts at learning our new language. My initial impression is that there are common patterns to English, and I can see the hermeneutic root in many of the words. As I was looking at kinder, a word for children, I was reminded that kindergarten was originally described as a garden for children. Interesting the roots of kindergarten are in Germany. Friedrich Fröbel began his career in educating young children. I found a striking quote from him: "Education consists of leading man, as a thinking being, growing into self consciousness, to a pure and unsullied consciousness and free representation of the inner law of Divine Unity and in teaching him ways and means thereto" (Fröbel, 1974, pg.2)

Fröbel set up his school that later became known as kindergarten (Headley, 1965). The teachers, called kindergarteners, were called to educate the children from the earliest experiences to become integrated and whole people (Fröbel, 1967a). This system emphasized play and later progressed to more complexity. From here kindergarten moved to the United States and Canada. I find this fascinating and extremely timely in my current contextual thinking about education. Today, kindergarten curriculum is a full day cognitive based program that includes reading and writing in addition to technology. We have lost Fröbel's initial concept, which was to allow children to socialize while at the same time learning concepts needed for school. We have rushed children into "doing school" and paid a tremendous cost in terms of wellness and social development. I believe we need to return to these original ideas of the school as a social institution where all the flowers in the garden are permitted to bloom together in beauty and brilliance.

Hermeneutics is calling me. Perhaps time to revisit Gadamer, Heidegger, and Kant amongst others. The Universe is sending me in this direction to study the root. Today I feel I have so much to learn. The need for knowledge and growth is compelling. Perhaps the impending move halfway around the world is inspiring my Spirit to awaken again to all the wonderful things that are possible.

With deep love,

Kimberley

On Jan 12, 2019, at 2:48 PM, Leggo, Carl <carl.leggo@ubc.ca> wrote:

Sounds very exciting, Kimberley!

I think Germany represents an opportunity for you and your family to engage with some European adventures that will fill you with "old newness" and "new oldness." Germany is an amazing country! Enjoy!

I love the work of Fröbel —he understood education as child-centered.

And, yes, hermeneutics is calling you. Of course! Hermeneutics is significantly located in German philosophy and theology.

I send hope for "astonishing silence."

With love,

Carl

From: Kimberley Holmes <kaholmes@ucalgary.ca>
Date: Saturday, January 12, 2019 at 8:54 PM
To: "Leggo, Carl" <carl.leggo@ubc.ca>
Subject: Re: Connecting

Dear Carl,

The juxtaposition of old newness and new oldness greatly intrigues me. I think perhaps the horizons are beginning to merge, and the work and my lived experiences are beginning to all become part of the whole. The need for contemplative awareness and contemplative silence is deep, and I hope this indeed may result in something quite astonishing.

I am excited to be entering the birthplace of hermeneutics in a month and eager to look more at the work of Fröbel. I seek to contemplate child-centered learning and the understandings of the interconnected complexities of the whole.

Today my husband bought me a new but old pair of diamond earrings. We found them at a jewelry consignment shop in the collection of estate sale pieces. Sparkly and beautiful, this "set" held intrigue as the diamonds are not a perfect pair. One is an old European diamond, perhaps over a hundred years old that the jeweler thought had originally been a stone in a wedding band. The other was a Canadian diamond that had been chosen to match the European diamond to create the imperfectly yet perfectly matched set of earrings. Hence this pair of earrings has one stone from Europe and one from Canada. I took the finding of this unique set as a sign, and now am proudly displaying them in my earlobes. They shall twinkle in the light and remind me to seek the connections.

With contemplations on the journey and focused awareness,

Kimberley

On Jan 13, 2019, at 10:15 AM, Leggo, Carl <carl.leggo@ubc.ca> wrote:

Endearing stories, Kimberley!! Exactly the kind of stories we need to share and hear and live!! May there continue to be many similar stories, wherever we live.

You are preparing yourself and your family for a grand adventure. I love the story of your husband's buying the diamond earrings! And, yes, "we share the same stories."

Continue to linger in contemplation, filled with hope for possibilities. With love, Carl

THE SPACES IN BETWEEN

From: Kimberley Holmes <kaholmes@ucalgary.ca>
Date: Sunday, January 13, 2019 at 6:23 PM
To: "Leggo, Carl" <carl.leggo@ubc.ca>
Subject: Re: Connecting

Dear Carl,

I hope that there will be interconnected stories as we proceed to this next part of the adventure. Today, I am feeling somewhat overwhelmed and apprehensive. It is funny how one fluctuates between excitement and fear. The fear leaves me feeling quite tired and sleepy, perhaps a primitive response to retreat. I think it is because I am caught between two worlds. I spent most of the day sorting and evaluating my English 30 students so they can have a final grade prior to writing their provincial diploma exam tomorrow. I need to be at the school by 8 to set up for the provincial exam and then have 6 long hours of supervising students while they sweat their way through the writing prompts. Writing on demand is such a strange concept and not how we work in the real world. I suppose we are simulating working and thinking under pressure with these tasks, yet I cannot help but wish I was just teaching in the morning. I know what they have learned and how they are growing. I do not need a standardized test to confirm my results. Really perhaps the tests are to confirm that the teachers are capable and professional, for if the student fails to learn the lesson then the teacher is to blame. The three weeks of exams are long and boring and simply do not seem to be a good way to spend the time. The stress level and misery are palpable as we trudge through January. Second semester starts February 2nd, but I am not anticipating being there. I am still awaiting confirmation of my leave so feeling somewhat disoriented and slightly concerned that it may not be approved.

The next month will be challenging as my husband is leaving Tuesday and the boys and I will be navigating the transition. There are so many little details that need to be attended to before we leave.

Intermingling Worlds

Eight am the bell sounds to begin the diploma exam and students tentatively trudge

Like snails to school to prove proficiency in their prose with perfect punctuation

Metaphorical images, symbolic messages, and insight into our human condition

My children study German language and culture in anticipation of their next adventure

Following along online with the program of studies and learning a new language

As they await the plane that will take them to the next experiences of learning

I hold one foot in one world and tentatively step towards another land

Where hermeneutics and deep philosophy await and Checkpoint Charlie calls

As the wall between America and Mexico is waiting to be built juxtaposing the Berlin Wall coming down

Our lives are but a series of juxtapositions and compositions of complexity

The metaphors and the experiences developing into a complex thesis

That unpacks an essential question and defends it in five concise paragraphs

To be or not to be that is the question reflecting on to thine own selves be true

Don't be a coward and go to war or you will be slowly overtaken by the horses of the night

Paul steps in front of the oncoming train as his ideal illusion outpaces his raw reality

The fear of the journey is felt deep in the gut yet the call to adventure is strong

The familiar is safe and the strange an adventure, yet both hold an appeal to the heart

Where the horizons will meet and when understanding will begin to address us

On Jan 14, 2019, at 9:54 AM, Leggo, Carl <carl.leggo@ubc.ca> wrote:

Dear Kimberley,

I trust all will work out for your grand family adventures in Germany! Embrace the possibilities!

You are certainly now living in the midst of challenges, but we are almost always living in the midst of some kind of challenges. May each day unfold with a keen sense of excitement for what might happen next!

Feeling "off balance and unsettled" is not such a strange feeling. I feel that way most/all the time! I love the following line from your poem: "Our lives are but a series of juxtapositions and compositions of complexity."

Sending love for making decisions,

Carl

From: Kimberley Holmes <kaholmes@ucalgary.ca>
Date: Monday, January 14, 2019 at 7:44 PM
To: "Leggo, Carl" <carl.leggo@ubc.ca>
Subject: Re: Connecting

Dear Carl,

I am trying to trust but am varying between excitement and terror about all the possible things that could go wrong. As our recent brief jaunt into Mexico was somewhat disastrous, I am tentative in my ability to have faith that all will be well. The yogic concept of surrender is one that I am struggling with today, and as my husband prepares to leave tomorrow, I can feel my body tensing up for a month of single parenting and the various responsibilities that come with steering the ship alone. I am preparing to be in charge, to be responsible, to be the sole guardian of this small family. It makes my shoulders feel heavy, and I need to focus on the steady pattern of my breathing.

I understand our lives are filled with challenges, and without these challenges we fall into a bored depression where life lacks meaning and purpose. We lose opportunities and experiences to the security of familiarity. To be the same day after day is not healthy, and I need to openly embrace the possibilities which have been presented before us. It was so much easier when it was just me to worry about. Once, I was just a girl with a backpack and a dream and life was only about me. Life is so much more complicated with two teens and a dog in tow as the bounds of the family are sometimes quite heavy. Tris's medical issues impact things significantly. We may have to return to Canada monthly for his IVIG and need to determine if the medication he takes is available. Such are the various obstacles we shall need to face. On a significantly smaller scale, the dog refuses entrance to her travel kennel so she will put up a battle. The boys refuse to travel without her, so somehow we need to convince her that her traveling cage is not so bad.

I supervised the diploma today, and the question was a derivative of "discuss how our experiences impact our life choices." Our experiences are our lives and our lives our experiences. Sometimes they leave us feeling exhilarated, and at other times we feel like a melting muddy puddle of snow slowly disintegrating into the ground in a mess of nothingness. Fluctuations of the seasons of our life: a series of growing, freezing, melting, and starting all over again.

Today I feel neutral as I am deeply tired. Supervising an exam for 6 hours drains me as does uncertainty. Time to take rest and consider the moments and how they may unfold. I am practicing being the observer. I am observing my thoughts and my emotional response and trying to practice non-attachment. I am watching the fluctuations of my mind to seek patterns and find direction.

Fluctuations

An exhilarating opportunity presents itself and we are breathless with anticipation

As only seconds later the fear and doubt strike presenting all the possibilities of darkness

Light turns into dark and then stars spark in the blackness illuminating hope

A possibility for an adventure unfolds yet the pathways are filled with cutting thorns

Pricking one causes the possibility of deep bleeding or even death to those who dare

The life blood flows through the body always aware of the potential for silent stillness

The teen flips through the pictures on the web page wondering and dreaming

The glossy photos mesmerize the mind yet speak of places unfamiliar and far away

Temptations calling to seek the unknown and home offers its sacred secure space

The secure sanctuary of what is known and comforting and what we call home

Tempted by the images of what lies beyond the cocoon of current existence

Seeking and searching adventure yet yearning for the safety of the familiar

Fluctuations

On Jan 15, 2019, at 9:49 AM, Leggo, Carl <carl.leggo@ubc.ca> wrote:

Dear Kimberley,

"Fluctuations" is a good title for your poem—always so much give and take in every day, even in the most ordinary of days!

You are looking forward to some big adventures, and those adventures will shape you and your family in significant ways. Embrace the adventures!

The details will work out, or they won't work out! Or most likely, the details will work out with fluctuations! That is how life unfolds and emerges in story.

I send love for making wise decisions that will fit with all the circumstances of your lives.

Carl

From: Kimberley Holmes <kaholmes@ucalgary.ca>
Date: Tuesday, January 15, 2019 at 6:54 PM
To: "Leggo, Carl" <carl.leggo@ubc.ca>
Subject: Re: Connecting

Dear Carl,

Yes, every moment of our lives offers different possibilities. We cannot change the daily events that comprise our experiences, only our inner response to the world around us. This is the quest of the enlightened to learn to control the fluctuations of the mind. To learn the power of the breath to soothe the body and the spirit.

My husband left today about 3:45 for Berlin. I was at work dealing with details of final grades, and the boys were home with their dad to say goodbye. Just prior to Ken's departure Tris had a seizure. I was anticipating this as he has been quite upset about his father leaving ahead of us, and emotional distress is a strong trigger. The fluctuations of the mind and the emotional surge overtook his spirit, and his body spoke out. I often wonder if he suffers from some type of PTSD, some residue memory of being left alone in ICU. His fear of abandonment and separation from his family is evident. I wonder what type of childhood memories are trapped within his strong and powerful 17-year-old body. The body holds our memories, our emotions, and our fears deep inside our core. When the build-up is too much they erupt in physical manifestations. Stomach pains, headaches, body pain, and, in Tris's experience, seizures. When the spirit is frustrated the body speaks.

Tris is currently sitting on the sofa across from me processing his feelings and emotions. He knows the anxiety he feels feeds the seizures, but he does not know how to control it. I find it a strange coincidence that I named him Tristan. *Tristhana* is the yoga trinity of *prana* (breathing), *asana* (movement) and *drishti* (focus). It is almost as if in naming him I determined the path he must follow and master. He must learn to control the fluctuations of the mind, and I must be his teacher. To be able to be the teacher I must also master my own fluctuations and be the observer. I must learn to watch the world and my emotional responses. I can feel myself observing tonight, focusing and preparing myself mentally to be the one in charge. I am aware of my breathing and the feeling of it traveling through my body. I am thinking about all the things I have learned from my teachers and how I must now teach my son. I am learning to breathe and breathing to become.

We have many vast and complicated experiences before us in this journey of life. Some will be amazing and others extremely difficult. We shall need to accept them all for what they are. This is the challenge of human existence.

Surrender

The busy world demands our attention as the details of life intersect and compete

The phone blinks, the computer pops up messages, and the bell rings to hurry up

And begin the busyness of the day and the important work that calls to us

My mind swirls and begins to daydream of walks in the mountains and sun-filled days

Of lazy afternoons in my pajamas with a cup of steaming coffee in my hand

The exquisiteness of empty nothingness calling me to recognize its value

As the lights flash, things beep, humans struggle, and the body begins to speak

The messages are mixed into patterns of rapid flight or vicious fight for survival

The inflammation races through the body a fire of passion igniting all systems

The body speaks out in fear as the flames of inflammation course through the system

Burning brightly leaving the sizzling embers hissing hysterically in the remnants

Of the furious surge of powerful passions and exuberant emotions

The breath calls to the body to cool the flame and gently soothe the sizzling embers

Slowing the rapid heartbeat and calming the fluctuations of the frenzied mind

Whispering silently to the Spirit of the sanctuary of the surrender

On Jan 16, 2019, at 9:38 AM, Leggo, Carl <carl.leggo@ubc.ca> wrote:

Good-morning, Kimberley,

I appreciate your understanding of "breathing to become." You named your son well, and he now lives with the rhythms and resonances of his name.

May you and your family always seek and know: "Whispering silently to the Spirit of the sanctuary of the surrender"—beautifully expressed!!

With love,

Carl

From: Kimberley Holmes <kaholmes@ucalgary.ca>
Date: Wednesday, January 16, 2019 at 6:56 PM
To: "Leggo, Carl" <carl.leggo@ubc.ca>
Subject: Re: Connecting

Dear Carl,

I am hopeful that we will all breathe to become as we begin our journey. Today I have been thinking of the hero's journey and the call to adventure. I remember reading a book as an undergrad entitled Giovanni's Room and the line, "are you willing to say yes to your adventure?" Joseph Campbell's "follow your bliss" is also running through my mind. What does it mean to follow your happiness? Today, all though completely exhausted and somewhat overwhelmed, I feel fully alive. There are things to organize, anticipate, and contemplate. Life is a mystery awaiting unpacking and decoding. I think dealing with complexity and being busy in meaningful and authentic ways is what makes me happy. Perhaps it is what makes us all happy. Life is about a balance of finding silent reflective spaces and engaging fully in the complexity of life.

Tomorrow I shall attempt to finish assessing and sorting my students. It is quite unpleasant work really and not where my heart lies. I would have rather had an extra two weeks with my students learning. I am still waiting to see if my leave from the school board shall be granted. I am a bit apprehensive as all the wheels are turning without confirmation. We are also waiting to determine access to medical treatment. We may need to fly home monthly for our IVIGs.

With anticipation of the quest,

Kimberley

On Jan 17, 2019, at 9:23 AM, Leggo, Carl <carl.leggo@ubc.ca> wrote:

Hi, Kimberley,

I wish you and your family many advantages and clear paths in your plans!

I admire your commitment and conviction and calling!

And I certainly admire the positive way you look at how events can transpire!

Writing with lots of exclamation points!

Sending love, Carl

From: Kimberley Holmes <kaholmes@ucalgary.ca>
Date: Thursday, January 17, 2019 at 8:10 PM
To: "Leggo, Carl" <carl.leggo@ubc.ca>
Subject: Re: Connecting

Dear Carl,

Today has been a crazy busy day with students and driving my own boys to various places and spaces. You don't realize how essential two parents are until you are a single parent. I have utmost admiration for those who parent alone as it is challenging to keep up with all the details of life. I have been up since 5:45 am for an early swim practice for Tristan and have just managed to make it to sit down on the sofa and reflect now.

Perhaps tomorrow will allow for a cross country ski across the sparking snow through the park. I think gliding peacefully through the winter wonderland may help me process all the things occurring around me. It seems somewhat dreamlike tonight: "If we shadows have offended think but this, and all is mended. That you have but slumbered here while these visions did appear" (*A Midsummer Night's Dream*). But then again perhaps life is simply a temporary illusion, and who really knows what is real?

THE SPACES IN BETWEEN

Visions

One moment and the world seems a dreary and mundane routine
One-minute marching mindlessly into the next in a series of patterns and tasks
That seem never-ending and a frenzied march to unbounded boredom

One moment everything shifts and the possibilities swirl and merge in synchronicity
Moments rushing by quickly as the to-do list gets longer and possibilities expand
Opportunities are overwhelming and excitement pulses powerfully through the veins

The world changes in an instant and each significant second offers an opportunity
For a second chance, a different perspective, a possibility to change the view
Shifting visions of opportunity and experiences that slowly shape the illusions of life

Out out brief candle life is but a walking player that dances and struts upon the stage
A tale told by an idiot full of sound and fury but signifying everything that is possible
Vibrant visions sputtering and sparkling with the perpetual promise of a dream

On Jan 18, 2019, at 1:03 PM, Leggo, Carl <carl.leggo@ubc.ca> wrote:

Dear Kimberley,

You are a courageous woman—ready for the events and exigencies that percolate in each day! Always seek the hopeful and vibrant lessons/perspectives/conclusions that emerge!

I love the last line of your poem: "Vibrant visions sputtering and sparkling with the perpetual promise of a dream." May the dream never cease!

With love, Carl

From: Kimberley Holmes <kaholmes@ucalgary.ca>
Date: Saturday, January 19, 2019 at 9:06 PM
To: "Leggo, Carl" <carl.leggo@ubc.ca>
Subject: Re: Connecting

Dear Carl,

I am not sure if I am courageous or have just chosen to stop trying to control the way that life unfolds. For so much of my life I needed to be in control, to have things perfectly unfold as they should. I realize now that was a key catalyst to my unhappiness as the events of our life are far from controllable.

I should probably be alarmed as my leave from the school board is still not approved and we have not figured out the details of Tristan's medical treatment. Hence this whole adventure could be but a dream at any moment. However, being concerned about this will not help these things to happen. Worrying is such a useless emotion. All it does is work the psyche into a frenzy, which results in personal unhappiness. It makes your stomach turn and your head throb as you fight emotionally with things you cannot control. We need to learn to surrender to what will be and hope the lotus will eventually emerge from the mud.

I am thinking about the idea of a dream. Interestingly, it is of Germanic origin, relating to the old English dream, which meant "joy, mirth, noisy merriment," and also "music." It can also be defined as the sequence of images or illusions passing through the mind of a sleeping person and hence the verb dreaming. I think of Hamlet's "to die, to sleep…perchance to dream—ay, there's the rub, for in that sleep of death what dreams make come." Hence the lack of the dream is a symbolic type of death of the Spirit. We need to seek the joyful merriment that comes with living a full human life. If we spend our life "sleeping," which many of us do when we are not engaged in the mirth of life, all our life is but an illusion. Are these shadows of illusion simply the gatekeepers of the mind, stopping us from seeking the pure pleasure that could be found if only we surrender to the experiences of our lives? How can we make the illusion, the perpetual dream, our reality?

Perhaps our journeys may result in peril. Things may turn out badly, very badly, or maybe they won't. If we don't dare to indulge in the dream, we will never know what might await once we become fully awakened. We will never undertake our hero's quest; we will ignore the call to adventure, and eventually, although our physical bodies carry on, our Spirits will cease to exist.

I am currently reading The Untethered Soul (Singer, 2007), which is inspiring much of my current thinking. It mirrors much of the yoga training with the ideas of harnessing the fluctuations of the mind to allow the untethering of the soul. The word yoga means to yoke or harness. Hence if we harness the mind, we are allowed true freedom of the Spirit. Without our spiritual Muse our lives indeed become "a tale told by an idiot, full of sound and fury, signifying nothing" (Shakespeare).

Of course, these are concepts I understand in theory but am far from mastering. I wonder what a free soul would feel like, what it would do, and what illusions may appear while it slumbered. I think I shall contemplate this on the eve of the full moon.

<u>Tether</u>

The mind frets and stutters upon the stage screaming outrages and agonies

Inflicted upon it by the cruel and vicious world that does not allow critical control

The body cramps and seizes in pain, the muscles tense and prepare for the battle

Only to emerge without victory as these things cannot be darkly diminished

The Spirit watches the frenzied fluctuations of the mind as the neutral observer

It sees the highs and lows and the impact of the mind's rage upon the body

Tired of the drama and the pain the Spirit takes control of the frightened flight of the mind

And allows the breath to surge through the body in deep and grateful breaths

The mind becomes harnessed and tame and, in many ways, harmless and hopeful

Free to enjoy the simple merriment and mirth of each experience and episodic moment

The Spirit sings out in joy as it begins to float freely though the lunacies of life

In the sweet and unconditional simplistic sanctuary of surrender

With love and reflections under the gaze of the moon,

Kimberley

On Jan 20, 2019, at 10:17 AM, Leggo, Carl <carl.leggo@ubc.ca> wrote:

Hi, Kimberley,

I admire your perspectives on the Spirit and the mind and dreaming and the call to adventure! We need to acknowledge how open our imagination is, how active our creativity is.

Your contemplation on the eve of the full moon is filled with possibilities for learning to live with heart.

Onward with love, Carl

From: Kimberley Holmes <kaholmes@ucalgary.ca>
Date: Sunday, January 20, 2019 at 7:56 PM
To: "Leggo, Carl" <carl.leggo@ubc.ca>
Subject: Re: Connecting

Dear Carl,

The moon must be manipulating my emotions as I found myself quite moody and edgy today. I woke up early in a somewhat panicked state. It is funny how our fears haunt us in the wee hours of the morning. Often when I find myself perplexed or distressed about something, it is between 3-5 am that my mind decides to fret about it and awake me with feelings of anxiety and dread. I tried to work my way through it, but the twinges plagued me all day as I watched the swim meet and sorted the metals and ribbons for the competitions. I am nervous about not getting a leave, and I am nervous about leaving the country with a man-child who seizes. I don't know how to travel with a dog and am not sure how I will manage a pet in a two-bedroom apartment in downtown Berlin. My imagination has been busy creating all the possible recipes for disaster today, and tonight I am sitting quietly with a cup of peppermint tea trying to calm my mind's fluctuations and surrender to the process.

I often wonder what impact the full moon has upon our minds, our bodies, and our spirits. It is said that the full moon is a time of reflection and release, so perhaps today was all the residual worry that needed to bubble over the pathways of my mind and release into harmless vapor. It is also said a full moon is a time for releasing inhibitions, to step out into the world noticing what is coming to fruition in your life and to receive support for what you are up to. This is the stage where the seeds we plant at the new moon start to blossom in the light.

With love and affection,

Kimberley

On Jan 21, 2019, at 9:38 AM, Leggo, Carl <carl.leggo@ubc.ca> wrote:

Hi, Kimberley,

May you always be ready to say "yes" to adventures!!

It is good to consider the effects of the moon in our lives.

I enjoyed a quiet weekend. I have 4 more radiation treatments this week. I am learning to wait patiently!

I send hope for calm in making decisions.

With love,

Carl

From: Kimberley Holmes <kaholmes@ucalgary.ca>
Date: Monday, January 21, 2019 at 7:49 PM
To: "Leggo, Carl" <carl.leggo@ubc.ca>
Subject: Re: Connecting

Dear Carl,

Is this the last of your radiation? What is the plan for you after this week? I assume you are feeling quite tired as well. I hope you are managing to find quiet and reflective spaces to rest and to heal. Tonight, I shall ask the power of the moon to send you healing rays of energy and shine its luminous hope. Be strong!

With love,

Kimberley

On Jan 22, 2019, at 9:44 AM, Leggo, Carl <carl.leggo@ubc.ca> wrote:

Thank you, Kimberley, for your heartfelt thoughts. May the moon shine with healing hope! For both of us!

My radiation will end on Thursday. I will then wait about 6 to 7 weeks for the results. The journey continues.

Always with hope, Carl

From: Kimberley Holmes <kaholmes@ucalgary.ca>
Date: Tuesday, January 22, 2019 at 5:38 PM
To: "Leggo, Carl" <carl.leggo@ubc.ca>
Subject: Re: Connecting

Dear Carl,

The moon is luminous and bright tonight and speaks of healing hope and fresh beginnings. Its surface gleams a brilliant white, glistening brightly in the darkened sky and creating an illusion of safety and protection from whatever might lie lurking in the dark shadows. 'Tis a perfect evening to moon bathe under its glimmering reflections of the sun itself.

I am glad your radiation will end on Thursday. It has been a difficult January for you as you were consumed by the fire and inflammation. I hope the results are positive and that time is on your side. We never know what each day may bring us, and we must "gather our rosebuds while we may." Time is indeed flying by, although this week has seemed somewhat longer than usual—I think because I am restless, ready to move forward, yet still harnessed to the commitments of the past and the many obligations that connect me to my day-to-day existence. The journey does continue, sometimes quickly and sometimes tediously, depending on what is anticipated: it's the passage of time.

Tris's new therapy is now in its second week. It is too early to determine its effectiveness, but we are hopeful. If it tames the seizures, we will come off the epilepsy medication, which has serious cognitive implications. I am hopeful we are healing, growing, and perhaps re-emerging as a stronger version. Only time will tell what the final state will be, and all we can do is focus on each day and visualize the light.

Was the radiation process painful? I hope you and your family are finding strength within one another.

Sending love and luminous light. Kimberley

On Jan 23, 2019, at 9:47 AM, Leggo, Carl <carl.leggo@ubc.ca> wrote:

Hi, Kimberley,

After 2 more radiation treatments, I will wait for about 6 to 7 weeks for another MRI, which will tell us whether the radiation did any good! The radiation is not painful. It typically takes about 5 minutes to complete. Driving to and from the BC Cancer Agency is the only challenge!

I am tired, but generally I feel fairly well. The tiredness is hard because I have never really had much experience with feeling tired. In general terms, I am in good spirits—hopeful, poetic, full of longing!

I hope that Tris's new therapy works well!

May we continue to find rest, even peace, under the moon!

Sending love,

Carl

From: Kimberley Holmes <kaholmes@ucalgary.ca>
Date: Wednesday, January 23, 2019 at 7:14 PM
To: "Leggo, Carl" <carl.leggo@ubc.ca>
Subject: Re: Connecting

Dear Carl,

I love that you are "hopeful, poetic, and full of longing." It seems like that might be what we all need to be to live our lives well and with purpose. I unfortunately have a great deal of experience with feeling tired; in fact, sometimes I think it is my perpetual state of being. It started when I first became pregnant with Tristan. I remember this deep bone-penetrating exhaustion unlike anything I had ever experienced. Prior to becoming a mother, I was always moving, always engaged and constantly seeking. Now motherhood combined with teaching often leaves me deeply exhausted in an all-consuming and powerfully penetrating way. I suppose part of this is living with a teen who has been so sick, the constant fear of seizures, and the need to be on guard all of the time. Perhaps my body has been in a constant state of flight or fight, always anticipating taking rapid action to protect my young.

I am glad you feel generally well. Your spirit and hope inspire me, and I am optimistic that the MRI may bring some brightness and renewal. I have known many individuals who have fought these impossible battles and yet emerged victorious. I believe it has much to do with the strength of the human spirit. Even though our spirits can become weary and tired, they do not fully lose their light if we continue to long for what might be and reflect with our poetic hearts and souls.

With poetry and peace, Kimberley

On Jan 24, 2019, at 3:14 PM, Leggo, Carl <carl.leggo@ubc.ca> wrote:

Dear Kimberley,

Thank you for your wise words, full of a keen understanding of the complexities of being human! Always reflect on your resources and gifts and hopes! Reflecting will show us the ways we can journey.

I linger always in poetry. I know poetry will show me the ways I can journey.

Hold fast to your family and hopes and know that our lives are precious. With love, Carl

From: Kimberley Holmes <kaholmes@ucalgary.ca>
Date: Friday, January 25, 2019 at 7:30 PM
To: "Leggo, Carl" <carl.leggo@ubc.ca>
Subject: Re: Connecting

Dear Carl,

Our lives are indeed an interconnected and complex process that all come to the same end. As Hamlet reflects, "what is a King but to travel though the guts of a beggar." In the end, we all become food for worms and begin anew the cycle of human life. We need to spend our time mindfully and "gather ye rosebuds while ye may."

I was intrigued by the root of the word poetry. I found medieval Latin *poetria*, from Latin *poeta*, "poet." In early use the word sometimes referred to creative literature in general. Hence a poet is a maker or a creator. Perhaps poetry creatively reflects upon this complexity we call human life. It is a human attempt to make a complex conundrum or excessive emotional exchanges and vivid images and memories understandable to others. It is indeed metaphorical and lyrical reflections on the journey.

My family is in a bit of a holding pattern waiting for our adventure to begin to unfold. My husband has not been in Germany for 10 days, and the boys and I are failing back into the patterns of our life. Ken should return in a week or so, and we will all be in a holding pattern. The school board still has not approved my leave, although we have changed my teaching assignment to better suit a beginning teacher and are anticipating a changeover. The details of Tris's medical plan are still to be determined; hence, we are waiting patiently to see what might unfold.

Anticipation

As a child one cannot wait to grow up, to drive a car, to get a job, and to be a teen

The teen cannot wait until it is time to graduate, walk the stage, and be an adult

The adult seeks their first job and works towards bigger and better things seeking glory

Not realizing that the quest itself is the only thing that matters in the end

The grandmother rocks in her chair patiently knitting the rows of a multicolored hat

No reason for the creation except to simply create something and use the mind

The needles clicking rapidly and the artistry falling down into the lap of the knitter

In swirling interconnected patterns that reflect the cycles of a life well lived

The teen scrolls through the internet seeking satisfaction and inspiration

The fingers fly over the keyboards typing messages to others sitting alone

Waiting for life to happen, for the adventure to unfold and the messages to appear

Not realizing that the opportunities are just beginning, and all is possible if they look up

The mother sits quietly after cleaning up the evening dishes and walking the dog

Awaiting the next need for movement, for action, but desperately seeking reflection

As the pieces of life swirl around her in interconnected patterns of family relations

Anticipating the journey and yet mindfully aware of the importance of the drive

With love,

Kimberley

On Jan 26, 2019, at 9:55 AM, Leggo, Carl <carl.leggo@ubc.ca> wrote:

Hi, Kimberley,

Your poem "Anticipation" holds the eagerness of waiting and hoping while also understanding how little control we have over all the anticipating. It is a lovely poem that sings with a kind of active stasis or static activity!

Hold all the possibilities, and trust that events will unfold/emerge in ways that will hold you and your family secure in the adaptability of each day.

With love,

Carl

From: Kimberley Holmes <kaholmes@ucalgary.ca>
Date: Saturday, January 26, 2019 at 1:45 PM
To: "Leggo, Carl" <carl.leggo@ubc.ca>
Subject: Re: Connecting

Dear Carl,

Today the Universe is challenging me to trust and surrender. I am sitting on the love seat outside of Tris's room. While I was out running errands this afternoon, he suffered a seizure at home. He was in his room folding laundry when he stumbled to the laundry room and found his brother. Drooling and incoherent, he moved towards where he knew his brother was standing, seeking the help that he knew he would need. Jayden responded and reacted, controlling the seizure and following all the right steps. Then he called me, politely requesting I come home, which I did immediately. Currently we are dealing with the migraine headache and the vomiting and waiting to see if he will come out of this one. I am also trying to ensure Jayden is okay as I know this stress is impacting him immensely. He is only 14 and has had to deal with so much already. It is just too much to surrender too sometimes, yet what else can one do?

I am fearful the Kineret will not work and this demon will continue to plague us, but I know I must be hopeful and mindful. I must visualize that life will go forward, all will be well, and this too shall one day come to an end. I hate the lack of control, the inability to tame this dragon and find a solution to this problem. No matter how much I read, how much I study, or how much I learn, the seizures remain a complex enigma connected to the inflammation that courses though his body. There is nothing I can do, nothing I can control. All I can do is sit and try to be present within our story as it unfolds around us. I can pay attention and be mindful.

Inflammation is the root of so much illness, but the question that needs to be answered is what causes this inflammation to burn through the human body? What is the body reacting to externally or perhaps internally? What is the catalyst, and how we can treat the essence of the problem? Why are so many people being "consumed by fire," and how can we tame this ring of flames? The questions run deep through my mind, but answers are illusory or perhaps completely non-existent. There is only the never-ending stream of questions. It is the cycle of life unfolding around me, and it is so difficult to simply surrender to this process, yet I know that is all that we have the power to do.

Helplessness

The inflammation courses through the central nervous system wreaking havoc on the brain

One moment the teen is dancing to music and folding his laundry in mundane normalcy

The next moment the mouth is twitching, drool running down the face and seizure overtaking him

Language and communication eliminated suddenly lost when desperate for help and human connection

Instantly rendered helpless to the demon that attacks the system and seizes all conscious control

The tumor grows in the remaining breast tissue that flaps after the mastectomy
In spite of careful diligence, proper diet, and daily exercise mindfully undertaken
The stress of the world has taken its toll and manifests into ugly illness
The cancer breeds in the body and yet another dark demon demands its dues
Leaving the human helpless to the process of illness and the darkness of disease

The fingers fly through the pages of the medical research desperately scribbling notes
Seeking a solution, an answer, a root, or anything that might aid in the solution
Of this complex conundrum of inflammation that sets fire to bodies destroying all in its path
Of the raging inferno of burning and seizing and manifesting the darkness
That threatens to diminish all that is hopeful and all that is luminous light

We fight with the temporary tools that western modern medicine has to offer
The potions, the injections, the radiation, and the removal of all offending pieces
We fight with our soul to calm this blazing inferno and soothe the demon
Yet he still rages on destroying the humans and all those that love them
Melting all our candlesticks to the ground yet we still keep on hoping

Hoping one day we may not feel so helpless but perhaps will receive what is needed
To heal not only the inflammation of the body but the wounds of the hopeful heart
That pounds out its powerful melody as it struggles to keep dancing and dreaming on

The heart that screams to the demon to be gone and release the human

The helpful heart that forever beats on in the rhythms and patterns of luminous life

With hope of overcoming the helplessness, Kimberley

On Jan 26 2019, at 3:45 pm , Leggo, Carl <carl.leggo@ubc.ca> wrote:

Dear Kimberley,

Your experiences are complex, and they are both demanding and commanding. I am glad that you are able to hold open the spaces that Tris needs, and you are able to stand in those places, ready to assist and support Tris as you can. You understand how we often need to surrender—to give up, to deliver over—even when we definitely do not want to surrender. In surrendering, we are not giving up on our loved one—instead we are participating in the story that always stretches beyond our imaginations and abilities and spiritual reserves. We offer what we have, and we don't pretend to be more than we are, or to have more than we have. We live honestly with truth and patience and courage and care. Always believe in your "power to help."

Your poem "Helplessness" is the call of the victor—a song of triumph, a psalm of healing, a testimony of heartbeats!
Sending love, Carl

From: Kimberley Holmes <kaholmes@ucalgary.ca>
Date: Sunday, January 27, 2019 at 8:13 PM
To: "Leggo, Carl" <carl.leggo@ubc.ca>
Subject: Re: Connecting

Dear Carl,

Yes, demanding and commanding are apt descriptors for the current context of my lived experience. I am called to pay attention yet to yield to forces beyond my ability. Tris suffered two more seizures yesterday. One was a partial complex and one absent. We were at my parents' for dinner when they both occurred within a few hours of each other. What was compelling was the look of utmost terror on his face. This look terrified me and shook me to my soul as it was unlike any of the other events he has had. It is almost as if he is facing some terrifying demon deep inside his soul, that he knows he needs to battle but is intensely frightened of. I know there are many complexities swirling within him, built up section by section by the intersecting experiences of his life. Yet I don't know how to tap into anything. My portal to the world is language and word, and ironically this is the place of his blockage, the part of the brain the seizures impact. His temporal lobe is impacted, robbing him of language and his ability to communicate. With this portal blocked I am unsure how to access what lies trapped deep within him; I am unsure how to unlock the gates and release what needs to be purged from his mind and his body. Without words and language to soothe and heal, the enigma struggles to unravel. He has no poetry to protect him, yet I shall still strive to offer it.

I watch as Tristan works on his English homework. This type of work is a struggle for him, and it makes my heart bleed to watch him complete the insignificant tasks his teacher assigns to him. His teacher misses that the purpose of our curriculum is to unpack the complexities of our human stories, to explore the individual's response to adversity, and to triumph over the impending forces of darkness. Perhaps if we could teach our curriculum as our lived human experience it would help my son face his own dragons and find light.

Again, I find myself questioning the purpose of school. We should be learning how to live our lives well, to face the challenges on the journey and to move forward. For this is all there is, and all that will ever be.

Educating the Youth

The young child skips to school eagerly anticipating learning, growing, and being

Rapidly defeated by the day-to-day drill of disconnected bits of knowledge

Signifying nothing and taking away the possibilities of all that could be

The teen trudges mournfully as he proceeds to the institution we have placed him in

Giving up the freedom of creativity and imagination to the rules and regulations

That society has bound around him, requesting he fill in the bubbles to become a man

The young adult crosses the stage in the sacred cap and gown in pomp and circumstance

The parents and grandparents clap as victory of completion is celebrated and honored

The system has completed the process and the education has been lost

With deep thought on the process, Kimberley

On Jan 28, 2019, at 10:31 AM, Leggo, Carl <carl.leggo@ubc.ca> wrote:

Oh, Kimberley! How much suffering can we endure? Your observation, "What was compelling was the look of utmost terror on his face," is a memorable testimony to your relationship with Tris. Always love him, always walk with him! Always share poetry with him! And, indeed, love both your children with a boundless heart!

Your poem "Educating the Youth" reminds me how much we invest in education and educating—with the constant sense of loss!

May we hold fast, always, to hope for our commitments and efforts! With love, Carl

From: Kimberley Holmes (kaholmes@ucalgary.ca)
Date: January 28, 2019 at 6:42 PM
To: "Leggo, Carl (carl.leggo@ubc.ca
Subject: Re: Connecting

Dear Carl,

It is quite remarkable what we can endure. Human resiliency is a remarkable thing. How often our diploma prompt evolves around the question, "discuss the individual's response to adversity amongst compelling conditions." The literature explores the common human story, yet I wonder if the learners truly understand the message.

We need to teach students to live their lives, to understand the complex inner turmoil, and to find a way to tame the dragons that constantly threaten to take flight and burn our worlds into smoldering piles of nothingness. We need to write to understand our own feelings and ideas, to unpack the messy business of our human lives, and to try to soothe our weary souls. This is the essence of literature. This is the essence of our interconnected and immensely complicated human existence.

I have journaled over the years somewhat sporadically. I chronicled the details of my story in fragmented pieces in different spaces and places. It was only in a graduate class writing assignment that I finally allowed the words to flow. Without opening that portal, I have no doubt I would have perished.

Our correspondence has also been a bit of a lifeline. I never think about what I am going to write; I simply let the word drip from my fingertips as they need to. Generally, when I am done writing I feel better. I have not solved anything or moved any closer to a resolution, but the writing provides a type of release, a point of surrender where I can share my thoughts and feelings and have another bear witness to the journey. This is why we write; this is why we communicate. Through this portal we understand we are not alone in our stories but are the chapters of the greater story of human existence.

Stories

The baby is born and takes his first breath of air screaming in rage at the invasion

Of the safe and quiet space that he was floating within that has been disrupted

Abruptly interrupted for this brief interlude sometimes referred to as life

The toddler wobbles his first shaky steps and then screams in victory and glee

As he learns to walk and then to run, taking careful steps and then leaping in the air

Learning how to travel through the pathways of life using his own resources

The child awaits the arrival of the Easter bunny after filling the basket with painted eggs

Dreaming of illusions and myths that hold together the mystical magic of youth

Enjoying the process and not rushing to the future

The teen stalks through the kitchen seeking some type of satisfaction

Bored and disengaged he seeks a challenge in the world that no longer amuses

Keen to move forward and begin the more exciting stage of the journey

The adult looks back on the process and reflects on all the stories

That spun tight webs around him and wove the strands of the alchemy around him

The significant stories that braid this complex tapestry of human life

With reflection, Kimberley

On Jan 29, 2019, at 10:14 AM, Leggo, Carl <carl.leggo@ubc.ca> wrote:

Dear Kimberley,

You are a writer! And you know intimately the challenges and joys of writing. We are all learning how to live all the time.

I admire your understanding of being a parent—"when one had a child your heart was never fully your own again."

Your poem "Stories" is superb! You evoke the tangles of each stage of life with vivid images that feel true.

Keep on writing!
Sending love, Carl

From: Kimberley Holmes <kaholmes@ucalgary.ca>
Date: Tuesday, January 29, 2019 at 7:49 PM
To: "Leggo, Carl" <carl.leggo@ubc.ca>
Subject: Re: Connecting

Dear Carl,

Perhaps I am a writer. I remember being in elementary school and writing stories. I can still remember what they were about. One was about a young boy dying of an illness, another about magical creatures who had power to change the world. Even as a child I was writing about our complex human conditions and attempting to find alchemy to soothe the whips and scorns of time. I have never been trained as a writer. However, I read all the time and I always have. I grew up a "rink rat," the sibling of a brother who played hockey and spent endless hours in an arena. I did not like the cold damp smell of hockey so often retreated to the Bowness library, conveniently located across the street. I spent hours immersed in books, flipping through pages and pondering the power of the words. No one taught me to do this. I was called to the pages in some strange way, seeking something that innately entranced me and called for me to pay attention. It is through my friendship with books that my own voice emerged. It was strong when I was younger, unafraid and bold, but became softer and quieter as I worried about making errors. I received mixed reviews as an undergraduate, ranging from "brilliant" to "illiterate," and was never sure which assessment to believe. I now understand the precarious predicament of assessment and no longer worry about those who think I am an idiot. They are free to think what they want, and I am free to write what I need to write. I was always taught that writing poetry and stories was frivolous and not something one did to make a living. I was instructed to find a good job with benefits. Yet without words and poetry my day job quickly became pale and weakened my spirit. Without creativity and the making of poetic alchemy all become dull, flat, and colorless.

There is so much about teaching and education that needs to be addressed. The work is so deep, and I am unsure how to approach it, how to carve the pathways for authentic learning and real-life application. The old guard of teachers stands strong with their rules and their memorizing. They daily suck the souls of young learners with the objective of doing things right, of reaching the standard, and of putting individuals into identical boxes. The boxes are suffocating, and we need to kick our way out of them, creating new spaces and places for our young to grow and flower.

Poetry

The words drip from my fingertips in a consistent and pleasant melody

Spinning softly off the tongue in tantalizing images and metaphors

That rise unbidden in the folds of my mind without rule and regulations

The five-paragraph theme still reigns as god for an essay or a doctoral dissertation

Put the comma in the right place, careful with the run-on sentence and use APA

The structure is tight, and the process is foolproof for obtaining the elusive A

Yet the poetry squirms through the structure, seeping into the sentences

Merging and swirling with metaphors and images that refuse to be silenced by rules

Speaking softly of the stories that need to be told and the whispering of the heart

The rules and regulations will get you the educational grade shiny and bright

But the poetry will seep through your pores igniting your Soul and sparking your Essence

Even though the teachers will tell you that what you are doing is not right

With poetic rebellion,

Kimberley

From: Leggo, Carl <carl.leggo@ubc.ca>
Sent: January 30, 2019 9:43:20 PM
To: Kimberley Holmes; Leggo, Carl
Subject: Re: Connecting

All beautifully and powerfully expressed, Kimberley!

You are a remarkable writer, and I trust that you will continue to write, and explore writing, and teach writing. Writing is a way of living, being, becoming!

In your poem, the heart of your writing is held in the following line: "But the poetry will seep through your pores igniting your Soul and sparking your Essence"—so strong!!

I am moved, delighted, and rendered more hopeful!

With love,

Carl

From: Kimberley Holmes <kaholmes@ucalgary.ca>
Date: Thursday, January 31, 2019 at 8:23 PM
To: "Leggo, Carl" <carl.leggo@ubc.ca>
Subject: Re: Connecting

Dear Carl,

Thank you for your kind words and your faith in my writing ability. I love to write, time stands still when I am immersed in the process, yet I still am not sure "that I am doing things right." I don't know if this is just the remnants of school and the battles with APA or just my own insecurity in my wisdom and my power.

I received approval for my leave from the board today so officially will be off duty February 15th till summer. I also started the second term with new classes. I have a small class of Canadian studies. This is 20 new immigrant students who need to learn how to be Canadian, and—for many of them— how to speak English. The textbook is dull and boring, and I need to find ways to make them laugh and allow them to play with language. If I follow the deadly boredom of the prescribed curriculum, they will not thrive. I also started two new English 10 classes. They are keen and eager to learn, and many of them selected me as their teacher based on recommendations from their older siblings. I feel somewhat guilty passing them to a new teacher. However, I am hopeful the new teacher will be bright and shining and able to inspire enthusiasm and engagement. This is where the critical work lies—in our teacher education programs. We need to bring forth a new generation of teachers that understand interconnectivity, authenticity, and relevance. Otherwise learning is but fragmented shards of glass glistening with sharp edges ready to wound the soul of a frustrated child. We need to teach in relevant and meaningful ways. We need to teach with the heart to the hearts of others in mindful and compassionate ways. The work is deep and complicated.

<u>*To Teach*</u>

To teach or not to teach that is the question that most English majors consider

When wondering what to do with the Shakespeare, Atwood, or even Whitman

Who contemplates the song of himself in an existential crisis of living and being?

In this complex yet interconnected world of swirling, spiraling, synthesizing stories

That make up the ink marks that merge and blur into the patterns of our lives

The novel provides insight into our experiences, and characters are the people in our neighborhood

Who face the daily trials and tribulations that cascade around us in a tightly woven web.

The modern play puts it all on stage so we can feel the pain and see the tears of sorrow and of joy

Short stories are a mini version offering some irony or perhaps some satire to make us think

And poetry is the balm that soothes the soul and frees the angst from the fingertips of the writer

Can you see the patterns that emerge from the stories that are swirling in the sunrise?

Are the human connections evident and can you create the synergy to bring it all to life?

These are the deep questions for consideration and contemplation dear thespian

When you consider to teach or not to teach the essential questions of the tapestry of our humanity.

With deep reflection,

Kimberley

On Feb 1, 2019, at 12:23 PM, Leggo, Carl <carl.leggo@ubc.ca> wrote:

Hi, Kimberley,

It has taken me most of 65 years to acknowledge that while my writing is not everything I want/hope it to be, it is also just fine! My writing is always in process, always ready for revisiting, always open for new interventions, always incomplete, always broken off, always hopeful, always reaching out with open hands and arms and heart, calling for interconnections. Your writing is like that. Don't be fooled by evaluative voices that fail to offer the generous spirit of acknowledging how rich and diverse and poignant your writing is! You are a marvelous writer. You have the gift of writing, and you have devoted much of your life to writing. So, of course, you are an exceptional writer!

And you are an exceptional teacher as well. You understand how teaching is offering the heart to other hearts. Indeed, "The work is deep and complicated."

Your poem "To Teach" is a heartfelt and well-lived call living with others in humane ways that will support all of us to find our stories on the journey!

With love,

Carl

From: Kimberley Holmes <kaholmes@ucalgary.ca>
Date: Friday, February 1, 2019 at 7:22 PM
To: "Leggo, Carl" <carl.leggo@ubc.ca>
Subject: Re: Connecting

Dear Carl,

I suppose learning to accept your talents and your trials is all part of the complexity of slowly acquiring fragments of wisdom. We are always gathering the strands of the pieces that swirl and tumble around us and trying to braid them into some type of tapestry that recognizes our Essence. I look forward to the day when I finally discover what it is that exists at my center, what my core is, and what sustains me. I suspect it has something to do with writing, with teaching, with speaking, all working towards living well and making the planet a kinder, more sustainable place for all to inhabit.

I think often of what children, teens, and even adults need to thrive. I look forward to experiencing Europe in a few months and observing and participating in a different culture and way of being. I hope for inspiration and new chapters to add to my story. At this age and stage, I finally understand the line "gather ye rosebuds while ye may." Life is short and blooms for only an instant. We truly need to seize the beauty that presents itself. I just heard on the radio that the tulips are blooming in Vancouver. Have you seen the signs of spring already?

Curriculum

The seedling is planted deep in the earth awaiting the rain and the kiss of the sun

Its roots burrow in the safety of Mother Earth and its fingerlings begin to reach upwards

Curving, spiraling, growing to one day burst into bloom and brilliance

The child walks to the bus stop and awaits entrance to this placed called kindergarten

A garden for children where one may expand the roots and grow to the sky

A place where tendrils of tiny seedlings intertwine and connect with one another

Sharing the stories of letters, of numbers, of stories, and of growing older

The children stretch their fingertips up towards the sun as they chatter on the playground

Creating experiences and memories that will one day burst into brilliance

With love and thoughts of seedlings,

Kimberley

On Feb 2, 2019, at 5:51 PM, Leggo, Carl <carl.leggo@ubc.ca> wrote:

There are many signs of spring on the West Coast, Kimberley, but it is still fairly cold (or at least chilly)! Vancouver hasn't really engaged with winter this year. Perhaps it will. In the meantime, we are all enjoying the blue skies and slow days.

I'm glad to hear that you have enjoyed a non-school day! We need more of those days!

Each of us finds our way in our teaching careers—at least most of us, and those who cannot find their way often move on. I am always so impressed by the teachers at my granddaughters' school, teachers who are full of enthusiasm and joy and hope! Mirabelle, who is celebrating her 8th birthday this week, has a teacher who could retire but who has chosen to spend another year or so. She is perfect! A gift for Mirabelle, and for all her class!

Your time in Germany will be filled with leaning into new adventures and learning from new stories.

I admire your understanding of curriculum as a seedling. In this way we can dream about the possibilities.

In dreaming mode,

Carl

From: Kimberley Holmes <kaholmes@ucalgary.ca>
Date: Saturday, February 2, 2019 at 6:54 PM
To: "Leggo, Carl" <carl.leggo@ubc.ca>
Subject: Re: Connecting

Dear Carl,

I am glad there are signs of spring appearing. This is not the case in Calgary as we are currently experiencing a polar vortex, which is a euphemism for frozen hell! Currently it reads minus 25 on the thermometer on our deck, but with the wind chill we are going down to -35 tonight!

I am thrilled Mirabelle has a master teacher who is continuing to share her gifts and talents. Jayden had a teacher like that for grade 5 and 6. I wonder if this is the key difference between my boy's ability to find success in school. Jayden was inspired by a master teacher, and Tristan was crushed by teachers who were simply putting in time. I wish the teachers that taught Tristan had moved on, but they were simply counting their days until retirement at the cost of the souls of the young students. I wish we had more teachers like Mirabelle's and fewer of the ones who simply don't care.

I am not sure what our European adventure may hold for us. It is a bit of an enigma!

Dreaming about cherry blossoms and spring,

Kimberley

On Feb 3, 2019, at 10:21 AM, Leggo, Carl <carl.leggo@ubc.ca> wrote:

Hi, Kimberley,

I like your comparison of Calgary weather to "a polar vortex, which is a euphemism for frozen hell." I can't quite imagine a "frozen hell," but I like thinking about the possibility.

I guess schooling will always be a lottery for most children, at least much of the time. We just continue to live our parts in the story.

Keep on dreaming!

I trust that the Germany adventures will be rich with possibilities.

Sending love,

Carl

From: Kimberley Holmes <kaholmes@ucalgary.ca>
Date: Sunday, February 3, 2019 at 7:48 PM
To: "Leggo, Carl" <carl.leggo@ubc.ca>
Subject: Re: Connecting

Dear Carl,

The temperature continues to plummet here, and the city is immersed in a cold fog of misery. Last check at the temperature was at minus 27 with a wind chill of minus 40. Hence tomorrow we will be forced to drive instead of our usual walk, and life will become more challenging. I suppose we have been lucky as this is our first deep freeze this season, but I cannot help but wish for the more moderate temperatures. I am not sure how people live in places that are this cold all the time. I guess we all adapt to our environment if we have to.

Schooling is indeed a lottery, and the lucky ones get the good teachers. The rest do their best to survive. Life itself is a bit of a lottery or even a game. Clichés abound like "he was dealt a poor hand" or "she is not playing with a full deck" or the "deck was stacked." It all seems to come down to luck, chance, and a little bit of manipulation of the cards. When we are dealt a bad hand, we need to figure out how to play it well enough to make it to the next round.

This polar vortex should lift by Wednesday. In the meantime, we need to "learn how to deal" with the weather and any other obstacles that attempt to freeze us in our tracks.

With dreams of spring and sunshine,

Kimberley

On Feb 4, 2019, at 10:30 AM, Leggo, Carl <carl.leggo@ubc.ca> wrote:

Dear Kimberley,

We woke up to snow this morning! So odd! Also, so beautiful! Lana and I will go for a walk soon.

I wish you well with navigating the winter conditions! And, of course, also with navigating the plans for traveling to Berlin! I always like the word "navigating" for thinking about how we will traverse each day's bumps and meadows!

Dreaming onward,

Carl

From: Kimberley Holmes <kaholmes@ucalgary.ca>
Date: Monday, February 4, 2019 at 8:16 PM
To: "Leggo, Carl" <carl.leggo@ubc.ca>
Subject: Re: Connecting

Dear Carl,

Snow is beautiful. This morning the trees were draped in a silver frost, which was quite magical. I must admit I love to walk in the sparkling snow and watch the crystals dance in the air. Although the cold bites at my face and threatens to freeze my cheeks, it makes one feel fully alive.

Today my new students and I spent some time watching large groups of birds in the trees outside our window. There were hundreds of them moving in unison from tree to tree, almost as if they were putting on a performance for us. I don't know if they were simply trying to keep warm or this is some type of ritual they do. My bird knowledge is minimal, but the observation time was well spent. My grade 10 students were mesmerized by the graceful patterns and synchronized movement. When I asked them why they thought it was important to watch birds, their response was, "It is just beautiful." We can always find beauty if we seek to discover it.

I hope you and Lana enjoyed your walk and the sparkle of the snow filled you with joy.

On a cold winter's night,

Kimberley

On Feb 5, 2019, at 10:06 AM, Leggo, Carl <carl.leggo@ubc.ca> wrote:

Dear Kimberley,

Winter has its challenges, but also its wonderful delights!!

How lovely that you and your students watched large groups of birds outside your window!! The beauty is always here and there!

Lana and I enjoyed a sumptuous walk yesterday morning—cold, clear, full of life!

Sending love, Carl

From: Kimberley Holmes <kaholmes@ucalgary.ca>
Date: Tuesday, February 5, 2019 at 8:11 PM
To: "Leggo, Carl" <carl.leggo@ubc.ca>
Subject: Re: Connecting

Dear Carl,

It is another deep freeze day today, but the sky was blue and the frost on the trees resembled something painted on a Victorian Christmas Card. My international students gazed out the window at the natural beauty, contrasting the stark white of winter and the brilliant blue in wonder. This is a new experience for them as they have not seen snow or frost or felt the extreme cold. We made Tim Horton's hot chocolate and marshmallows this morning as we explored "What is a Canadian?" Some thought the sticky sweet drink was wonderful, and others made faces and requested hot tea. All of us laughed at the need to hold onto something hot to become warm inside. Some of the students are terribly homesick while others are entranced by the enigma of this new place where they have chosen to study. I admire their courage and their tenacity. Some are fluent in English, and others can barely string together a few sentences. All of them speak softly and slowly with great care. We bow our heads to each other at the end of the class in respect and gratitude. They are a joy to work with. I also have a special needs First Nations student who joins us as he wanted to participate in a social studies class in his grade 12 year. He is our authentic native Canadian and is teaching us all words in Blackfoot. He is also going to help me teach the sections of the curriculum on the FNMI people. It is a beautiful thing to have him join our learning community and offer his insight and voice.

My two grade 10 classes are engaged and thoughtful as we prepare to explore the deep questions in our literature and our writing. It is so much fun to observe their growth in high school and watch them develop into amazing human beings. The work of education is fascinating and deeply touches the heart if the practice is mindful and authentic.

I am struck by how much I am enjoying my days now that I know I have very few left. You don't realize how much happiness something brings you until you are leaving it. I thought my days of teaching high school might be done, but now I am not sure. I think it was the endless routine that was crushing me. With a break from routine upcoming I am finding more joy in my teaching and with my students. Mandatory time off to do new things might be something that would help heal a tired teaching profession.

I have a group of students that are regularly "visiting" and spending time with me. All are in grade 12 and I think recognizing our paths are about to diverge. We have much left to talk about, and I am trying to ensure them that paths continue to cross in strange ways and those that have touched your heart never truly leave you. It is never truly goodbye but until we meet again.

Life is truly a full and vibrant journey. So much to look forward to and so much to simply enjoy in the present moment.

Kimberley

On Feb 6, 2019, at 4:31 PM, Leggo, Carl <carl.leggo@ubc.ca> wrote:

How wonderful, Kimberley!! May you and your students continue to enjoy all the pleasures of winter!

I never have enough time to respond in the ways I wish I could. So, I will just respond with a HEARTY HELLO!

And trust that all our plans will be met by cheerfulness and generosity!

Carl

From: Kimberley Holmes <kaholmes@ucalgary.ca>
Date: Wednesday, February 6, 2019 at 7:10 PM
To: "Leggo, Carl" <carl.leggo@ubc.ca>
Subject: Re: Connecting

Dear Carl,

Today everyone was tired and somewhat crabby. Perhaps something to do with midweek, third day of cold and the start of a new semester. Many of my international students are homesick, and many of the grade 10 students difficult to engage. Such is the pattern of teachings. Some days are wonderful, and others make one want to retire early. Today is a retire early day.

I am hoping to find some spaces for creativity and joy. Onward!

OX

K

On Feb 7, 2019, at 1:27 PM, Leggo, Carl <carl.leggo@ubc.ca> wrote:

May you find those "spaces for creativity and joy," Kimberley!

Embrace the duller days! Anticipate they will turn to fuller days! After a few days of my feeling besotted with illness, Lana and I went to the emergency of Vancouver General Hospital where I spent about 5 hours. I had some tests, and I was given a drug. I went home around midnight—feeling rejuvenated and hopeful! I am feeling much better today!

With hope for fuller days!

Carl

From: Kimberley Holmes <kaholmes@ucalgary.ca>
Date: Thursday, February 7, 2019 at 6:44 PM
To: "Leggo, Carl" <carl.leggo@ubc.ca>
Subject: Re: Connecting

Dear Carl,

I am happy to hear you have triumphed once again over the obstacles of illness and are feeling rejuvenated and hopeful. Although I am not a firm believer in Western medicine, it does have its place and can soothe the body enough to allow the healing process to occur. I have spent many a night in emergency. In the boy's early years, it was generally for croup, which I now realize I should have phoned an ambulance for. As they grew older it was for various broken bones that we visited the emergency room. Tris's seizures brought us there a few times but always by ambulance. I have utmost respect and gratitude for EMS as their arrival at my doorstep helps my sanity and my own ability to breathe. It is a wonderful feeling to be able to pass responsibility to someone else and be the observer.

I shall enjoy the more mundane days ahead and look forward to the upcoming experiences. The mundane is required for the highs to appear.

I hope your wellness continues to grow and flourish.

Much love

Kimberley

On Feb 8, 2019, at 11:02 AM, Leggo, Carl <carl.leggo@ubc.ca> wrote:

Hi, Kimberley,

In spite of the toll on your daily life, I hear the hopefulness in your words! You live with energy and love! I am glad that Ken is now home and that you can plan your next leg of the adventure side-by-side.

I enjoyed a wonderfully well-measured day yesterday! Always glad for every day that feels in any way like "normal"! I hope that today will be much the same.

Sending love,

Carl

From: Kimberley Holmes <kaholmes@ucalgary.ca>
Date: Saturday, February 9, 2019 at 12:45 PM
To: "Leggo, Carl" <carl.leggo@ubc.ca>
Subject: Re: Connecting

Dear Carl,

I am glad you enjoyed a wonderful day. It is funny how in times of crisis each day that feels normal is a gift. I often wonder what it might be like to live a normal life, a life without illness and obstacles, but then I wonder if such a thing even exists. Life is full of obstacles, and we need to manage our perceptions of our reality to keep ourselves well. This is challenging when faced with complexities, but I suppose the work of being human.

It is still bitterly cold here, and I feel very tired. Although the sky is a brilliant blue, there is something about the unrelenting cold which exhausted me. I also don't really like the feeling of being in a "holding pattern." I have three days left of teaching, but we probably won't head to Europe until the first week in March. Although I am sure there is much to do that I have not thought of, I feel myself agitated at the delay. I should be grateful for the space, the open time, but I feel like a racehorse blocked at the gates, prancing and fretting in a need to run quickly towards new things. The urge to move forward is overwhelming yet intimidating at the same time.

<u>At the Gate</u>

Feet stomping, head tossing, the nostrils flair at the scent of the adventure

The gate is closed, access blocked, forcing a type of patient waiting

The mare tosses her head in frustration and tries to focus on the proces

The need to run, to burst into a new way of being and belonging is strong

The heart races in anticipation and they stutter and struggled at the barricade

Unable to enjoy the moments of silence that sits quietly before the exhilaration

Nostrils flare and air is breathed deeply through the lungs and surges in the body

Calming and soothing the anxious anticipation and forcing the mare into reflection

The mind calms, trying to focus as the foot continues to stamp restlessly in the dust

K

On Feb 9, 2019, at 2:23 PM, Leggo, Carl <carl.leggo@ubc.ca> wrote:

All truly and clearly expressed, Kimberley! You are at a kind of crossroad in your living experience, and everything feels kind of frozen and flexible—you are ready, but the circumstances are not yet calling out the freedom! Soon!

I know only the experience of waiting, hoping, coping, longing…. At least, I am in process. I have been in many places in my life where I have been overly taxed with longing for something, but now I feel a kind of lightness in waiting, even in longing.

I recommend that you call on your mind to calm and "focus as the foot continues to stamp restlessly in the dust," but do not let the foot only "stamp restlessly in the dust"—let the foot dance restfully in the dust.

Sending love, Carl

From: Kimberley Holmes <kaholmes@ucalgary.ca>
Date: Saturday, February 9, 2019 at 7:48 PM
To: "Leggo, Carl" <carl.leggo@ubc.ca>
Subject: Re: Connecting

Dear Carl,

I like the idea of dancing instead of stamping. I would like to be lighter, more fluid, and more flexible as I move towards new things. Yet I still feel like a restless racehorse, tossing my mane in eager anticipation and pawing at the dirt in a desire to start the race. It is a juxtaposition to your place of waiting, hoping, coping, and longing. We are at different points in the journey, and your experience reminds me of the significance of grabbing for the brass ring as it spins quickly before me. In an instant everything can change, and I don't want to regret.

<u>Dancer</u>

The music calls and the sounds swirl around as the dancer stands ready to leap
Gracefully into the air twisting and turning in elegant movement
Landing softly on bruised and broken toes forced into point shoes
That make the dance brilliantly beautiful and gruellingly graceful

Her grace and poise are stunning as her aura shines out into the audience
Breathing hope, radiance, and longing into the crowd who admire her flow
While her toes slowly start to bleed through the silky satin slipper

Her heart spins and twirls matching the patterns and movements of her body
Her breath quickens and she spins in anticipation of the crescendo
Her feet numb of all feeling as they spin strongly through the air

On Feb 10, 2019, at 11:58 AM, Leggo, Carl <carl.leggo@ubc.ca> wrote:

Hi, Kimberley,

You understand well the tension and conflict that erupt in your body. All your desires are rich with hope, and some desires call more loudly than others. Embrace all the desires and see how they will unfold!

I love your poem—full of movement and precision, learned from hard work and devotion. I especially like the phrase: "gruellingly graceful."

Continue to lean into the dance!

Love,

Carl

From: Kimberley Holmes <kaholmes@ucalgary.ca>
Date: Sunday, February 10, 2019 at 4:14 PM
To: "Leggo, Carl" <carl.leggo@ubc.ca>
Subject: Re: Connecting

Dear Carl,

The body speaks in a variety of ways. The gut tightens, the voice quivers, and the shoulders brace for an attack, sometimes seizing in a tightly wound rage. Some moments the gut is only a whisper, a primitive way of knowing that tells you to pay attention. It silently speaks to you of deeper ways of knowing and being in the world. Sometimes the gut erupts in spasms and brings the mind to the state of a pounding headache. The entire body rages, seeking to be heard and acknowledged. The messages of the body are diverse and powerful.

I think this also applies to teaching and parenting. We appear to be fully capable while balancing on bloodied toes, the pain seeping through our body. Our daily accomplishments appear effortless but have taken years of practice, reflection, and contemplation. The exhaustion runs deep through the body, yet we override so no one can see the struggle. How often my soul still bleeds while I smile brightly in front of my young charges. Yet smile and spin gracefully I must as I continue to dance the complex patterns of the cycle of life.

With love, Kimberley

On Feb 11, 2019, at 9:46 AM, Leggo, Carl <carl.leggo@ubc.ca> wrote:

Good-morning, Kimberley,

You understand well how the body speaks in diverse ways that can be hard to interpret and translate. Much of our living practice is sorting out how to respond!

May we always understand how each day's living experience is a way of embracing all the adventures and moving here and there in artful ways!

I will see the oncologist today. I am looking forward to her report.

With love,

Carl

From: Kimberley Holmes <kaholmes@ucalgary.ca>
Date: Monday, February 11, 2019 at 8:34 PM
To: "Leggo, Carl" <carl.leggo@ubc.ca>
Subject: Re: Connecting

Dear Carl,

I hope the report from the oncologist brings positive hope. These visits to medical professionals are always a conundrum. I want to have faith in their science yet seek the power of the human spirit to transcend the obstacles. We have had so many negative predictions in our lives, yet somehow, we still manage to exist, to proceed about the day-to-day business of living. It is almost as if the spirit refuses to acknowledge the science, or maybe the science is not a science at all. What will be will be, in spite of all our human efforts to control our destiny.

I am not sure I understand what the body wants or needs, but I have learned to listen. I recognize the anxiety and the anger and have learned to sit with it, honor it, and allow it to pass through my body. If I repress it, I find it rears up in more severe, louder, and painful ways. Hence, I sit with the rumblings, the throbbing, and the uncomfortableness and try to figure out what in my life is causing me the distress. Usually, when my body speaks it is signaling some type of conflict, almost a warning system that things are going to become rocky. It senses the danger and puts me on high alert. My body is sensitive to the environment, to the energies and to the various personalities that swirl around me. It is an intuitive vessel always aware and wary of the surrounding waters.

Limbo

The call of adventure awaits, and the seeker is eager to begin the journey

Yet attendance must be taken, student records organized, and data recorded

Initial assessment and sorting must begin although the process will not be continued

They will be organized and established and then handed over for future care

The business of school is being accomplished without the commitment of the heart

Which holds itself back aware of the need to be free from all attachments

As the call to adventure must be heeded and attachments cause hesitation

And a need to return to safe places where all is known and organized and categorized

Hence the heart keeps a safe and mindful distance so when the call echoes

It is ready to answer the musical crescendo to dance in new and unknown spaces

Knowing always that after undertaking the adventure and traveling new pathways

We return to our starting place and the heart always finds its way home

Sending warmth on a frigid cold night,

Kimberley

On Feb 12, 2019, at 1:53 PM, Leggo, Carl <carl.leggo@ubc.ca> wrote:

Hi, Kimberley,

Many keen thoughts about life and living! Thank you!!

I did not receive good news yesterday from the oncologist. She will try a couple more drugs in the near future, but the prognosis is not good. I and my family are making plans as we anticipate what the future might hold.

I especially like the last line of your poem: "We return to our starting place and the heart always finds its way home."

Sending love, Carl

From: Kimberley Holmes <kaholmes@ucalgary.ca>
Date: Tuesday, February 12, 2019 at 7:57 PM
To: "Leggo, Carl" <carl.leggo@ubc.ca>
Subject: Re: Connecting

Dear Carl,

I am so sorry that you did not receive good news from the oncologist. I suppose there is hope in drugs, but certainly not what you were hoping for. How does one make plans in anticipation? I am sure this is a very difficult time for you and your loved ones, and my heart feels sympathy and sorrow for you all. The process of life always ends in the return to Spirit, yet I have no idea how we prepare for this ultimate event. The pathway is vague. I can only listen to the stories of Others and hope to one day understand.

When my grandmother passed last summer, it was after a stroke and relatively quick. Although painful the process was only about a week. The pain came later, at Christmas and birthday parties when her absence was evident. It came with the family conflict over the estate and the estrangement of my cousins. The loss of my grandmother and of the family connections still bleed.

When my best friend's mother passed of a brain tumor the process was long and hard. I tried to support my friend and help but did not know how, as each day brought new challenges and small moments or understanding. In the end, she and her family managed to face the inevitable and bind together to survive. I guess this is what we do, and we continue to live on through one another. Although it is very difficult and painful, those who are left go on and survive with a hole in our heart.

Perhaps you may be "returning to your starting place." Maybe we are all just energy that temporarily takes up a physical body and then returns to energy of the Universe or maybe even home to God. I don't know if I believe in a God, but I would like to. My logical mind denies the possibility, but my heart yearns for something beyond this temporary state of human existence. My heart hopes we are all continuous energy that thrives on forever and is recycled into another form or existence. My heart hopes that there is something magical that happens when the Spirit flows out into the Universe and that it is joyful.

I remember watching my grandmother as she took her last breath. The sun was slowly setting, and my uncle asked me to open the curtains on the window. It was like he sensed it was time to release her to the Universe. She took one slow deep breath in, and then all breathing stopped. She was still and peaceful, and the room was solemnly silent. There was no struggle or pain. My mother believes that my grandfather came to get her as a small smile played across her face during her final breath and her skin shone radiantly. She looked like a young girl. It was very odd as her skin was almost luminous and healthy looking in her final breaths. I don't know where she went, or if she can still see us. I like to believe that she can, and sometimes, when I am afraid and frightened, I talk to her, asking for her support. It makes me feel better to call upon all my grandparents for support, and although they are all in Spirit now, I feel they are somehow still with me. I like to believe this, that they are now my special angels helping me care for my family and protecting us from harm. It allows me to find light amidst my sadness and hopefulness within my longing to talk to them again.

Sometimes I see them in my dreams and seek the messages. Sometimes I depend on them to manage things that I cannot and allow them to carry the weight of responsibilities I find too heavy to bear.

Tears fall freely down my face as I write this now. I am not sad but deeply emotional in a way I cannot describe or understand. I am simply human and have no understanding or comprehension of what lies beyond. I just know that something does, and when you love someone, they never truly leave you. We carry the echoes of our ancestors in our blood, their stories in our memories and their love in our hearts. Their genetics, their memories, and their essence stream through me as my heart pounds and keeps me alive. I cannot help but think of Findley's words in the novel The Wars: "To my daughter Laurene, I am alive in everything that I touch. Touch these pages and you touch me. Nothing dies, everything lives forever. I am your father always."

With reflections on forever and perpetual cycles of energy and possibilities for transformation,

Much love,
Kimberley

On Feb 13, 2019, at 10:27 AM, Leggo, Carl <carl.leggo@ubc.ca> wrote:

Thank you, Kimberley, for all these personal and precious words! We each live into our endings (and hopefully new beginnings) in our own ways! I appreciate the ways you have lived into the endings (and hopefully new beginnings) of your grandparents and others! Much to be learned!!

I probably have a few more months—time to sort out my office, make plans financially with Lana, and mostly organize the transition of leaving. It sounds like a big job, but really it is not—just more stuff that needs to be cared for and grieved and celebrated. Always there is so much to celebrate!!

With love,
Carl

From: Kimberley Holmes <kaholmes@ucalgary.ca>
Date: Wednesday, February 13, 2019 at 9:26 PM
To: "Leggo, Carl" <carl.leggo@ubc.ca>
Subject: Re: Connecting

Dearest Carl,

I am struck by your words "organize the transition of leaving." I am currently trying to organize us to move to Europe, and you are organizing to move to possibly a completely different space and place, far beyond my mere human comprehension or understanding. There is indeed so much to be celebrated in a beautiful life well-lived that has touched so many and impacted the whole. Yet also some deep and painful grieving and human souls that will need to be cared for. Although we all understand that the passage to spirit is inevitable and even desirable, under certain contexts it is not something we are ever fully prepared for. Time goes so swiftly when we realize that the moments are coming to an end.

I remember way back to 10 grade, and age 15, when I had my first experience with loss and the death of my first grandparent. My grandfather was plagued with prostate cancer and spent much time in pain in the hospital. My grandparents lived in the Crowsnest Pass at the time. While Grandfather was in the hospital in Calgary, Grandmother stayed with us, and I remember hearing sounds of stifled sobs in the middle of the dark night. I was frightened and afraid for what was about to happen, for I had not lost anyone before. The experience was new, and raw.

Yet the night my grandfather passed something quite remarkable happened. I remember distinctly awakening in the middle of the night and seeing Grandfather sitting on the edge of my bed. He was wearing his blue hospital gown and was peaceful and serene. I was not afraid and in my sleepy state remember asking him why he was in my room. His answer was he just came to see me and say goodbye. I embraced the familiar figure on my bed and went back to sleep, falling into a deep comforting space where I knew all was well. The goodbye did not alarm me; it was just something that had occurred.

To this day I do not know if it was just a dream, a strange coincidence between my imagination and the time of my grandfather's passing or a visit from his Spirit as it traveled between spaces. When I awoke the next morning, I learned my grandfather was gone. At this point I broke into tears and explained to my mother my "dream." Through her tears she smiled and said that she had also seen my grandfather in the night. He did not talk to her but bent over my father and kissed him softly on the forehead. Then he was gone.

I did not "see" my grandfather ever again. He did appear however to Jayden when Tristan was critically ill. Jayden called him "the man in the blue light," and we all assumed, since he was only 4, the man was some type of imaginary friend. The man talked to him when Tristan was in the hospital and comforted him. Every night Jayden would report the man was sitting on his window bench and "talking to him." The rest of us saw nothing other than the empty bench and assumed Jayden's imagination was creating a coping mechanism to deal with his brother's illness. Tristan was in ICU for many days intubated so he could breathe through the swelling of his throat.

It was a terrifying time, and his possibility of death haunted our every hour. We did not know if the swelling would stop, or if he would ever return to us again.

One evening the man in the blue light had a message for Jayden. He told him Tristan was able to breathe now and that he would be coming home. Jayden burst into my bedroom in the early morning announcing Tristan would be better today. And he was, as a few moments later the ICU unit phoned and said the swelling was subsiding and they were planning on removing the breathing tubes. Tristan began to breathe on his own once more.

Weeks, possibly months later, while at my parent's house Jayden came across an old photograph printed upon a large button. It was a photograph of my grandfather as a young child. Jayden was thrilled with the discovery, as he told my mother that was "the man in the blue light." He had no idea the photograph was my grandfather.

Perhaps these events are all just strange coincidental moments in time, but I don't think they are. I think when you truly love someone and they know that you need them, there is a way to cross through the barriers between the physical being and the spirit. We have not seen my grandfather since, but I sense the presence of my angels all the time.

With deep thoughts on transitions, Kimberley

On Feb 14, 2019, at 6:51 PM, Leggo, Carl <carl.leggo@ubc.ca> wrote:

Thank you, Kimberley, for all your precious words which sustain our spirits in these challenging and precious times!

Happy Valentine's Day! Carl

From: Kimberley Holmes <kaholmes@ucalgary.ca>
Date: Thursday, February 14, 2019 at 8:02 PM
To: "Leggo, Carl" <carl.leggo@ubc.ca>
Subject: Re: Connecting

Happy Valentine's Day, dear Carl. I hope you are surrounded by those whom you love. Our fragments of life are but brief slivers that sparkle in the sunlight and then splinter into new and diverse forms. The fragments are the sparkling images embodied within our stories, our hopes, our dreams, and our love. Each fragment merges with others and becomes a part of the greater whole. A single story becomes a part of the interconnected stories of our humanity. It is the interconnected stories of love, of adversity, and of hope that allow us to persevere even the darkest of moments. Hold fast to the love that surrounds you and let it illuminate your Spirit. Love is all that there is, all that we have, and all that will ever be.

"Love is patient, love is kind. It does not envy, it does not boast, it is not proud. It does not dishonor others, it is not self-seeking, it is not easily angered, it keeps no record of wrongs. Love does not delight in evil but rejoices with the truth. It always protects, always trusts, always hopes, always perseveres. Love never fails."

1 Corinthians 13:4-8 New International Version (NIV)

With hope in the power of love, Kimberley

On Feb 15, 2019, at 10:26 AM, Leggo, Carl <carl.leggo@ubc.ca> wrote:

With a poet's commitment to love and words and living, you understand how to reach out to others, Kimberley!!

With gratitude,

Carl

From: Kimberley Holmes <kaholmes@ucalgary.ca>
Date: February 16, 2019 at 11:46 MST
To: "Leggo, Carl" <carl.leggo@ubc.ca>
Subject: Re: Connecting

Dearest Carl,

You told me long ago when I reached out to you via an email that "poets call to one another and that we always answer the call." We do not know how our stories will unfold, but we know that we are always alive in our poetry. No day will be exactly as we want but filled with possibilities. As my headache subsides, I contemplate the slowly falling snowflakes on the mountainside and the magic of life itself. May we always linger in poetry and know poetry will show us the way that we can journey as we hold fast to the understanding of life as an interconnected emerging process.

Much love,

Kimberley

From: Kimberley Holmes <kaholmes@ucalgary.ca>
Date: February 19, 2019 at 3:40:46 PM MST
To: "Leggo, Carl" <carl.leggo@ubc.ca>
Subject: Re: Connecting

Dear Carl,

It has been three days since I have had an email from you. I hope desperately that all is well but recognize the fragile reality of our tightly interconnected strands. I fear your lack of response signifies that the transition to the next stage of existence has begun....

Your strand is slowly unraveling, and I am tasked with continuing to weave the web and keep us all strong. I must continue to write, continue to share stories, and continue to allow the poetry to seep through my pores and provide healing to those who are left in the shadows. This seems a deep and powerful task, and I am overwhelmed with the responsibility. I am not ready to move forward alone but realize I do not have a choice. Our moments are but fleeting and infinitely precious.

Today is a mystic full moon day. It falls in the sign of Virgo, which is my zodiac sign and is said to be the strongest super moon of the year. As the moon shines brightly in the sky tonight, it is said we will feel the energetic effects and pull of the moon vibrating to the depths of our soul. I can feel this energy building and am awaiting something. Perhaps an awakening, an inspiration, or an understanding of this infinite energy we are all a part of. Tonight, I shall reflect on the moon and listen to the message it may have for me on how to move forward with the work, with my life, and with all the interconnections that are needed to sustain us through difficult times.

I understand that things the human mind grapples with, the things we find terrible or unbearable, perhaps are our Souls seeking to rejoice at the lessons. Perhaps it is a chance to engage in a celebration of the emotional intensity of the human journey and acquire wisdom through this complex process of becoming a fully actualized human. Life is filled with adversity, with tragedy, and eventually with death. This is all there is. We need to honor, perhaps even embrace, all of it as all are strands in the interconnected webs that bind us to one another. In the end, we all return to where we began and start anew.

"In the sweat of thy face shalt thou eat bread, till thou return unto the ground; for out of it wast thou taken; for dust though art, and unto dust shalt thou return."

Genesis 3:19 - *King James Version*

"For someone who was never meant for this world, I must confess I'm suddenly having a hard time leaving it. Of course, they say every atom in our body was once a part of a star. Maybe I am out leaving...maybe I am going home."

Vincent (*Gattica*, 1977)

I feel great sadness as you move closer to death because I will be losing a master teacher. I realize this is incredibly selfish, but you have been such a significant impact in my life as both a scholar and as a human being. I cannot help but feel angry at the potential loss of you but also incredibly grateful that our pathways had the opportunity to intersect and that you touched my Soul. May our atoms continue to mingle and intermix, and may we always find our way home to the stars....

Intersection

A fleeting moment of time and a poet calls out into the night in fear and isolation

Only to be answered by another Soul that understands the magnitude of the journey

And is willing to be a guide through the darkest passages of the cold and bitter night

Lives intersect, stories collide, children become ill, and conflict arises in daily occurrences

Pain and suffering are evident and evidently Death rears the stallions on his fierce chariot

And comes to claim the brilliant energy that was only brought to Earth as a temporary gift

The gift is precious and will live long after the physical body has departed for Greatness

The words linger on, the poetry speaks of passion, and the call echoes through the night

Poets call passionately and vibrantly to one another— and they always answer

With poetry, peace, and deep love, Kimberley

Final Note

Carl Leggo suffered a seizure shortly after his last email on February 15th. At this point he began his final transition to the other side. My heart weeps at this cruel twist of fate, but I know that he lived his story with faith, hope, and love for as long as he was possibly able to do so. Dr. Leggo lived with love and was my committed teacher to the very end. His life was a love story that shall live on in all those he touched and inspired.

The email chain entitled Alliance was never meant for publication—it was two poets seeking a way to live well in the world, through the braiding of stories and the sharing of hearts. We were writing together about living well in the messiness of the world that we live in. We used our poetic braids to seek answers, understand complexity, and unpack this complex journey of our shared human experience. I realize now this was significant work and my teacher's final gift to me. He was teaching me how to write by capturing the fragments of my life and braiding them tightly with the fragments of others, capturing my "heart of wisdom." He reminded me daily that empathetic inquiry is the most compellingly theorized and conceptualized process of the practice of life writing. Life writing, for "life writing involves a recover, of well, Life" (Smith, 2012, p. xv). It is a mode of educational inquiry where I have earned a "heart of wisdom" as I struggled with Carl through the tensions of learning, teaching, and being in the world. Experience is the only thing that we share, and through this sharing of experience we came to an understanding of the complexity and beauty of human life. I will be eternally grateful for Carl's teaching and his light.

As Griffin (1995) reminds us,

If human consciousness can be rejoined not only with human body but with the body of the earth, what seems incipient in the reunion is the recovery of meaning with existence that will infuse every kind of meeting between self and the universe, even in the most daily acts, with an eros, a palpable love, that is also sacred. (p. 9)

Writing authentically about our life experiences is a journey not only in language but deep into the complexity of our shared world. This world is far from perfect, and often we fall deeply into the dark night of the soul, the world pressing so heavily upon us it feels as if we may never emerge into the light again. At this point it is critical that we bind the threads of our stories with those of the Other and hold on to all that is still light, all that is still good in the world.

I understand the need to embrace the darkness and anger when I need to and to let the poetry pulse through the portals of my Spirit, cleansing and purifying along the way. If I do not practice and honor this process, I will die emotionally, spiritually, and possibly even physically. I also know, as my teacher taught me, that there is light, abiding light, and I must always lean into the possibilities. We do not know how our stories will unfold, but we must hold fast to gratitude and grace. Love is healing, soothing, interconnected energy, and I am alive in poetry, always and forever.

"May we always hold fast to the understanding of life as an emerging process. I will live the story with faith, hope, and love, and I will live the story as long as I can. We will never know all we need to know, think we might need know, hope we can know! We just keep on moving in the living process, learning as we lean into the next moment, always interconnected with all the moments just left behind, or imagined or dreamed"
Dr. Carl Leggo (1953-2019)

References

Aoki, T. (2004). Towards curriculum in a new key. In W. Pinar and R. Irwin (Eds.), *Curriculum in a new key*. New York, NY. Routledge, Taylor and Francis Group.

Berry, W. (2001). *In the presence of fear: Three essays for a changed world*. Great Barrington: The Orion Society, 2001.

Breit, S., Kupferberg, A., Rogler, G., & Hasler, G. (2018). Vagus nerve as modulator of the brain-gut axis in psychiatric and inflammatory disorders. *Front Psychiatry*, 9. 44.

Cahalan S. (2013). *Brain on fire: My month of madness.*

Campbell, J. (1991). *The power of myth.*

Findley, T. (1977). *The wars.*

Griffin, S. (1995). *The eros of everyday life: Essays on ecology, gender and society.* New York: Doubleday.

Hasebe-Ludt, E. Chambers, C.M., & Leggo, C. (2009). *Life writing and literary métissage as an ethos of our times.* New York: Peter Lang Publishers.

Hillman, J. *The Force of Character and the Lasting Life.* New York: Ballantine Books, 1999.

Huxley, A. (1932). *Brave New World.*

Kogawa, J. (2016). *Gently to Nagasaki.*

Leggo, C. (2016). *A Poem Can: Poetic Encounters: LEARNing Landscapes Volume 9*

Leggo C. (2019). *The Pen. Toasted Cheese Literary Journal.* Tclj.toasted-cheese.com

Holmes, K. & Leggo, C. (2019). Places of the heart. In E. Lynn (Ed.), Identity landscapes: Contemplating place and the construction of self. Yorkville University.

Lewis, C. (1950). *The chronicles of Narnia.*

Orr, G. (2002). *The blessing*. Tulsa: Council Oak Books.

Singer, M.A. *The untethered soul: The journey beyond yourself.* Oakland, CA: New Harbinger Publications, Inc.

Smith, D. (2012). Spiritual cardiology and the heart of wisdom. *A heart of wisdom.* New York, NY: Peter Lang Publishers.

Smith, D. (1999). *Pedagon: Human sciences, pedagogy and culture.* New York: Peter Lang Publishers.

Requiem

Living Writing

Poetic Fragments for Living Life Well

Kimberley

The Greeks defined "practical philosophy" as engagement in the activities of interpreting our lives and the world around us. This act of interpretation, specifically the interpretation of biblical texts, is rooted in the study of hermeneutics and offer us a unique type of insight. Gadamer (1989) reflects,

> Insight is more than knowledge of this or that situation.
>
> It always involves an escape from something that has deceived
>
> us and held us captive. What (we) learn through suffering is not
>
> this or that particular thing (but) insight into... the experience
>
> of human finitude. The truly experienced person is one who has
>
> taken this to heart. (p. 357)

This deep insight into the experience, a true journey to the heart, is the epiphany of human existence. As we learn through our suffering, we develop a type of heart wisdom that allows us to embrace the obstacles, feel the pain, and then transcend to another way of being in the world. This transcendence is required for us to master the fluctuations of the mind, to control the anxiety and depression that is brought on by the attachment to the illusion. Only when we recognize the illusion, or the shadows, are we fully able to embrace the possibility of the light seeping through the seemingly unending darkness of adversity. If we don't face the dark we are unable to move forward as "what we fear, we repress, and what we repress comes over and over to haunt us, in our dreams, in our compensatory actions, until the day comes when we can no longer fun away from it, and we have to make friends with it, and embrace it as part of what sustains us" (Smith, 1999, p. 23). Our recognition of the light is based on our ability to interpret the experiences connected to the human understanding of interdependence. When embracing the philosophy of hermeneutics, "the concern must always be with life as it is lived, with a desire to understand the same, interpreting it in a way that can show the possibilities for life's continuance" (Smith, 1999, p. 47). Our ability to thrive within our stories of life depends on our ability to understand the constraints and conditions of our day-to-day existence in relationship to the interwoven web of life. Life itself is a text, an intricate story that has multiple chapters and is full of possibilities. The text of life is readable and interpretable and helps us understand our selves and our world in vastly interconnected and philosophical ways.

This hermeneutic philosophy challenges us to inquire, to consider, and to wonder about the vast intricacy of our human journeys and the experiences encountered through the process. As humans seeking meaning, we are constantly contemplating our world, our experiences, and our personal ontological framework. This philosophy is linked to the Greek messenger, Hermes, who carried complex messages from the gods and made them accessible to mere mortals. Hermes helped understand complexity through metaphor, through illusion, and through our commitment to living well using the alchemy of words. Illusion allow us to shift our perspective, and our language is essential to our perception. As the words tumble from our fingertips and onto the page, the magic is evident. As we focus on both introspection and the examination of the self and other, the magic of worlds allows us to braid our stories together, identify common themes and patterns, and come to a significant realization that we are but one small part of a much greater whole. Life writing is an alchemical reaction between the body and the spirit that involves a recovery of life itself. It ensures our singular memoirs do not wither in isolation but are bound with the experiences of others, anchoring us to something much greater. As Chambers et. al (2012) reflect, "Through our writing and our willingness to share our writing with others, we perform our commitment to living with careful intent, critical exploration and thoughtful awareness (p. xxvii.). The thoughtful awareness is a type of awakening, an understanding of the illusions that shift our perceptions and cause us to struggle and question the human journey. That awakening is a type of magic that happens when we learn together what might be and explore reflectively what currently is. It is the magic of interconnectivity, the strength shared through the exploration of the story, and the recognition of the part as only a segment of the greater whole. None of us have ability to independently write our stories, as the stories are already written, awaiting us to discover the voice within. We do not live in isolation but in relation to all the interconnected components that compose life itself. Once the voice is discovered in the individual, it can become part of the woven tapestry of vibrant colors representing the magnitude of exquisite experiences that encompass the chapters of human life.

Hermes guides us through the process of inquiry and wonder. He reminds us that education is indeed a curriculum of imagination and interpretation. A hermeneutic endeavor is therefore the practice of interpretation and engagement in the making of meaning in vastly complicated and interconnected ways. The hermeneutic circle, as a method of interpretation concerned with human problems and the exploration of human actions shows us the spiral loops that compose meaning and identity. These understandings are relevant as we write, read, and reflect upon the text. The circular exploration of the text and its interconnections with the whole spins in a spiral of creativity and interpretation as we unpack the complexity of language in human understanding, and then examine the interplay of the part and the whole in the process of understanding as we make meaning and find a "heart of wisdom" (Chambers et al., 2012). It is a spiral process that mirrors the journey of our human lives, as language both encourages and constrains our understanding of existence and being. Language is confusing and complicated, much like human life itself. We use our language to define us, yet still are confounded by its limitations. Hence, we journey between the parts of the hermeneutic circle, creatively using our language and our understanding to bridge the boundaries between the parts and the whole. We journey to find completeness, to keep the circle spiraling in an interconnected circle of love and hope. We journey together, keeping the circle strong and embracing the possibilities of Oneness. We trust the process and know that regardless of obstacles the circle never ends but continues to spiral in powerful and interconnected ways and patterns of being.

Gadamer (1960/1989) states, "understanding begins when something addresses us" (p. 299). Being addressed by something is a powerful push towards an understanding that we have been called to, sometimes an understanding that we are not ready or willing to take. Understanding begins when something calls for our attention, reminding us repeatedly to be present and attuned to the manifestations materializing around us. It will keep calling to us until we pay attention and address it. Based on the philosophies surrounding this hermeneutic school of thought, we recognize that inquiry rarely has a starting or an ending point but evolves around the experience of being addressed personally about something in one's life. Gadamer's hermeneutics "supports all the recent [sic] work in narrative and story, which proceeds from an affirmation of the traceably constitutive nature of human understanding and its roots in recollection and memory" (Smith, 1999, p. 34). Writing about our lives, our memories, and our experiences is part of the hermeneutic journey as we struggle to interpret experience and emotive events in a complex quest to find deeper meaning in our human existence. We write to understand this journey of life, and we read to recognize the other seekers who travel beside us and share the experience.

Dewey (1916) reminds us that "education is not preparation for life, education is life itself" (p. 239). We become educated by our life experiences, through the experiences that color the journey and impact the root of our essence and ultimately our understanding and perspective of the world. Westover (2018) writes her personal and emotional memoirs as she explores, through vignettes of her life story, the process of "becoming educated." She understands that her education is her life story, reflecting, "You could call this selfhood many things. Transformation. Metamorphosis. Falsity. Betrayal. I call it Education" (p. 329). Orr (2019) in his work *The Blessing* reflects on his life experiences as blessings gathered through the accumulation of many wounds. Through his written reflections he challenges our reasons for being in rage, despair, and all-consuming frustration: "Either this was a meaningless and horrible universe and this woman's ideas were a lollipop she sucked in the dark, or as there was a divine plan, but it was not benevolent" (p. 16). Our human journeys are often fraught with moments of adversity, portals of darkness where seeking even the slightest sliver of light seems a daunting and overwhelming battle. Yet these battles with both their victories and failures encompass the human journey. It is Campbell (1949) hero's journey, the classic story structure that appears as a frequent literary motif. The tale of the character who seeks to find their purpose and what they need, then faces significant adversity and ultimately triumphs over the conflicts, is a common strand in our human story. We all seek meaning and purpose, we all seek connection, and we are all in a type of wonder with regards to how our stories will unfold. The stories of our lives are our education, and our education should be based on the braiding of those stories with those of the other people, the Environment, and the complex system of living creatures that we dwell within. It is our stories that bind us, connect us, and sustain us.

It is through the explorations of the events and experiences of our lives that we come to an understanding of who we are in the world and our interconnected space within it. One way we explore this experience is through the writing process. We live our lives in stories and words, fragments tumbling and jumbling together in a symphony of stories that create the tapestry of our humanity. These fragments divide and then intersect, creating the patterns of the whole, the tapestry of the Muse, a brightly woven creation of stories, words, and wonder that help us live our lives well in spite of overwhelming complexity.

The process of teaching writing and reading is one that is debated and deliberated amongst educators, specifically English language arts teachers. We have strategies for teaching kids to read, yet are not prepared to differentiate when reading does not occur. We don't account for academic readiness, the possible impact of trauma, or socio-economic and cultural conditions. For the most part, teachers follow a standard protocol that is not questioned. If the child fails to learn to read and write, it is assumed that there is something wrong with the child. We do not consider that the fragmented and isolated pieces do not make sense to the child and that we need to return reading and writing to its essential purpose. We need to understand literacy as a whole process derived from the fundamental need to connect and share our human stories. As educators, we need to recognize that the text is rooted in storytelling traditions that acknowledge "the truth about stories is that that's all we are" (King, 2003, p. 2). Our human species thinks in metaphors and learns the lessons of our lives through the telling and sharing of stories. One only begins to understand the complexity of writing a curriculum for writing by examining the series of fragments derived from years of teaching writing and living daily within the confines of the classroom. Writing is fundamentally a human process used to explore and record the human journey or the spaces between life and death. Yet, in spite of this fundamental understanding of the humanities' need to focus on "purposeful living, manifesting a spiritual creativity in the broadest sense, creating culture within historical continuity" (Husserl, 1965, p. 150), the debate continues to rage in educational institutions today regarding how we approach writing and literary studies. Many still cling desperately to the antiquated factory model of education where tests are standardized and students are treated much like products on an assembly line...as teachers break things down into little pieces, charging students to memorize the pieces, and then reproduce the pieces into tiny bits of discombobulated knowledge void of meaning and authentic learning (Jardine, Clifford, & Friesen, 2008). As educators, we organize, categorize, and use formulas such as the standard five-paragraph essay required to pass most college and university entrance exams. This type of writing skill is important and has its place in education, but if it is the only type of writing we do, it has particularly harmful consequences with regards to the study of the humanities and human life itself. It renders the act of writing a simple formula for analytical reasoning and neglects the need for writing to trace the patterns of what it means to be a human being in complex and variable conditions of life, neglecting the important consideration "that the heart of pedagogy is becoming fully human" (Leggo, 2015, p. v). The study and extrapolation of life unravel this vastly complex process of becoming fully human within complex circumstances. Curriculum exploration is not standardized or formulaic but an interconnected spiraling process that twists and turns in vibrant and wonderful wandering ways. This is not something that can be memorized and regurgitated but something that must be fully embodied and actualized. It involves a deep and powerful love for the playful and inspirational nature of words, allowing us to turn thoughts and emotions into stories which we then share with Others. It is process that must be practiced and embraced as we explore the complexity of our human journeys and recognize that the heart of pedagogy is indeed this process of becoming human in deeply emotional and spiritual ways. Without this pedagogical process our holistic wellness is threatened and diminished. Dr. Shelby Hague, the Islamic Chaplain at the University of Alberta, reflects,

> We have a billion-dollar health care system (which ought to be called a disease care system) which treats people after they become physically sick; what they really need are spiritual cardiologists who can help humans cure the disease of our spiritual hearts.

(http://www.uofaweb.ualberta.ca/chaplains/islamic.cfm)

(Smith, 2012, foreword)

Humans are complex beings, and the journey to understanding is fraught with conflict, pain, and sorrow. Currently, mental illness is on the rise in our schools and universities with increasing rates of anxiety and depression as "according to Marcia Angell (2011) former editor of the *New England Journal of Medicine,* in North America 'mental illness is now the leading cause of disability in children'" (Chambers et al., 2012, foreword). Mental health is now a significant cause of human suffering in North America. Many are troubled and burdened by the complexities of our fast-paced modern world, trapped in a digital world that connects yet disconnects through use of illusion and complex manipulation of human thought and emotion. Many are lost and seeking connection, seeking a bond, looking for a similar story to help them understand their own experience. There is laughter and joy, but there is often also tears and suffering. Mental illness is a leading form of human suffering in North America, and we need to pay attention to the call to connect with others and gather our strength together in vibrant communities of care and love. We need to recognize all that life bestows experiences upon us, and writing is one way to find our way towards deeper understandings of living and being in this world. Through the process of writing and sharing our writing, we are offered a deep and meaningful support through emotional and spiritual growth. Through story we understand our world, the way we live in the world, and the way we live in the world in relationships to others. We are our stories, and our stories are deeply intertwined with the story of the Other. Writing opens portal for sight, and the process of poetry takes us even deeper into the embodied and intertwined journey of our human condition. It allows spaces of reflection to open up for us, portals of peace that allow us to understand and be still in the current situation and simply allow things to happen to us. When we allow the experiences to just happen, our lives are blessed with the ability to find some grace, gratitude, and mindfulness.

We all dwell daily in the spaces between living and dying. That space is all there is and all that will ever be. Sometimes our death is imminent and at other times a slowly creeping shadow that brings us closer and closer to the other side. Yet, in the end death is what awaits us all. Hence, we need to spend our time celebrating these spaces in between we call life. Life is all we have, and we need to learn to embrace both the beauty and the pain of human existence. As educators it critical we understand the precious and finite circle of life as we teach who we are (Palmer, 1998), and without understanding that our own existence is precious we cannot transfer that understanding to our learners. Hence, the most important thing we need to develop is the ability to "feel fully alive and become increasing authentic as an individual, and in relationships" (Cohen, 2015, p. 12). One way we do that is to write, for writing is a transformative process whereby we learn to live gracefully and with more peace in the midst of the tangled mess that weaves around us. We are part of the web of life, and we need to learn to embrace and accept our strand within the great whole. Additionally, educators need to have a strong understanding of empathy "as rooted in emotion, passion, imagination, sympathy, and vicarious identification" (Chambers et al., 2012, p. xxiv). This empathy develops through writing about our experiences, "often in vulnerable, confessional and personal ways" (p. xxvi), a process which allows us to join the conversation of compassion uniting our human circle.

Poetry is a particularly potent tool for opening spaces for understanding. Poetry is a portal to our humanity, a way to connect deeply with others, and a special type of alchemy made possible through the combinations and permutations of words and ideas, as "many poet-researchers consider poetry as an excellent means to present data about the human experience and consider poetry an ideal way to capture and present this experience in a more easily 'consumable, powerful, emotionally poignant, and accurate form than prose research reports'" (Faulkner, 2009, p. 22). Poetry portals capture the essence of our human experience, bringing us to a deep and embodied way of knowing that transcends traditional research methodology as it seeks stronger, more insightful ways of knowing and being in the world. Poets engage in a dance of discourse as they play with their words, leaping and swirling their ways towards complex understanding of thoughts, ideas, and emotions.

Jane Hirshfield (1997) believes that poetry has the power to clarify and magnify our human existence as "each time we enter its word-woven and musical invocation, we must give ourselves over to a different mode of knowing: to poetry's knowing, and to increase the existence it brings, unlike any other" (p. vii). This mode of knowing is not something that can be directly taught but something that must be inspired, a type of opening of the inner state of being, allowing what exists within to emerge outwards via the transmission of sounds and energy. The precious threads of poetry provide lifelines that ground and anchor us to ourselves and to each other. Orr (2002) reflects on poetry as a tool to "find my way out of the labyrinth of my own consciousness" (p. 143). The labyrinth of the human mind is a complex and intricate maze, and its ability to darken or illuminate our conscious understanding is profound.

> *True to poetry's laws of dream and metamorphosis it changed in my*
>
> *hand as I held it. Sometimes it was the thinnest of silk filament, so*
>
> *fine that it almost cut my palm simply resting there. Other times,*
>
> *thickened and became slick as with blood, all warm and wet, and it felt*
>
> *like my own guts paid out and now had to be followed back toward*
>
> *the source or exit*
>
> Orr, 2002, p. 143)

As writers, we often do not know what will emerge but learn to trust the process and wait for the pieces to appear upon the page. Those who aspire to write poetry need to pay careful attention and listen to the voices in their head. As voices swirl in our consciousness providing clarity and transformation, poets experience a type of schizophrenia where voices clamor to be heard, calling from some place deep within to be recognized and actualized. Often writers such as J. K. Rowling use metaphors to capture thoughts and feelings; for instance, depression is the root inspiration for the Dementors in her Harry Potter series. Our experiences and feelings shape our world, and our use of language, symbols, and images allows us to bring others into that world and travel with us. The more we read, the more we understand the stories, see the interconnected patterns, and learn how to write our own stories. Reading and writing are parts of the whole and should not be separated. We read to write, and we write to allow others to share in our journeys, for "the task of the writer is to allow the reader to experience fully the lives of people other than themselves" (Herring, 2007, p. 39). The human connection is evident when readers recognizes a piece of themselves in the story they are reading. Through stories we recognize our light and our darkness and find the innermost essence of our Soul.

> *Yes*
>
> *Burden and blessing---*
>
> *Two blossoms on the same branch*
>
> *To be so lost*
>
> *In this radiant wilderness*
>
> (Orr, 2002, p.1)

We write to address the major events and thresholds of our lives, to honor them, to embrace them, and to process the experience, allowing us to find a type of peace that is only accessible to those who are willing to face what exists within, who are willing to be lost wandering in the wilderness without fear. Poetry presents a pathway to recognizing that as human beings we really don't know very much and need to undertake this complex journey of understanding and the quest for wisdom. Smith (1999) reflects, "in Wisdom traditions, it is accepted that everything begins and ends with the mind, or in Chinese, hsin, the heart-mind, which expresses the essential unity between thought and emotion" (p. 91). This is the type of practice that writing allows us to undertake "a journey into language and into the world and through our writing and our willingness to share our writing with others, we perform our commitment to living with careful intent, critical interrogation and thoughtful awareness. None of our stories are ours alone" (Chambers et al., 2012, p. xxvii.). There is so much more to our stories than the telling of them. As each reader reviews the ramblings of the rants and rages, they begin to seek fragments of their own struggle, their own voices echoing in the emptiness as they seek the answers. Through our writing we realize that we are never alone; we are only interconnected strands in the spinning, spiraling stories of life.

Life has beginnings and endings, and writing helps us find our way through both. Writing is about healing from pain and suffering, finding the reason for each season. Through our words we began to understand the process, the pain, and the eventual passage to the next stage of being. It helps us understand the art of deep and thoughtful introspection. In the fourth century Saint Augustine set a precedent for this autobiographical work; as Smith (1999) writes, Augustine's "*Confessions* were an experiment in the art of introspection, being the means by which to unravel and describe all the ways that the human soul could be devious in the search for its true, divinely inspired identity" (p. 12). We write to understand ourselves and to heal from the onslaught of experiences that threaten to overwhelm us.

Through writing we learn to live creatively in the world as we attempt to live well within the world. We write to seek health and healing as "stories present possibilities for understanding the complex, mysterious, even ineffable experiences that comprise human living" (Chambers et al., 2012, p. xx). When health eludes us and we are angry and bitter, we write to heal. We write to find our ways to new possibilities and to record our stories. We write to move forward despite the obstacles. We write to recognize the fact that we are still alive, that we can breathe, that we can create, and that we are able to record the fragments of the journey through the woven words on the page. Many of us have blocked the energy flow at our throats, trapped our voices within us, and stuffed our feelings deep inside. This causes bitter stagnation and stifled energy, which impedes our physical wellness. It causes separation between the body, the mind, and the spirit. Deep writing is more than communication with others; it is a conversation with the Self that unites the three parts of the whole, bringing our mental, spiritual, and physical Essence into balance. Writing helps us understand and helps us heal our pain. Through the process of writing, we discover and remember the stories and poetry of our lives. We begin to see new perspectives, gain clarity, find solutions, celebrate accomplishments, notice and change patterns of behavior and refine our understanding of life's experiences. In this process we make meaning though our stories, constructing who we are and who we are becoming." (Cutler, Monk, & Shira, 2014, p. 2)

As we write we grow as writers and as human beings. The writing process itself is the only way one becomes a writer, as it is a practice. Through careful practice we begin to understand the process, we begin to see the patterns, and we begin to make magic with our worlds. Writing is a type of alchemy that has the power to shape and change our perceptions and our world. As educators, we need to consider the possibilities of poetry as contemplative practice, as a means to explore identity and connection and trace the various strands of what it means to be a human as "the ongoing discovery and inquiry into the purpose of a person's life and how to live well is core to all education" (Cohen, 2015, p. 7). Authentic education is about learning to be well in our world in whimsical, wonderful, and intensely interconnected ways in spite of the challenges of human existential crisis.

Yet, in school we play a type of game of obeying teachers' rules and following their direction. School has convinced us that the teacher knows all, that we need to follow the template and do as instructed. We need to write in a certain way that follows the rules and stick to a standardized structure. Granted, this is the type of writing expected in post-secondary academic work, but it is certainly not the only type of writing we should be experiencing. Writing should allow us to

> take risks, engage innovatively with a wide variety of genres, push limits in order to explore creatively how language and discourse are never ossified, but always organic, how language is used integrally and inextricably connected to identity, knowledge, subjectivity and living. (Leggo, 2006, p. 70)

Language should allow us to live, and life itself should be a luminous, living language. We use language to extrapolate and explore the infinite mystery of being human which allows us the ability to "find ourselves in poems" (Richardson, 1989, p. 459). Poetry allows us to show our humanity and to recognize moments of truth as we transcend through the chaos and become well.

Unfortunately, many teachers of writing are still obsessed with assessment and evaluation and lose sight of the powerful process of discovery and awakening. We feel the constant need to critique what is written and how it was written. When seeking adherence to the template we lose sight of the process. We disregard how much the writing touches us and focus on the technical errors. We miss the message of life in the quest for a grade and believe our purpose in education is to prepare for the standardized test in contrast to preparing for a life well lived. We create stress, anxiety, and depression through the constant critique and evaluation, preventing the writer from blossoming, growing, and discovering their own inner essence and purpose of being. We bleed our red pens upon the page and suck the life blood out of the writer. Our pedagogy is a ploy to pluck the spirit and erode the quest for self-understanding and peace. As Jardine (2012) reflects, "a pedagogy left in peace is no tranquil and passive spot. It is the peace had in being who we are, the peace in letting things and words and topics and ourselves show themselves as they are" (p. 134). Writers should be free and wild, interpreting in their own ways and discovering their own stories. They need to be awakened to a deeper way of knowing and Being that goes far beyond the five-paragraph structure into a world of wonder, or reflection and authentic engagement with the process. The structure has its place as a tool, but it is not the entire writing process. To write well we need to care about our writing, we need to have something to say, and we need to be engaged in the process without fear of negative assessment. Writing is a portal to human connection and wellness and needs to be embraced as such. It cannot be reduced to simple methodologies but must be embraced as a quest for wisdom.

Smith (2014) reflects, "a true teacher is one who honors not just the child who is 'present' but also the human being who is yet-to come" (p. 54). We are all in this process of Becoming, and educators need to move beyond the scope of grading and assessment towards the acquisition of wisdom. Teachers need to honor the intuitive wisdom they have acquired from years of working with writers, "involving an understanding of how each child brings to the classroom a different life story with its own particular ways of proceeding to meet the world" (Smith, 1999, p. 9). Each person has a unique story to tell, a unique understanding of their world and a perspective to unpack, repack, and explore. Educators "need to be awake, put in sufficient effort at initiatory moments, have a feel for what the optimal intervention is at the moment and within the context, and have the ability to stay within the process" (Cohen, 2015, p. 6). Human beings and life itself are a process of growing, being, and becoming. We need to use our language as a tool to extrapolate and explore process, to play with words and create meaning. Through this process of engaging with the mystery of language we become readers, writers, and fully developed human beings, expressing what emerges and offering opportunities to embrace multiple perspectives. We must embrace the mystery and continue to grow through the disjointed process of discovery and interconnectedness. We must write for ourselves with little thought of how the writing will be reviewed. We must write with the heart, to allow us to touch the heart and acquire our own "heart of wisdom" (Chambers et al., 2012), interacting in the spaces and places in between and embracing the possibilities.

Poetic fragments

The words merge into ideas and expressions encompassing the power of the human Soul

Spiritual souls intersect, ideas clash and merge in bizarre patterns and systems of Being

Belonging to part of life's story yet remaining an independent separate enigmatic entity

Fingers clicking on the keyboard in a quest to find the answers in a world of broken dreams

Out out brief candle for your moments on earth are but a fleeting frenzied instant

Gather ye rosebuds while ye may

Brains seize and die of disease while humans contemplate the magnitude of eternal existence

Amidst the sorrow, pain, and suffering of broken dreams the neon light flashes brightly

Promises of a new tomorrow and a chance to start again amongst the ruins of destruction

Illness rages and cancer breeds its vile form through the vibrant human body, and we recognize

That one day we shall need to say goodbye or perhaps until we meet again in another space

The cracks and portals and spaces in between our patterns of time and being

Words, wonder, wander, white light and other forms of protective magic

Health, healing, happiness, and hope in harmony with the rhythm and patterns of the Universe

> *Waves crashing, snow falling, soft footsteps along the garden path seeking the flowers*
>
> *Buried deep within the snow awaiting the awakening and the new signs of life*
>
> *The process, the journey, the portal of poetry slipping through the cracks of the darkness*
>
> *And offering hope to live life well wandering towards wellness*

We need a luminous love to call out quietly and guide us through this deep darkness

Finding the words to help us balance on the tightrope and protect us even if we fall from grace

Slowly into slumbering darkness and mystery and mazes and problematic patterns

Of old familiar stories and familiar patterns of a tale awaiting to be told around the fire

Life's sweet simple powerful patterns and never-ending cycles of endings and new beginnings

A baby cries out as it takes its first breath gasping in bewildered wonder

Never-ending fragments written between the gaps and cracks and spaces of living and Being

In a world that is and will always be filled with luminous lamentations and incredulous inquiry

Writing as a discovery that never ends at the bottom of the page but only is part of the cycle

Seeing the everyday things with new eyes open to perspective and possibilities and hope

Knowing that in the end love and human connection will guide us through the process

As we travel the mysterious and intriguing spaces in between

No day will be exactly what we want but each day is filled with possibilities. Lean into the possibilities. Carl Leggo

References

Chambers, C., Hasebe-Ludt, E., Leggo, C., and Sinner, A. (2012). A heart of wisdom: Life writing as empathetic inquiry. New York, NY: Peter Lang Publishing.

Cohen, A. (2015). Becoming fully human within educational environments: Inner life, relationships and learning. Burnaby, BC, Canada: The Writing Room Press.

Cutler, W. J., Monk, L., & Shira, A. (2014). Writing alone together: Journalling in a Circle of Women for Creativity, Compassion and Connection. Salt Spring Island, BC: Butterfly Press.

Dewey J. (1916). Democracy and education: An introduction to the philosophy of education. New York: Macmillan.

Faulkner, S.L. (2009). Poetry as method- Reporting research through verse. Walnut Creek, CA: Left Coast Press.

Gadamer H.-G. (1989). Truth and method (2nd rev. ed.) (J. Weinshemer & D. G. Marshal, Trans.). New York, NY: Continuum. (Original work published 1960)

Herring, L. (2007). Writing begins with the breath: Embodying your authentic voice. Boston, MA: Shambhala Publications.

Hirshfield, J. (1997). Nine gates: Entering the mind of poetry. New York: HarperCollins.

Husserl, E. (1965). Phenomenology and the crisis of philosophy (Q. Lauer, Trans.). New York; Harper and Row.

Jardine, D., Clifford, P., and Friesen, S. (2008). Back to the basics of teaching and learning: Thinking the world together (2nd ed.). New York, NY: Routledge Press.

King, T. (2003) The truth about stories: A Native narrative. Toronto: House of Anansi Press.

Leggo, C. (2006). End of the line: A poet's postmodern musings on writing. English Teaching: Practice and Critique, 5 (2), 69-92.

Leggo, C. (2015). Poetic Ruminations on Pedagogy: Toward a *Forward*. Becoming Fully Human within Educational environments. Burnaby, BC: The Write Room Press.

Orr, G. (2002). The blessing. Tulsa: Council Oak Books.

Palmer, P. (1998). The courage to teach: Exploring the inner landscape of a teacher's life. San Francisco, CA: Jossey-Bass Publishers.

Smith, D. (1999). Pedagon: Interdisciplinary essays in the human sciences, pedagogy and culture. New York, NY: Peter Lang Publishing.

Smith, D. (2012). Spiritual cardiology and the heart of wisdom. A heart of wisdom: Life writing as empathetic inquiry. New York, NY: Peter Lang Publishing.

Smith, D. (2014). Teaching as the practice of wisdom. New York, NY: Bloomsbury Publishing.

Richardson, M. (1998). Poetics in the field and on the page. Qualitative Inquiry 4, 451-462

Westover, T. (2018). Educated: A memoir. Toronto, Ontario, Canada: HarperCollins.

About the Authors

Carl Leggo, originally from Corner Brook, Newfoundland, was an accomplished poetic scholar. A professor in the Department of Language and Literacy Education at the University of British Columbia, he was renowned for his dedication to living poetically and playing with the power of words. His research interest included life writing, a/r/tography, narrative inquiry, poetic inquiry, creative writing, contemplative practices and arts-based research. The Canadian Association for Curriculum studies awarded Dr. Leggo the *Ted T. Aoki Award for Distinguished Service* within the field of Curriculum Studies. This award recognizes individuals who make major contributions through research, teaching, and/or professional service in the field of curriculum studies in Canada. He received the prestigious Killian Award for Excellence in Mentoring Senior level for supervising a remarkable cohort of doctoral and master's students and was a superior mentor. Published books include: *Life Writing and Literary Metissage, Growing up Perpendicular on the Side of the Hill, Teaching to Wonder, Come by Chance, View from my Mother's house, Sailing in a Concrete Boar, Hearing Echoes and Speaking of Learning; Recollections, Revelations and Realizations.*

Kimberley Holmes, from Calgary, Alberta is a poet and a scholar. She is adjunct assistant professor at the Werklund School of Education, The University of Calgary and an educator at the Calgary Board of Education. She is committed to living poetically and telling the truth critically and creatively. Her research interests include; educational neuroscience, literary neuroscience, narrative inquiry, poetic inquiry, creative writing, contemplative practices/mindfulness, FNMI storytelling and arts-based research. She was awarded The Canadian Association of Teacher Educations dissertation award for her contribution to teacher education. Her work evolves around the nexus between mindful pedagogical practice and educational neuroscience bridging the world between the arts and science. She has numerous publications in narrative inquiry, contemplative inquiry, teacher education and educational neuroscience.

CPSIA information can be obtained
at www.ICGtesting.com
Printed in the USA
BVHW040317231221
624661BV00004B/41